Expressions of Sufi Culture in Tajikistan

FOLKLORE STUDIES
IN A MULTICULTURAL
WORLD

The Folklore Studies in a Multicultural World series emphasizes
the interdisciplinary and international nature of current folklore
scholarship, documenting connections between communities and
their cultural production. Series volumes highlight aspects of folklore
studies such as world folk cultures, folk art and music, foodways,
dance, African American and ethnic studies, gender and queer
studies, and popular culture.

Expressions
of Sufi Culture
in Tajikistan

Benjamin Gatling

THE UNIVERSITY OF WISCONSIN PRESS

Publication of this volume has been made possible, in part, through support from the Andrew W. Mellon Foundation.

The University of Wisconsin Press
1930 Monroe Street, 3rd Floor
Madison, Wisconsin 53711-2059
uwpress.wisc.edu

3 Henrietta Street, Covent Garden
London WC2E 8LU, United Kingdom
eurospanbookstore.com

Printed in the United States of America

This book may be available in a digital edition.

Library of Congress Cataloging-in-Publication Data
Names: Gatling, Benjamin, author.
Title: Expressions of Sufi culture in Tajikistan / Benjamin Gatling.
Other titles: Folklore studies in a multicultural world.
Description: Madison, Wisconsin : The University of Wisconsin Press,
    [2018] | Series: Folklore studies in a multicultural world
Identifiers: LCCN 2017046465 | ISBN 9780299316808 (cloth : alk. paper)
Subjects: LCSH: Sufis—Tajikistan. | Sufism—Tajikistan. | Tajikistan—
    Religious life and customs.
Classification: LCC BP188.8.T3 G38 2018 | DDC 297.409586—dc23
LC record available at https://lccn.loc.gov/2017046465

To
MANDY

Contents

Illustrations

Acknowledgments

I first want to thank the men who graciously welcomed me into their homes, served me food from their tables, and did their best to teach me what it meant to be Sufi. It is their stories that fill this book, and I regret that their names cannot openly grace its pages. My hope is that what I have written does not stray too far from what they entrusted to me. I am similarly thankful to the many patient Tajik civil servants, *imoms*, and scholars who took time out of their schedules to share with me their experiences or the results of their research.

I am deeply appreciative of the many friends and colleagues who offered their steadfast support, incisive remarks, and good humor, chief among them Margaret Mills. She has been my *pir* since I first bought a copy of her yellow book in a Kabul bookstore. Ray Cashman meticulously read and perceptively commented on numerous drafts. He prodded me toward greater analytical precision and more artful prose. Morgan Liu and Dick Davis have been sage intellectual guides and deserve special recognition for their generous support since the earliest iterations of this project. Debra Lattanzi Shutika, Joy Fraser, and others at George Mason University have made the English Department and the Folklore Studies Program a collegial and supportive environment to work, and for that I am grateful.

I owe a debt of gratitude to those who read the manuscript in whole or part and generously offered their astute feedback. They include David Montgomery, Maria Louw, Amy Shuman, Christian Bleuer, Sheila Bock, Tim Thurston, Ed Lemon, and Daniel Beben. I also want to thank the ever-helpful Raphael Kadushin and Amber Rose at the University of Wisconsin Press. Thanks too go to Sheila Leary. Due to her confidence and encouragement, I was privileged to participate in the Mellon-funded Folklore Studies in a Multicultural World workshop and profited immensely from the perceptive critiques of workshop participants. I express my gratitude to them—in particular Grete Vidal and Dana Weber—for their careful attention to several shoddy, early chapter drafts.

Books like this one would not exist without financial resources for research and writing. I gratefully acknowledge the U.S. Department of Education's Fulbright-Hays program, the Mershon Center for International Security Studies at the Ohio State University, the International Research and Exchanges Board (IREX), the Thompson Writing Program at Duke University, and George Mason University's College of Humanities and Social Sciences for their support.

Mandy sacrificed the most for the labor encapsulated here. She uprooted her life, traveled to Central Asia, and endured the project's ebbs and flows. This book is dedicated to her. Our children—Gray, Aram, and Evie—deserve credit for their hugs and understanding patience even when I had to shut my office door.

A Note on Transliteration and Translation

I have done my best to transliterate terms like the Sufis with whom I worked might. All technical terms for Sufi practice appear according to their local usage and standard Tajik spellings, many of which differ from their Persian, Arabic, or Turkish analogues. Even so, transliteration of Sufi terms and phrases sometimes highlights the differences between colloquial Tajik and literary Persian and unnecessarily calls attention to orthographic shifts between Tajik's modified Cyrillic alphabet and Persian script. In these pages, I have tried to chart a balance between precision and readability. I have transliterated all Tajik, Russian, and Uzbek words according to the Library of Congress transliteration system, while Persian transliterations follow the conventions used in the *International Journal of Middle Eastern Studies*, except for words with accepted English spellings (e.g., Sufi, Tajikistan, Dushanbe, Qur'an, Muhammad, etc.). At the same time, I have omitted almost all diacritical marks in the body of the text. Diacritics only remain in some notes, the reference list, and in parentheses when a word first appears. At several points, readers may find the same word transliterated in two different ways, one as it was spoken or written in Tajik and another as it appears in a Persian-language source. I hope readers will be patient with these inconsistencies. A full list of Tajik terms and phrases can be found at the end of the book. Italics in transcriptions mark singing. Unless otherwise noted, all translations are my own.

Expressions of Sufi Culture in Tajikistan

Introduction

The short, grainy video shocked most who saw it. Men writhed on the ground. One growled like a wounded animal, clutching his chest, his face twisted. Others flailed in an erratic dance as if possessed. The shifting camera angles and the glare of the lights gave the video an eerie feel. Its poor quality made the men's cries seem like otherworldly screams or the caws of birds.

"Was the video real?" I wondered aloud.

"Yes, for sure. Someone filmed it on a mobile phone," Parviz replied. "It was at the master's brother's house."

Parviz would have known. He had been participating in similar ceremonies for the better part of a decade. He had been a disciple of many Sufi masters (*pirs*) at one point or another. He had visited them occasionally as a child with his father in the 1970s, but it wasn't until he came back from Russia in the early 2000s that he started going of his own accord. In that regard, Parviz was like a lot of the Sufis I met—a synthesis of the new and old. He boasted about the devotion of his ancestors. Parviz could even name their pirs. That is where it ended. Parviz's father may have sought pirs' blessing, but he wasn't a disciple. It was only recently that Parviz took on an initiation and began attending rituals. Parviz betrayed little of that history. To most people, he didn't seem overly pious. He didn't wear special clothes. He went to weddings and circumcisions. He even sipped a little vodka when his hosts offered a toast. Many of his neighbors didn't even know he was a Sufi.

Men like Parviz were all around but not always recognizable to those around them. So when someone uploaded the video in response to a radio program, entitled "Does Tajikistan Have Any Sufi Pirs?," the reaction was

3

typical.[1] Sentiments online ranged from incredulity to rage. Secularized Tajiks decried the lack of civility. Muslim reformists bemoaned its heresy. Those who posted comments on the website claimed that the men depicted were deranged, apostates, foreign, backward, or even demon possessed. Others simply wondered who the men were and what they were doing. Parviz and his friends didn't see what all the fuss was about. It was just a clip of a ritual they participated in at least once a week.

"Did anything come of it? Did anyone get in trouble?" I asked.

"Nobody ever came after them. They're still doing it." Parviz paused and seemed to reflect on the controversy. "Until you become a Sufi and taste it, you can't understand God's grace."

By Parviz's estimation, I hadn't tasted it. Before graduate school, I spent a number of years in Kabul, Afghanistan, working for a nongovernmental organization (NGO). Through an acquaintance, I stumbled into a Sufi circle and afterward rarely missed one of its Friday morning gatherings, many of them much like the one the video depicted. In 2010, now trained as a folklorist and ethnographer, I came for the first time to Tajikistan. Tajikistan was not Afghanistan. Although the countries shared historical legacies, languages, and aspects of Persianate culture, the Bolshevik takeover of Russian-controlled Eastern Bukhara created a border between people who lived on opposite banks of the Amu Darya River and its tributaries. Seventy years of Soviet rule had left an indelible imprint. During the early years of the Soviet Union, the Tajik republic as a political entity was only in its infancy. The Tajik Soviet Socialist Republic (SSR) did not assume full union status within the Soviet Union until the end of 1929 and the beginning of 1930, well after Moscow had delimited the territory of the other Muslim-majority republics of Central Asia (Bergne 2007, 100–118). The territory within the Tajik SSR's boundaries included sparsely populated high mountain plateaus, only one large population center—Khujand—whose closest affinities were to places outside of the new republic, and distant rural valleys. Even Tajik, a language separate from the Persian and Turkic dialects of Central Asia, wasn't at the time a distinct linguistic category. Over the next sixty years, Soviet nation-building efforts remedied these omissions, and by the end of the Soviet period, Tajikistan had a capital—Dushanbe—a national language, history, literature, and folklore consistent with its republican status within the Soviet Union.

Dushanbe, unlike Kabul, was a relatively new city, filled with communist era monoliths and gray apartment blocks. In recent years, developers had bulldozed some of the city's oldest buildings, only dating to the first Soviet decades, and cut down many of the trees along the city's verdant main avenues in favor of gleaming glass structures, like an aspirational Dubai in miniature. In the place of the city's Soviet era Lenin monument sat a statue of Ismoil Somoni, a ninth-century king, the progenitor of the country's latest national mythology. Dushanbe similarly boasted a new national library, museum, and palace, the erstwhile tallest flagpole in the world, and the foundations for what had been billed as Central Asia's largest mosque.

The frenzied pace of change in Dushanbe contrasted sharply with the reality of life in the villages surrounding the city, some of them among the most impoverished in the former Soviet Union. In 2010 as many as a million of Tajikistan's approximately eight million people worked abroad, mainly in Russia, making Tajikistan the most remittance-dependent economy in the world (Danzer and Ivaschenko 2010). Crumbling state farms and irrigation canals, lack of access to basic health care, and a teetering Russian economy escalated villagers' poverty. For many of the men I encountered, state development efforts, like campaigns to fund construction of what promised to be the tallest dam in the world, seemed like either an economic boondoggle, destined to deprive them of what little resources they still had, or a panacea, providing the country with a viable export and reliable electricity.[2]

I didn't know it at the time, but my arrival in Dushanbe marked an escalation of another sort. That weekend, twenty-five inmates escaped from a maximum-security prison in Dushanbe, setting the security services on high alert and precipitating a wave of violence. The escapees had been sentenced for their alleged roles in narcotics trafficking in a part of the country where civil-war-era opposition leaders still wielded some power. Tajikistan's civil war had begun shortly after the dissolution of the Soviet Union, an event that had left the Tajik SSR with a fragile political order based on competition between different regional factions, all seeking control of what state institutions remained (Hierman 2010). In 1997, after as many as one hundred thousand had lost their lives and two hundred and fifty thousand had been displaced as refugees, government forces, led by collective farm boss turned president

Emomali Rahmon (1952–), finally reached an accord with the opposition, of which Islamist groups formed a significant bloc.

The prison break and its resulting violence became one of many pretexts Rahmon used to consolidate his power (Heathershaw and Roche 2011). He wisely framed continuing intra-elite struggles, like control of drug-trafficking routes, in terms of a global Islamist threat (Lemon 2014), a fact made all the easier because of the composition of the opposition and by the specter of a global "War on Terror" being waged along the country's southern border in Afghanistan. That is why I questioned the authenticity of the video and the poster's motives, not that there was anything particularly malicious in it, apart from its cinematography. In Tajikistan, Islam was a matter of state, and any deviation from state-accepted norms was conveniently marked as radicalism or a dangerous import from abroad (Nozimova and Epkenhans 2013). Too often, scholars and security analysts have echoed government claims about the dangers posed by so-called resurgent Islam in their policy papers, NGO reports, and media appearances (Zanca 2004; Montgomery and Heathershaw 2016). The online controversy over the video highlighted a number of these polemics—of violent extremism, alleged foreign political ideologies, the securitization of Islam, and renewed religious fervor. These are the same dynamics that *Expressions of Sufi Culture in Tajikistan* explores as I discuss how men like Parviz constructed what a twenty-first-century Sufi life in Central Asia should rightly entail.

SUFIS AND ETHNOGRAPHY

The men depicted in the video didn't see themselves as radicals or heretics, but rather as followers of particular paths (*tariqat*) to God, what I've glossed, not unproblematically, as Sufi from a range of related terms the men used (e.g., *ahli tariqat, tariqatī, tasavvufī, Sūfī*).[3] While the particulars were different, most of the men I met imagined the Sufi way (*tasavvuf*) as an amplified accompaniment to the sorts of practices that other Muslims also engaged in, things like the five daily prayers, mosque attendance, life-cycle rites, and so on. Most Sufis took on special initiations and became the disciples (*murids*) of men called pirs or *shaikhs* (sometimes also *éshons*), who by virtue of knowledge, God's special favor, or lineage possessed special blessings. Initiates came to Sufi lodges (*khonaqohs*), learned recitations (*vazifa*), adhered to norms of comportment (*adab*), and performed rituals, some like the one on the video, all with the expressed purpose of specially partaking in God's grace. Pirs presided over gatherings (*halqa, hujra, mahfil*) for ritual and teaching and, as living saints (*avlië*), acted as nodes of blessing for those both on and outside the path.

The men's paths extended beyond Tajikistan; they were local iterations of transnational teaching hierarchies that traced their origin back to the Prophet Muhammad himself through chains (*silsila*) of pious masters. The men took a special pride in the fact that a number of paths had their origins in Central Asia. The Naqshbandiya, perhaps the most globally dispersed path, was formed in Bukhara in the fourteenth century, not far from where the men I met lived. Key early figures in its lineage were buried nearby and had shrines that the men regularly visited. For many, their direct connections to fourteenth-century Bukhara remained ambiguous; like Parviz, their fathers, uncles, and grandfathers, for good reason, had not always diligently practiced during the Soviet decades.

Even so, history gave many Sufis confidence that their devotion was unambiguously Tajik, not so much as an ethnonym, but as an orientation befitting a citizen of the Tajik state. That is also the way I use the word Tajik, as a descriptor for the citizens of Tajikistan, not as an ethnic identifier. Tajik identity remains a fraught concept and one not shared equally by all citizens of the republic (Schoeberlein-Engel 1994). The Sufis I met frequently invoked Tajikness in the normative sense, similar to the way Soviet nationalities policies had fashioned it as distinct from its Central Asian neighbors and separate from broader Persianate histories. There remains a tension in the book between the men's normative invocations of Tajikness and their efforts to connect Tajik to larger transnational discourses.

This is a particular story, as all ethnography is. For one thing, it is gendered. It is a story about men and homosocial events. There are female Sufis in Tajikistan, but as a foreign, male researcher I didn't have access to them.[4] In some spheres of Tajik life, interaction between unrelated men and women is common, but most of the men I met practiced strict gender segregation. I sometimes met a friend's wife, mother, or sister, but after our introduction the women would excuse themselves. At times I heard female events going on in close proximity to the male ones in which I participated, but my exposure was limited to what I could ask their husbands, fathers, and brothers, and as such I can't include them here. I hope someone else will take up that task.

This story is also limited geographically. *Expressions of Sufi Culture in Tajikistan* offers a composite picture of men from different paths who lived in Dushanbe and towns and villages in central Tajikistan, places like Hisor, Tursunzoda, Vahdat, Faizobod, and villages up to Gharm (figure 1). This wasn't so much an analytical choice, but a practical one. This is simply where the men I met lived. At the same time, it has a bearing on the histories they discussed (or didn't) and the notions of Tajik identity the men put forward. Their absolute numbers in central Tajikistan were small; perhaps active participants in the groups I studied only numbered in the low thousands. However, the men were not marginal. They included a hodgepodge of twenty-first-century Tajikistan: men who lived in the capital and villages, professionals (teachers, dentists, and government bureaucrats), laborers recently returned from Russia, farmers, shopkeepers in the bazaar, teenage boys, and elderly white-bearded men. They included both Uzbek and Tajik speakers. Some had practiced the Sufi way most of their lives, while others were new to the path.

Research for this book took place between 2010 and 2014. I lived in Dushanbe for one year between 2010 and 2011 and took several trips over subsequent years, during which time I spent countless hours listening to Sufi teaching, participating in rituals, and conducting interviews with disciples, pirs, and other figures within Tajikistan's religious establishment. Because early on the political situation made attending group teaching and rituals challenging, many of the Sufis I met encouraged me instead to focus my efforts on the books they read and used—poetry collections, hagiographies, prayer manuals, and histories—texts they saw as appropriate sites for scholarship as modeled by Soviet era Orientalists. As such, I regularly met informally with Sufis to read and study, a thread that runs throughout the chapters of the book.

I am not a Muslim, nor a Sufi. My Sufi collaborators were quick to point out that my ethnographic knowledge was not their transcendent truth (Narayan 1992, 56–62). Ethnography, too, bucks the norms of Sufi comportment. Sufi knowledge only exists within the context of an initiate's ongoing relationship with a pir. My deep respect for the mystical enterprise, love of Persian Sufi literature, and sympathetic engagement over the span of a number of years provided little remedy since awareness of the inner, esoteric reality only comes after years of careful study and intentional cultivation. One pir, on hearing that I was planning to write a book, told me that there are so many secrets that they would fill

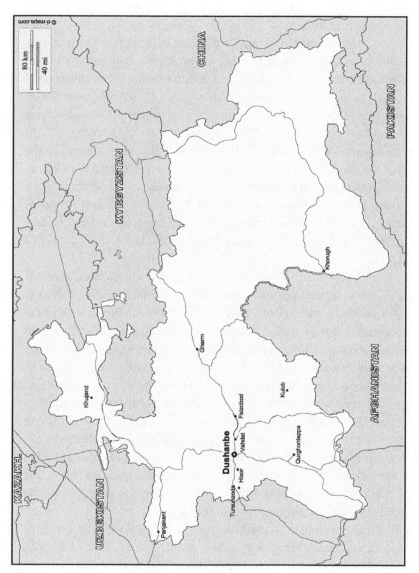

Figure 1. Map of Tajikistan

a multitude of books. If I submitted to his guidance, I would have to write two books, he told me, one with the products of my research and the other with the esoteric knowledge of the path. I readily admit that this book holds no purchase on the latter, and the former remains only partial and incomplete.

Even so, studying books alongside the men who revered them offered a serendipitous complement to other ethnographic methodologies and circumvented some of the challenges related to my outsider status. I could watch as my study partners used texts to offer commentaries on their present predicaments, commentaries to which I wouldn't have otherwise had access. I have filled this book with those conversations and the texts my conversation partners read. I also take comfort in the fact that the esotericism that remained beyond my grasp became immaterial to answering many of the questions that Sufis asked about their lives (Flueckiger 2005)—and by extension that I asked of Sufis. This gives me some confidence in the "aptness" of my attempts to understand Sufi life in Tajikistan (Mills 2008), apart from the hidden reality to which I didn't have access.

Many of the men with whom I worked wrestled with how to reconcile the infelicities of their present—the interference of a hostile state religious bureaucracy, the lack of jobs, crumbling schools for their children, a kleptocratic elite—with their visions of the sacred past. They struggled to connect what may have happened in both the distant and nearer pasts to what they experienced in twenty-first-century Tajikistan. Their anxieties carried over into the genealogies they constructed and the histories they told. They looked to the time of the Prophet Muhammad, centuries past, when Sufis commanded the attention of the powerful, and the late Soviet era, a time when teaching lineages flourished, to question their present circumstances. These are the questions that give this particular, even anecdotal, story its wider resonances, not just because it is a case study exploring religious life among one group in the countries of the former Soviet Union, although it is that too.

Still, some specialists of contemporary Central Asia may see Sufis as an obscure, small group within the wider constellation of Central Asian Muslims.[5] While for ethnographers Sufi may seem like an overdetermined category (Varisco 2005, 16–17). Sufis in Tajikistan are not important because they are generalizable. *Expressions of Sufi Culture in Tajikistan* does not so much offer a chance to extrapolate a "Tajik Islam," an untenable concept itself. The specifics of the Sufi lives I document instead critique sentiments like the ones posted in response to the video and similar ideas disseminated in policy papers, government reports, and media analyses with their accompanying narratives of religious revivalism, retrenchment, and danger (Liu 2011). Following the concerns of the Sufis with whom I worked, *Expressions of Sufi Culture in Tajikistan* seeks to understand the pastness of the Central Asian present—the condition necessary for revivalism and retrenchment even to make sense as analytical constructs—and the politics of the expressive cultures that give that past its life.

EXPRESSIVE CULTURE, PAST AND PRESENT

For many of the men I knew, the Soviet era stirred up some of their strongest feelings. Still, it has already been almost three decades since Moscow ruled Dushanbe directly. The majority of the population has no direct memory of a time when Tajiks held Soviet passports. The nearest past to which Rahmon and other governing elites harken is not a Soviet one but instead the 1990s and its civil war, a time of lawlessness to which they caution against a return. At the same time, institutional and ideological legacies left by the Soviet experience remain cogent features of the political landscape (Rasanayagam, Beyer, and Reeves 2014). I have already alluded to some. Soviet legacies loom large, not just in the architecture of Dushanbe's streets but in terms of the state's approach to Muslim life and how many Tajiks imagine the contours of nation and history (Thibault 2015). "Post-Soviet" is the frequent label, or more generally "post-Socialist," to account for what remains after the transition and the institutional afterlives of the Soviet experience (Verdery 1996; Hann 2002).

Post delimits rupture, a concept with a certain appeal. In many ways, 1991 was a watershed year. It ushered in new geopolitical orientations, a neoliberal economic transition, and, for Tajikistan, most significantly a civil war. At the twenty-fifth anniversary celebrations of independence in 2016, President Rahmon called independence "a life-changing and holy day . . . the most valuable achievement of the civilized Tajik nation."[6] Rahmon justifiably hailed the monumental changes that had occurred between 1991 and 2016. Independence Day, in marking the moment of rupture, seemed to capture the "post" moment neatly by celebrating the linear progress toward the sort of society Rahmon envisioned. Yet still, as the decades of state socialism become more and more distant from the present, the utility of *post-Soviet* as an analytical frame needs more justification (Boyer and Yurchak 2010), not least because it potentially limits the questions we ask and magnifies the alterity of those that still live it (Ibañez-Tirado 2015).[7] That is the critique that *Expressions of Sufi Culture in Tajikistan* builds upon, particularly because Central Asians' alterity exists as an order of magnitude greater when the object of analysis is Islam.

An emphasis on historical continuities and discontinuities has plagued ethnographic writing about Muslims in Central Asia.[8] Scholars have alternatively emphasized longue durée continuities or abrupt, post-Soviet discontinuities between what they see today, what might have come before, and the relationship of both to other places and times. The most egregious have argued that Sufis practice vestigial traces of historical shamanism (DeWeese 2011), while others have stressed the novelty of contemporary Islam, a-historically foregrounding its alleged distinctiveness and foreign influences. With respect to Sufi pasts, both modes remain fraught, obscuring the changes Sufis have continued to experience long after independence and the ways that past times have remained vital to Sufi self-understandings.

The Nobel laureate Svetlana Alexievich evokes just such a sentiment of lingering and relived pasts in her 2013 book *Secondhand Time*. Alexievich powerfully instantiates the present moment by chronicling her interlocutors' relived pasts. That is the same way many of the Sufis I met encountered their pasts, not as a simple choice between continuity and rupture. Indeed, both options take for granted the durability of the past. Sufis live in the present by partially reinscribing events from the Persian sacred and nearer Soviet pasts, calling special attention to others and attempting to account for the paradoxes that remain (Stoler 2016, 27).[9] These are plural pasts. Sufis judiciously invoke disparate pasts, even in the same interaction. They strategically inhabit multiple times: the paradoxical present, the Persian sacred past, and nostalgic visions of the Soviet era. It is an everyday that is pointedly asynchronous (Dinshaw 2012). Recursion emphasizes how Soviet and other pasts don't live on in wholes but only in part. That is one contribution that this book makes to Central Asian studies because neither explaining contemporary Islam in terms of its continuities with the past—no matter how near or distant—nor in terms of its distinctiveness fully captures how past times remain relevant.

Expressions of Sufi Culture in Tajikistan interrogates the persistence of the Sufi past in the present by exploring the specific expressive forms that animate it: memories, stories, artifacts, rituals, and embodied behaviors. The book's chapters successively consider each one. Although the past is deeply implicated in each form, these are not histories, nor are they manifestations of Sufi collective memory. They are more akin to "history-tellings" (Beiner 2007) or expressions of "communicative memory" (Assmann 2006, 1–30). This is significant because history-tellings and communicative memories exist in the interstices between people, in what folklorists call performances, marked situations, and settings that call special attention to acts of communication (Bauman 1984; Bauman and Briggs 1990). I focus on the events in which history-telling and communicative memory occur, for example, times when Sufis express memories, tell stories, enact rituals, participate in group teaching, and more.

Folklore studies has long been concerned with the durability of the past in the present, most often under the rubric of tradition (Ben-Amos 1984; Briggs 1988; Bronner 2000; Cashman, Mould, and Shukla 2011).[10] The performance turn of the 1960s and 1970s transformed folkloristic thinking away from artifact to process, from the thing of tradition to the ways in which humans traditionalize their presents (Hymes 1975). This wasn't so much an analogue to Hobsbawm's (1983) "invented tradition" as a recognition that there is no immutable heritage passed down from time immemorial and that the genuineness of any tradition is always judged in the present (Handler and Linnekin 1984).[11] Folklorists most often see tradition as a temporal ideology (Noyes 2009), an authorizing discourse (Howard 2013), or a potent means to expose discourse to critique (Mould 2005). In this vein, Henry Glassie (2003) complementarily described tradition as the making of the future out of the past.

Sufis do traditionalize the present, actively molding the future by mobilizing expressive building blocks from the past. Yet, the implied linearity of folkloristic concepts related to tradition doesn't easily encompass Sufi recursive histories.[12] The "temporal sedimentations" of Sufi expressive culture didn't always exist evenly (Stoler 2016, 339). Sufi history-tellings connected the men at once to multiple times, people, and situations (Dinshaw 2012, 36). *Expressions of Sufi Culture in Tajikistan* charts how Sufis expressively move in and out of the sedimentations of time and the visions of the present that such temporal linkages produce. This book seeks to expand tradition's rubric to include space for nonlinear modes of living, the sorts of alternative temporalities and asynchronies that characterize the Sufi present. A focus on Sufi histories and the expressive forms that support them doesn't just render moot the debate within Central Asian studies about historical continuity and discontinuity. It also forces folklorists and fellow travelers interested in expressive culture to take temporalities seriously. One additional disjuncture that the book attempts to mitigate is the implied hopefulness that runs in tandem with concepts of tradition as the past enables the construction of the future. For Sufis in Tajikistan, the future remains a difficult proposition.

The Politics of Expressive Culture

The state always lurked in the background during my interactions with Sufis. Just like with the video, Sufi memories, stories, artifacts, rituals, and embodied behaviors all bore traces of a malevolent other, real or imagined, waiting to strike. On a practical level, the ramifications were legion. When I first arrived in Tajikistan in 2010, the political climate had justifiably put everyone on edge. Security officials had begun indiscriminately shaving some men's beards on the street. Legislation had passed the year before expanding the state's already tight regulation of religious groups. Though enforced unevenly, the law effectively criminalized all unregistered religious activity. Sufis were reticent to welcome me to events in which the presence of a foreign researcher was conspicuous. Some pirs had dismissed their disciples entirely until circumstances proved more agreeable to meeting in public.

The situation modulated, and I was eventually able to build rapport. Still, many of the men with whom I worked were afraid, not so much of active surveillance or possible retribution, but mostly of what might happen if state security services co-opted the topics we discussed, to my knowledge something that never occurred. They talked candidly, sometimes shockingly so, in person, but worried about my recorder. As such, I have had to rely on my field notes to reconstruct many of the quotes that I use. To allay the men's fears, I have also changed all their names, with the exception of those outside the government's reach, already prosecuted, dead, or otherwise sanctioned, and altered a few details in several stories to protect my collaborators' anonymity. "The pir" in my ethnographic vignettes isn't a composite character, but each instance references a different man, eleven in total.

While it was impossible to ignore Sufis' anxiety about the Tajik state and its security services, it was less apparent how to account for their lurking presence in the memories, stories, texts, rituals, and embodied behaviors of my Sufi friends. It was tempting to see Sufis' asynchrony and the multiple temporalities that they inhabited as forms of expressive resistance to the overarching ideologies inherent in state modernizing projects, the sorts of temporal narratives that provided authorization for tearing down Dushanbe's Soviet era buildings, erecting new national mythologies, and securitizing Islam. Indeed, folklorists and anthropologists have frequently celebrated resistance (Noyes 2016, 182; Abu-Lughod 1990, 40–42).[13] The folk, understood as nonmodern others, wield their lore as a weapon of the weak (Scott 1985) to stand up to cosmopolitan elites and voice their opposition to homogenization, globalization, neoliberal integration, commodification, and so on.

This is not a story of resistance, if for no other reason than the Sufis with whom I worked would shudder to use the term.[14] *Expressions of Sufi Culture in Tajikistan* doesn't celebrate the Sufi will to exist, to refuse the will of the state security apparatus, or to shove off the pejorative characterizations that those who commented on the video put forward. Sufis like Parviz expressed bafflement—sometimes feigned, sometimes not—at the hostility they faced. They often insisted to me that their activities should not be construed as threats. After all, they weren't advocating for regime change, political parties, or specific government policies, a fact all the more significant due to the political legacies of Sufi history in Central Asia (Algar 1990; Gross 2002). In the centuries before the Soviet experience, Sufis did cultivate close relationships with rulers, commanding vast economic influence and shaping the sociopolitical landscape. Beyond cursory references to the saints, who embodied this synthesis of worldly and mystical power, most of the men with whom I worked never explicitly attempted to connect their activities to these larger histories.

Appeals to power or purposeful opposition were not how the Sufis I knew imagined their politics. Still, men like Parviz charted life worlds, at the least, notionally at odds with ideas put forward by members of the Tajik governing elite. That is the central paradox *Expressions of Sufi Culture in Tajikistan* attempts to unravel: how tradition—what I have glossed as the persistence of the Sufi past in the present—enabled forms of life that transcended the state and the lurking presence of its security apparatus, not as artful forms of resistance, hidden transcripts (Scott

1990), or performative masks (Yurchak 2006) but as media for action. Tradition articulated both the state's presence and what it meant to be Sufi in its midst.

The agency expressive forms lent symbolically restructured Sufis' experiences of the present (Jackson 2013, 35). It reconfigured the possibilities of action and changed the premises on which Tajik Muslim histories turned (Barad 2007, 214; Whitesel and Shuman 2016, 38). In moving in and out of the sedimentations of time, narrating asynchronies, and inhabiting multiple temporalities within the reflexive spaces of performance, Sufis ultimately transcended the times around them. This is the intervention *Expressions of Sufi Culture in Tajikistan* makes to folkloristic discussions about the relationship between expressive culture and politics. It was Sufis' expressive connections to past personages, situations, and worlds that gave them agency over the lurking presence of the state and its homogenizing narratives, enabling Sufis to deal with the exigencies of life in contemporary Tajikistan. Tradition provided agency's grammar.

PLAN OF THE BOOK

In chapter 1, we meet Muhammad Ali, a Sufi teahouse owner, and Ibrohim, an ex-Sufi academic, in order to think through the contours of the recent Sufi past. For both Ali and Ibrohim, the past worked as a potent communicative resource ever ready to judge the authenticity of the Sufi present. The chapter introduces the histories most resonant to men like them and the metrics of Sufi authenticity they saw as most valid—lineage, miraculous power, and mystical knowledge—through a discussion about some of the pirs they revered. Finally, Ali and Ibrohim's histories and notions of authenticity didn't exist in a vacuum. As such, the chapter also touches on how the political environment has inextricably shaped both.

Chapters 2 and 3 build on the temporal and political maps of the first chapter by focusing on the specific ways that Sufis talked about the past. Twenty-first-century Sufis face a paradox. All around them, they hear about their alleged freedoms. They supposedly live in a time of revival, a time when Islam has reentered the public sphere. Instead, they have experienced repression and declining numbers. Chapter 2 discusses the nostalgic memories of men like Firuz, an increasingly pious unemployed musician, disgusted over the relative paucity of devotion around him, and Khurshed, a businessman, who looked back longingly at the piety of his ancestors. The asynchronies of Firuz and Khurshed's nostalgia strategically bridged the paradoxes of their lives, even to the extent that for them nostalgia became a core feature of what it meant to be Muslim.

Chapter 3 begins with a story Firuz told me about a cat. Firuz's story and others like it were the primary expressive forms that Sufi nostalgia often took. Like memories, stories traversed the ruptures inherent to the contemporary moment. Firuz and his friends drew on resources from the Central Asian narrative tradition to lionize new saints and make nearer, atheistic pasts sacred. They manipulated the tools that genre and intertextuality provided to move through these distinct times. Their stories, which I term historical narratives, were affective histories that variously asserted visions of continuity and discontinuity and worked as persuasive counternarratives to the temporal ideologies expressed by the Tajik governing elite.

In chapter 4, we visit a shrine with Shavkat, a middle-aged bureaucrat struggling to make sense of the social changes occurring around him and his distrust of the government he served. Shavkat and I browsed the books for sale at the shrine day market and displayed inside the shrine. The focus of chapter 4 is these books, the texts Sufis read and write. Like narratives before, the books—poetry collections, hagiographies, prayer manuals, government-sanctioned religious histories, touristic shrine literature, and more—bridged asynchronous time. Chapter 4 demonstrates how Sufi books work as material communication. At the shrine, Sufi memory existed in tangible form, materializing all of its paradoxes. For Shavkat and others, books even materialized sainthood itself and carried with them special traces of saintly power.

Chapters 5 and 6 move into the intimate contexts of the Sufi lodge and build on the discussions of nostalgic memories, historical narratives, and books. Within the Sufi lodge, ritual performances and embodied behaviors like pious comportment and dress ultimately allowed for temporal transcendence—the creation of new Sufi times. Chapter 5 explores rituals like the one with which the book began. In ritual, the past came alive for many of the men with whom I worked. Ritual offered a reflexive space for change as pirs from the sacred past spoke directly into the men's present.

The final chapter opens on a mountainside not far from Dushanbe, where Sufis worked to construct the foundations of a mosque. It discusses the men's embodied nostalgias and anachronisms—their dress, manners of comportment, and quietist concerns, which were all so out of step with the rest of Tajik society. In earlier chapters, Sufis expressed visions of the sacred past in story, disseminated it through books, or invoked it within the bounds of ritual. In chapter 6, they cultivate an ethical life through participating in group teaching events. They embody memory as they learn how to be Sufi.

chapter 1

Sufis in Tajikistan

"How did you become a Sufi (*ahli tasavvuf*)?" I asked Muhammad Ali during one of our first visits together. We had been lounging all morning on cushions and chatting over plates of grilled meat and glasses of green tea. I knew Ali from a teaching circle I had visited several times before in his village. Ali and several of his close relatives ran an open-air teahouse adjacent to a busy district road. He was a practical man. He devotedly met with his pir, but he more frequently talked about the price of food or the harassment of the local police. He was the kind of man who took the Naqshbandi dictum to live in the world to heart, and our conversation reflected that. Between serving customers and tending skewered meat on the grill, we spoke about the economic hardships of village life, labor migration to Russia, and recent contacts between pirs and government officials.

"I've been a Sufi (*tariqati*) for about three years," he answered, looking away as if he were counting the years in his head. "I'd been reciting my daily prayers for years before that," he continued. "I'm the only one of my brothers in the teaching circle (*halqa*). Their hearts haven't yet accepted it."

"Why do you think you did?" I said.

"Well, the *shariat* helps you know God, but the Sufi way (*tasavvuf*) helps you know God better.[1] You get to save the Lord's light," he paused to turn several skewers of meat hanging above bright orange coals.

As if to sum up the distinction he was trying to make, he said:

"It's like this. One day, Iskandar was traveling with his cook, Luqmani Hakim. A healer (*tabib*) approached Luqmani Hakim with a special ingredient to

19

bake inside Iskandar's bread, so that Iskandar might become a Sufi pir. Luqmani Hakim agreed and began to bake the bread. Each time he attempted
to put the piece of bread on the side of the oven to bake, it fell off into
the dirt. Luqmani Hakim eventually gave up trying to make the bread with
the healer's special ingredient and instead made a fresh loaf for Iskandar.
Later in the day, Luqmani Hakim ate the leftovers from Iskandar's meal for
his own dinner along with the dirt-covered bread. All at once, Luqmani
Hakim's eyes were opened. Secrets were revealed. He was able to talk to
plants and animals. He gained healing powers. He became a Sufi pir. All
these wonders happened to the humble cook, Luqmani Hakim, rather
than to the healer's intended recipient, the world-conquering Iskandar.[2]

This chapter engages the same question as Ali's story: who in Tajikistan has tasted the gnosis the mystical loaf provides, in both the present
and the past. Of course, the two go hand in hand. The Sufis with whom
I interacted provided less a recounting of the past as they foregrounded
socially productive interpretations of their presents. Ali's story also
touched on another important aspect of Sufi life in the republic. The
political environment has inextricably shaped it. Sufi histories exist in
dialogue with the almost hegemonic force of state-sponsored narratives
concerning Muslim life. While men like Ali had already submitted to the
guidance of Sufi pirs and eaten metaphorically from the ashen loaf,
members of the governing elite remain, like Iskandar, outside mystical
wisdom's embrace, many openly hostile to forms of public religiosity
that exist outside their direct control.

HISTORIES OF TAJIK SUFISM

"The Sufism (Sufizm) you've read about in books isn't in Tajikistan,"
Ibrohim said. A respected Soviet-trained scholar of medieval Muslim
history, Ibrohim served as one of my frequent interlocutors in Tajikistan.
We often talked together about the historical nuances of contemporary
Muslim life. Despite his Soviet-inflected predilection for interpreting
Muslim life in classist terms, he was an astute observer of the relationships between Central Asian history and contemporary political life. He
was proudly unobservant himself, but he still celebrated the magnitude
of Muslim history or, as he put it, the "civilizational" achievements of
Timurid Central Asia. Looking back to the glories of the Central Asian
past, the present seemed to him to be but a mere shadow.

"This is what's going on in Tajikistan. The ones claiming to be pirs aren't really shaikhs. I used to have an interest in mysticism. When I was younger, I would go to pirs, kiss their hands, act all respectful. I can't do those things anymore. There's no Sufism here."

Ibrohim's Sufism was that of the Sufi lodges of Transoxania and Khurusan not long after the early Naqshbandiya spread their message throughout the cosmopolitan trading centers of Bukhara, Samarkand, and Herat and beyond to the greater Middle East and South Asia. It was a time in which Sufis enjoyed political patronage. Sufi scholars and rulers commanded respect from across the early modern Muslim world. Scions of important families apprenticed themselves to shaikhs, and pirs exerted vast economic influence in the form of pious endowments. In the Timurid court, mystical poets such as Jomi (1414–92) wrote some of the most widely acclaimed works of Persian literature.

Ibrohim wasn't wrong. The pirs Ibrohim knew personally didn't look like those he read about in his history books. For Ibrohim the flowering of the Muslim scholarship and literary output he respected so much was only preserved in fading manuscripts, stored on the dusty archive shelves, among which he had worked in the Oriental studies institutes in Dushanbe and Tashkent and the library in Saint Petersburg, where he had completed his doctoral work. Undeniably, contemporary practice might not compare to Sufi life in late medieval and early modern Central Asia. Even if the temporal axis were rendered drastically shorter, to the reigns of the last emirs of Bukhara, the pre-Soviet rulers of much of the territory now encompassing present-day Tajikistan, Ibrohim still might justifiably ponder the seeming incommensurability of living pirs with the mystical prowess of their forebears.

Ibrohim was by no means alone in his bleak assessments of Tajikistan's twenty-first-century mystics; I found his ideas echoed at almost every turn, especially by urban interlocutors unacquainted with the particulars of religious life outside of their social spheres. Each time I met an imom, a local political figure, or a foreign diplomat and described the focus of my research, I heard similar sweeping declarations: "There aren't any Sufis here. There may have been once, but not anymore"; "There's no Sufism in Rasht [or, alternatively, Faizobod, Khatlon, Panjakent, etc.]"; "The Sufis today aren't real Sufis"; "All of the pirs were killed"; or "There aren't any saints in Tajikistan, but there are a lot of them in Afghanistan [or, Pakistan, Iran, India, etc.]." These observers, no doubt, had good intentions. Most based their comments on comparisons they could readily make with other parts of the Muslim world or, for some, their copious readings in world history. Whatever Sufism they knew from somewhere or sometime else was not what they saw evidenced on the streets in Tajikistan.

While I can understand why Ibrohim and others said what they did, their declarations that "There's no Sufism here" better highlighted the contours of their own historical imaginations than they did the nature of present-day devotion for many of Tajikistan's Sufis. At the same time, many of the Sufis I met still expressed history-inflected anxieties, perhaps not so differently than ex-Sufi, Soviet-trained historians. Sufis often wondered how the infelicities of their presents related to what had come before. Their worries, though about history, were less about the Central Asian sacred past than they were about accounting for what they were experiencing today in twenty-first-century Tajikistan. Ibrohim's "There's no Sufism here" sentiment captured the feeling of this seeming disjuncture, between perceptions of the religious present and the imagined past, and tellingly suggested the magnitude of sociopolitical change many Muslims have experienced since the fall of the Soviet Union and the reintroduction of Islam onto the public stage.

As many Sufis were quick to note, for a time after Tajikistan's independence and the end to its bloody civil war, public religiosity seemed to proliferate: new mosques were constructed, or at least unregistered Soviet era congregations were allowed to serve worshippers openly for the first time; novel forms of pious dress were adopted; and previously proscribed religious literature saw publication. Many standard scholarly and journalistic treatments of Islam in Central Asia published in recent decades have invoked a revivalist trope to discuss the nature of public Islam after the end of the Soviet experience. Revivalism is predicated on the notion that Muslim life during the Soviet period was stifled and repressed and that what Islam remained after the ferocity of the Soviet assault was marginal or merely a curious holdover of backward-looking Central Asians (DeWeese 2011). In reality we now know that Soviet era Islam was much more complex. It is a truism to note that the Soviet experience for the Tajik SSR's Muslims was uneven, both temporally and geographically. Soviet strictures were applied haphazardly, and in different periods varying political imperatives brought with them waves of persecution and modulating periods of relative openness. Additionally, what occurred at the local level could at times be starkly different from what religious policy makers in Moscow envisioned.

Significantly, many Sufis I knew fought against a narrative of discontinuity between the present and the recent past. They stressed how facets of Muslim life continued almost unabated throughout the social upheavals of the Soviet period, despite state efforts at their elimination. Sufi teaching hierarchies persisted in transmitting mystical knowledge and performing ritual. Hagiography even celebrates covert state support for mystical initiation and religious patronage during the height of official antireligious campaigns (see Hokiroh 2010, 210–11). Some Cold War era Sovietologists went so far as to allege that Sufi groups served as strident bulwarks against militant atheism (see Bennigsen and Wimbush 1985). Others still imagined Sufis to be key repositories of "local or popular knowledge of Islam" in the face of Soviet era attacks (Shahrani 1991, 162–63).

At the same time, many Sufis bemoaned the fact that for others the scope and meanings of Islam dramatically changed as a result of shifting political currents. For some, this took the form of rendering Islam a marker of local identity vis-à-vis the weight of Soviet cultural hegemony (Khalid 2007, 82–83). Islam may have become more about local cultural heritage and customary tradition than wider, transnational channels of learned Muslim religiosity. For others, the spiritual significance of Islam might not have diminished, yet the opportunity for devotion decreased (Borbieva 2017, 159). Significantly, too, Muslimness and Sovietness did not exist as discrete categories (Sartori 2010; Abashin 2014). Self-identified Communists participated in Muslim life-cycle rites, prayed *namoz*, and surreptitiously recited the Qur'an. Their piety was not subterfuge, nor was their Communist identity a mask concealing hidden religious fervor (Rasanayagam 2011, 65–95). Rather, Soviet and Muslim existed together as complementary and interdependent frameworks for social action.

Soviet and Muslim

History was a common topic among the Sufis with whom I regularly interacted. Muhammad Ali and his friends told stories about past pirs whenever they got together. Pirs referenced episodes from Muslim history when they taught their disciples. Like Ibrohim, many Sufis relished talking about the golden age of Central Asian Sufism, but they invoked nearer pasts too. I frequently heard them talk about Sufi life in the late

nineteenth and early twentieth centuries and how life had changed between the present and the times of their childhoods, which went as far
back as the immediate postwar era. The history they didn't tell was the
trauma of the early Soviet decades: the 1920s to the 1940s.

Between 1926 and 1932, party authorities in Moscow orchestrated a
draconian, full-fledged assault on alleged "backwardness," the supposed
traditional practices of the inhabitants of their newly controlled territories in Central Asia (Keller 2001, 141–211). Such campaigns included
the *"hujm"*—the forcible deveiling of women—the closures of schools,
mosques, and Muslim courts; the arrests and executions of *ulamo* (religious scholars); the confiscation of pious endowments; and the forcible
collection and destruction of centuries-old religious manuscripts. Early
assaults on the institutional bases of Muslim life were wildly successful
in the sense that they often worked to sever the means of Islamic knowledge production (Khalid 2007, 81). For many Sufis, the practical effects
of such campaigns were silsilas rent asunder, lodges destroyed, and pirs
killed or ushered into forced-labor camps.

After quelling the partisan uprisings of the 1920s, government organs of
the nascent republic forcibly resettled thousands of mountain-dwelling
Tajiks to lowlands in the south, first to facilitate easier governance and
later as part of Soviet collectivization campaigns (Kassymbekova 2016,
55–65; Bleuer 2012, 76–77). The primary, yet not exclusive, impetus was
to relocate peasants living on nonproductive land in the mountain high-
lands to new farms in the warmer, lowland south to provide labor for
mechanized cotton monoculture. Additional waves of forced migration
occurred between 1947 and 1954, with the majority of migrants forcibly
resettled between 1949 and 1951 (Abdulḥaev 2009, 179–233).

The extent of social disruption is suggested in the fact that during the
1920s approximately 70 percent of the republic's population lived in
mountainous regions (Niyazi 2000), yet by the end of the Soviet period
the figure had been completely reversed, with 70 percent of the population of the Tajik SSR then living in cotton-growing lowlands. Demographic shifts dramatically impacted Sufi groups (Giehler 2014; Zevaco
2014). Local experiences were, of course, as diverse as the geographic
and historical conditions of each resulting collective farm, but in general
migration cut villagers' ties to pirs, created new rivalries among religious functionaries, and even expanded the geographic reach of other pirs

because after migration they could cultivate followers among both the new lowlanders and those that remained in the mountain valleys.

Apart from the decades-long lacuna of the 1920s and 1940s, Sufis often told me stories about their experiences during the postwar era. A number of key teaching circles that still wield influence date to the postwar period (e.g., Dudoignon and Qalandar 2014, 51–52, 100–101). By the 1950s, many murids no longer lived in the same villages as they had before. A generation of Sufis had died in Siberian prison camps or on the war's European fronts. Though remnants of the pre-Soviet religious elite had survived, most pirs of the 1950s were of a social station decidedly distinct from those of previous generations, and many Sufis instead traced their intellectual and genealogical pedigrees back to places, institutions, social relationships, and historical experiences different from those their spiritual predecessors might have claimed.

The mid-1970s marked another important watershed in the memories of the men with whom I interacted. This is when many of them began to assume positions of prominence among both accredited and nonaccredited religious personnel. Younger Sufis often looked back nostalgically on this era, imagining it as another golden age in which sociality and teaching flourished relatively unhindered by state interference.[3] I frequently heard Sufis talk about ritual performances, the circulation of religious literature, and the easy movement of disciples between pirs during the 1970s and 1980s. During this period, several key ideological shifts occurred. For one, many of the so-called young mullahs of the postwar generation began to propagate various competing strains of reformist views against forms of traditional Tajik religiosity (Mullojonov 2001, 226–29). Individual responses to new ideological perspectives were diverse, even as Soviet-inspired polemics conflated distinct theological imperatives as homogeneously "Wahhabist" in origin (Babadjanov and Kamilov 2001). For some factions of Tajik ulamo, the politicization of Islam enjoined them to work for political change, which would eventually, at the dawn of the independence era in 1991, lead to an Islamist coalition led by Saiid Abdullohi Nuri (1947–2006), one such acolyte of the reformist school, who would serve as the chair of the Movement for the Islamic Revival of Tajikistan (MIRT) and the United Tajik Opposition (UTO) against regional factions led by the current president, Emomali Rahmon (Heathershaw 2009, 27–30).

Both during and after the Soviet period, Sufi groups and the ulamo were not altogether distinct categories; both camps overlapped and were interdependent (Dudoignon 2011). Disciples moved between pirs and members of both the official and unofficial ulamo. Muhammadjoni Hindustoni (1892–1989), perhaps the most widely known representative of the ulamo in the Tajik SSR, and Eshoni Abdurahmonjon (1920–91),[4] the most important Soviet era Naqshbandi pir in the republic, shared networks of disciples (Hokiroĥ 2010, 218–19; Dudoignon 2011, 67–68). Even the small teaching circles (ĥujra, maĥfil, and ĥalqa) that proliferated among the young mullahs during the final Soviet decades were reminiscent of Sufi teaching lineages and used Sufi pedagogical models for teaching ethical poetry and comportment.

Many Sufis did operate outside the bounds of state-sanctioned religious networks, but Soviet era Sufism was not limited to the so-called "unofficial," "unregistered," or "folk" channels of Soviet era religiosity.[5] As the example of Hoji Akbar Turajonzoda (1954–), the last Soviet era head Islamic official of the republic and the son of an important Sufi family, illustrates, Sufi lineages were entwined with the bases of official Soviet era Islam and Sufi interactions with the political sphere did not end with the fall of the Soviet Union. Figures instrumental in the Islamist opposition during the civil war also cultivated relationships with Sufi lineages. Many UTO members were disciples of the Naqshbandi pir, Domla Hikmatollo Tojikobodi (1929–). Even, the first supreme mufti of independent Tajikistan, Hoji Fathullokhon Sharifzoda (1941–96), appointed not long after Rahmon began to assume power, was the son of a popular Sufi pir (Mullojonov 2001, 246).

Declarations that "There's no Sufism here" only make sense depending on which period becomes the basis for comparison. As my friends were quick to point out, by no means has Sufism been marginal to the Soviet and post-Soviet religious experience. Many Sufis argued that teaching circles don't now enjoy the same relative freedoms they did during the late Brezhnev era. However, Ibrohim's "There's no Sufism here" underscores particular histories and precludes others. If notions about the Sufi past suggest more about contemporary historical imagination than fantasies of historical objectivity, then invoking a revivalist trope similarly works as a potent rhetorical gambit. *Revival* is synonymous with *return*, yet many Sufi practices are not returns. Most Sufi accounts of Soviet era religious history vehemently reject discourses of revivalism and instead stress that the Sufi present shares much longer historical genealogies and strict continuities with earlier periods. In the place of revivalism, Tajikistan's Sufis engage a much more potent discourse related to authenticity. For many devotees, it is more important to determine who are the real Sufis, the ones who have tasted of Iskandar's mystical loaf, than to debate historical particulars.

REAL SUFIS

The pir's house sat on a narrow dirt lane framed by tall mud walls and uncultivated fields. The inside was a sparse affair—a large guest room, empty save cushions stacked along the walls and a coatrack on which several robes and a green, pointed prayer cap rested. In a much smaller room next to the larger one, the bearded pir sat cross-legged on the floor behind a small table. Compared to the larger, empty room, the smaller room was a sensory emporium. The scent of perfume wafted through the open door. Each wall had been decorated with glossy posters: a scene of an idyllic Alpine glade, a tropical waterfall, a deep red rose with a name of God on each petal, and a nighttime photograph of Mecca's Great Mosque. Behind the pir, an anatomical diagram and a poster cluttered with Persian text hung on the wall.

After a few perfunctory greetings, the pir didn't waste any time. "What are you doing? Why are you here?" he said.

"I've ccc ... come to learn about Sufism (tasavvuf) in Tajikistan," I replied. The pir radiated authority, which took me by surprise and made me stumble over my Tajik.

"You can learn about Sufism in books," he countered. "Where did you learn Tajik?"

"In Afghanistan. I was there three years."

"You were there three years and you still don't know Tajik?" the pir said, not attempting to hide his incredulity. The pir's tone jarred my concentration. I had only arrived in Tajikistan several weeks earlier, and this was the first opportunity I had had for an extended interview since I started my research. Still trying to get my cultural bearings, I had prepared a detailed interview guide and brushed up on relevant vocabulary, rehearsing potential lines of questioning in the best Tajiki Persian I could muster. In the moment, my good-intentioned preparations provided no remedy for my unfamiliarity with the intricacies of Sufi comportment.

"Yes, I was there three years and met many Sufis."

"What do you want to know?" he said.

Intimidated by the pir's unexpectedly terse interrogation, I ignored the list of prepared questions on the notepad in front of me. "What is Sufism?" I said, immediately regretting that I had asked. It struck me at once as naive and a waste of time.

"When the Prophet, peace be upon him, was in Medina, Salmoni Forsi was in the house,"[6] the pir said. It was almost as if the simplicity of my question had eased his mind about the purpose of my visit. "One night, Salmoni Forsi was sitting with others and reciting," the pir continued. "The Prophet, peace be upon him, asked, 'What are you doing?' 'I'm reciting zikr,' Salmoni Forsi said. 'Start reciting again because I saw grace falling on you,' the Prophet told him." The pir paused. "Salmoni Forsi said that if a man passes a night freeing slaves and another passes it in zikr, the second one will be better."

Perhaps sensing my confusion over his cryptic answer, the pir continued. "In any crowd, only a few will have pure intentions, will be real, the rest not. Because of the reality of the few, God accepts the actions of them all. That's the way it is with zikr," he said, returning to his anecdote about Salmoni Forsi and the basic ritual practice of Sufism, zikr—the ritualized recitation of the name of God. "The Naqshbandi practice silent zikr. That has merit, but congregational zikr draws people in.[7] Only some are truly intoxicated by zikr. The rest are doing it from their animal spirit," he said, pointing at the anatomical diagram above his head.[8] Then, gesturing at the other poster behind him, which was filled with Persian text almost too small to read, he said, "It's the same way with Ghavs al-Azam." The pir finished by echoing a refrain I would hear from many of my Sufi collaborators: "Unless you come in, it all seems like foolishness. Enter, pray your daily prayers, and you'll understand it. Your questions can't be answered from the outside."

The pir deftly used my misplaced question to highlight what distinguishes Sufis from the mass of Muslims: knowledge and ritual. He didn't stop there. Sufism was not simply a matter of voicing notional precepts or performing rituals. Only those with "pure intention" were real Sufis. Notably, the pir did not stress the relative importance of initiations into specific global teaching hierarchies or Sufi paths (tariqat), the predominant way scholars of Islam often differentiate between streams of Sufi practice. Historically, the vast majority of Sufis who lived within the territory of modern-day Tajikistan have subscribed to one of two paths, the Naqshbandiya or the Qodiriya. In the areas surrounding the Tajik capital, most pirs self-identify as Naqshbandi, while only a minority expresses exclusive initiations into the Qodiriya. The pir offered a bricolage of both. The anatomical diagram hanging on the wall came from the Mujaddidi tradition of the Naqshbandiya, whereas the story recounted on the cluttered poster came from the life of Ghavs al-Azam, an honorific for Abdulqodiri Jeloni (1077–1166), the eponymous founder of the Qodiriya. Most of the men I met spent little time parsing the distinctions between paths. They performed rituals from both and devoured teaching rubrics that conflated different teachings and histories. More frequently, the men proffered informal claims to group membership predicated on discrete circles of knowledge transmission, irrespective of their identifications with any specific transnational teaching hierarchy.[9]

Ibrohim's "There's no Sufism" notwithstanding, many of these men remained hidden in plain sight. Admittedly, Ibrohim suggested as much. Twenty-first-century Dushanbe might not stand as a ready analogue for Timurid Bukhara, yet thousands of Sufis pray, teach, and study across the city and in towns and villages in central Tajikistan. At the same time, the diversity of Tajik Sufism belies simple characterization as Sufis mark their authenticity through multiple and contrasting means. Some emphasize genealogical descent and their connections to historical figures from the Central Asian sacred past. Others stress the importance of miraculous acts and forms of pious comportment. Some Sufis rest their sole conviction on the varieties of mystical knowledge a pir possesses. Across these indexes of realness, pirs and their followers include adherents to new streams of religiosity, as well as those who share strict theological continuities with earlier epochs; pirs with both Islamist sympathies and those who enforce strict quietism among their adepts; and finally those who cultivate varying degrees of interaction with state-sponsored Muslim institutions and Tajik social life. The problem arises in determining who is truly intoxicated, to put it in the pir's terms, by what metric to judge the real.

LINEAGE

"God told me to become Sufi (*tariqatī*), comport myself, and do zikr," the man said.

"Did God tell you directly?" I asked him in clarification.

"No, of course not. The pir did. God acknowledges the pir. He doesn't acknowledge me because of my great sin. The pir told his assistant, who told me. I heard it from God by means of a chain, through the silsila."

The silsila, the chain of mystical transmission between master and disciple, proves to be among the most robust of Sufi claims to authenticity. As Ibrohim described silsila, "The shaikhs of Tajikistan can be divided into four groups: the *saiids*, *turas*, *makhdums*, and *khojas*." He said, "Eshon is just a term of respect for saiids. Saiids are the descendants of the Prophet, of the people of his household.[10] The khojas are people who have married into the line of the eshon. Tura is the same term for eshon but in Turkish, normally from the north of the country. Makhdums are people who have gained knowledge from the descendants of saiids, the knowledge of zikr, religion (*din*), jurisprudence (*fiqeh*), [have] received teaching authorizations, [and] have proceeded along the mystical path."[11]

Ibrohim's lengthy catalog of honorifics centered on genealogy. By Ibrohim's standard, what was important in marking the real was descent.[12] Along with chains of mystical transmission, Ibrohim's genealogy (*shajara*) legitimates claims to a wider mystical tradition, most often verified materially through written teaching authorizations (*khati irshod*), individuals received from their masters, and genealogical tables (*shajaranoma*), which verified their links by blood to spiritual forebears. This is the case with perhaps the best-known Sufis in Tajikistan, the Turajonzoda brothers, popularly known as Eshoni Nuriddin (1953–), Hoji Akbar (1954–), and Eshoni Mahmudjon (1960–). Turajon père, Eshoni Turajon (1934–2005), or, to comply with Ibrohim's terminological precision, Makhdumi Turajon, was an influential member of the Soviet era official ulamo and a Qodiri pir (Rahnamo 2009, 121–25).[13]

Nuriddin, heir and recipient of Eshoni Turajon's teaching mantle in the Qodiriya, succeeded his father and meets regularly with groups of village men, teaching ethical poetry and presiding over group ritual. However, the Turajon family's notoriety does not derive exclusively from its mystical initiations but rather because Nuriddin's younger brother, Akbar, served from 1988 to 1993 as head of the Qoziyot, the Muslim Spiritual Board of the Tajik SSR, the official body charged with supervising Muslim life in the republic, and later served as vice prime minister of independent Tajikistan. In a village several kilometers beyond the district center of Vahdat, not far from Dushanbe, the brothers served as patrons of a large mosque in which they hosted as many as ten thousand congregants for Friday prayers until the High Council of Ulamo (Shuroi olii ulamoi Tojikiston) moved against their influence and took away the mosque's congregational status (Nozimova and Epkenhans 2013). Their significant business interests as cotton producers and wheat import-ers—a concession given to the family as a result of the peace deal at the end of the civil war—also likely make theirs one of the richest families in the republic outside the president's clique (Epkenhans 2011). The reli-gious bureaucracy has marginalized the family since at least 2010, re-moving Hoji Akbar from office, taking away the brothers' leadership of the mosque, and possibly even setting fire to their cotton processing operations.

Not all Sufis who substantiate their place via lineage and descent remain as central to the country's social and political life. Another pir, the grandson of a widely respected pre-Soviet Naqshbandi shaikh who lived in the mountains of Rasht, northeast of the present-day Tajik capi-tal, still lives humbly in his family's mountain hamlet, far off the pro-visional road to Gharm. The saiid, to again use Ibrohim's taxonomic specificity, spends the majority of his time supervising a small madrasa. Local villagers send their young boys to him to learn the rudiments of Qur'anic recitation and the basic principles of mysticism. Women, vil-lagers, and others come to him seeking healing and intercession for their physical ills and spiritual remedies for the hardships of rural, village life. Despite the fact that the pir boasts exemplary genealogical bona fides and pristine silsila, he remains happily marginal to the wider sociopo-litical life of the republic.

Miracles and Comportment

"Do you know Shaikh Dovud?" I asked a few disciples of the Afghan pir, Khoja Abdulvakil Bahodir (d. 2015) one afternoon in their apartment in Dushanbe's western suburbs. It was a question I asked often because it invited my conversation partners to stress what distinguished their group from others.

"Dovud's disciples should be ashamed," one man replied. Another man added:

One of Dovud's descendants was sitting right here in this very room. He was saying how the pir was just doing sorcery and how our zikr was wrong.

There's a rule of the path that if you find a more powerful pir, you should go and give your oath of allegiance to him. Many of Dovud's disciples have come to Hazrati Pir and asked for a teaching authorization.[14] Hazrati Pir tells them they need to go to Afghanistan and serve for three months.[15] Many have come for that. Hazrati Pir tells them they need to follow the path in Afghanistan. Hazrati Pir does thirty or forty miracles a day.

In addition to lineage and descent, Sufis also judge pirs' authenticity by their miraculous behavior and exemplary piety. "I've seen miracles with my own eyes," one man told me. "I had a kidney stone once, and the shaikh touched me and pulled it out. Another time the shaikh switched the beards of two men. Another time the shaikh took water in his hand, blew on it, and turned it into medicine for a disciple." For Bahodir's Tajik followers the mystical project centers on miracles (karomot), saintly power (viloĭat), and spiritual grace (faĭz). By apprenticing oneself to Bahodir and his Tajik representatives, his followers hope to partake of his power.

Bahodir only cultivated Tajik disciples after the fall of the Soviet Union and the end of the civil war, yet his novelty did not concern most of the followers I met. "There was a prophecy during Soviet times that tariqat were going to come from Afghanistan," one man told me. "That is, they're going to come from Afghanistan. From Afghanistan, the path will reach its zenith."

In contrast to Bahodir's miracles, complete trust in God, or tavakkal, underlies the actions of the disciples of Eshoni Temur Khoja's, a Naqshbandi pir of Dahbedi Samarkand descent.[16] The total task of Temur's adepts at his home on a mountaintop west of the Tajik capital was to put off worldly entrapments in favor of cultivating love for the divine. They regarded the world as ritually unclean and embraced asceticism. Many of them eschewed employment and familial attachments. In one disciple's words, this entailed "Sleeping little at night, eating little, drinking little, talking little, reciting prayers often, doing zikr often." The disciples' comportment and ritual diligence indexed their inner spiritual attitudes. For them, real Sufis deny their earthly appetites and exclusively focus on ritual observance. Like the Turajonzodas, Temur has not escaped the attention of the governing elite. In early 2015, he was arrested and tried for polygyny and theft. He now sits in prison, his disciples scattered.[17]

MYSTICAL KNOWLEDGE

"A few months back, I was out toward Yovon," Ibrohim said to me on the same day as his "There's no Sufism here" pronouncement.

> I went to the Makhdum's teaching circle. I had come from the office, so I wasn't wearing a robe or prayer cap or anything. I sat down near the door. The room was filled with important folks, people from the government. They were all sitting there completely quiet, bowing, with their hands all folded. I eventually asked somebody for some tea, but it took a long time for him to bring me any. Finally, after some of the white beards had finished eating upstairs, they brought down some food. The pir started blowing all over it, and some of the old guys up front took it and put it in their pockets to take home. There was hardly any food left. That's the problem with the pirs. There's no real knowledge, no real mysticism.

Judgments like Ibrohim's mark the real not through lines of descent, miracles, or comportment but rather through mystical knowledge. In this frame, Bahodir's miracles are merely sorcery and Temur's comportment a mask hiding his ignorance of Muslim textual tradition. One day I told a prominent Dushanbe-based imom about a village pir I had met the previous week. The imom said, "I don't know who he is. He probably just spent a few weeks at a Sufi lodge in Afghanistan. There are a lot of them in northern Afghanistan. Then he came back and started doing the same thing here. Real Sufis have mantles invested by their pirs." The cleric echoed Ibrohim's suggestion about the pir near Yovon. Both Ibrohim and the cleric argued that Sufism is not primarily about miracles or pious comportment but intellectual experience.

Many Sufis living in and around the Tajik capital claim Sufi initiation through the most prominent Soviet era Tajik Naqshbandi pir, Eshoni Abdurahmonjoni Porsokhoja. Abdurahmonjon lived quietly in the Faizobod region, an hour or so drive northeast of Dushanbe, where he presided over a small circle of disciples, many of whom went on to occupy positions of prominence in the Tajik SSR and independent Tajikistan's religious field. Virtually all the Sufis with whom I regularly met claimed some kind of relationship with him and his teaching legacy. One of these men, the author of a popular book on the history of Islam in Central Asia, met me at his office in Dushanbe. An acquaintance at the Academy of Sciences had recommended him to me as someone who could facilitate introductions to various pirs around the city.

"I've been a Naqshbandi for twenty-seven years," he said after hearing about my work. His voice exuded pride. "I know many shaikhs," he added.

"Who is your pir?"

"My pir is dead," he said. "I was the disciple of Eshoni Abdurahmonjon. There's no one left as powerful as he was. I won't give my oath to another." The man was Sufi but had no pir. Like many of Abdurahmonjon's living disciples, the man practiced a kind of Sufism without a living group. His Sufism came from the knowledge he had received in the past from Abdurahmonjon.

One afternoon I was walking along a dusty road to catch a bus back into the city. I had spent most of the day with a village pir. I stepped into a dry goods store along the main road to ask the shopkeeper where I should wait for the bus. "What were you doing up there in the village?" the man said.

"I came to make pilgrimage to the eshon," I said. "Who normally goes to see him?"

"Some are really murids, they're practitioners (*vazifador*). Others just come for pilgrimage," he said.

As the man noted, some men merely interact with pirs on pilgrimage, seeking intercession and blessing. Others become practitioners, apprenticing themselves and submitting to complex teaching rubrics, ritual observance, and the intricate rules of comportment that follow. Still others limit their Sufism to the past, notionally affirming the importance of the Sufi way while shunning contemporary observance. Another man told me, "Ben, there are two laws of the tariqat: talk about the tariqat and do zikr. Those that do that are real." By his standard, it was common idioms and rituals that bound these diverse groups of men together.

Idioms and rituals do not exist in a vacuum. It was rare to pass time with Sufis when constraints on their open practice didn't enter our conversation. To describe the Sufi path in Tajikistan, one has to consider the role of the state in its articulation. The contemporary political environment has inextricably shaped Muslim life in the republic. Just as Sufis contest the authenticity of pirs, the governing elite tellingly attempts to offer their vision of authentic Islam, cloaked with tacit respect for the same grand Central Asian past that so captivated Ibrohim.

SUFISM AND THE STATE

During 2010–11, a billboard towered over the main east-west and north-south axes of Dushanbe, which featured the Tajik president meeting with a number of white-bearded men (figure 2). Its caption read, "Don't go without the protection of a pir," the first half line of a well-known verse of folk poetry. The billboard did not include the second half line, "Because each one [of them] is the Alexander of the age."[18] The billboard ostensibly suggested that even the president of Tajikistan submits to the guidance of his elders. For Sufis the billboard also held an unmistakable religious resonance: Rahmon seeks the advice of imoms, eshons, and pirs because such figures are the Alexanders of the age. The billboard's sentiment could not be farther from the truth. Rahmon does not seek insight, mystical or not, from the republic's religious establishment.

Like the billboard, the president's speeches, publications of the religious bureaucracy, specials aired on state television, and newspaper articles reference and celebrate Sufi figures, yet their visions of sacred

Figure 2. Billboard on a Dushanbe Street (photograph by the author)

history and devotion contrast sharply with the living activities of Tajikistan's Muslims. The difference becomes especially acute at shrines.[19]
Long a feature of Central Asian Muslim life, shrines exist as sites of
blessing where individuals come to fulfill religious vows, gain remedy for
both physical and spiritual ills, and benefit from the spiritual power of
the figures honored there. Shrines map Tajikistan's spiritual geography,
linking the local to larger Muslim histories and bridging the past and
present (Gross 2013; Louw 2007, 16).

Shrine days are raucous affairs. Bazaars often envelop sacred sites.
Shopkeepers tend overladen carts teeming with dried boughs of wild
rue to be burned or jugs of water and freshly baked bread to be blessed.
Booksellers sell prayer manuals, dream interpretation guides, and prayer
beads. Outside the shrine wall, the chronically infirm sit in wheelchairs
or hunch over wooden crutches. Impoverished widows wearing frayed
shawls hold out their hands in eager anticipation of pilgrims' charity.
Inside, extended families, children in tow, wait patiently for their turn
before an imom. The hopeful place items on the altar and stand sol-
emnly as the imom raises his palms in supplication, offering a prayer of
blessing for fertility, to cure an illness, or for financial success as a labor
migrant in Russia.

Shrine days in Kulob, a southern city contiguous to the region of
Rahmon's birth and the center of his early political support, most of the
time were different. Kulob city boasts the grave of Hazrati Amirjon (figure 3), better known to Muslim history as Mir Saiid Alii Hamadoni
(1314–84). Celebrated for his missions to convert Kashmir to Islam, he
traveled widely in Central and South Asia, eventually setting up a lodge
in Kottalan, present-day Kulob. Hamadoni, himself an initiate and pir in
the Kubraviya path, figures prominently in the silsila of Central Asian
Naqshbandi Sufis. I heard from many in Kulob how the shrine's efficacy
comes from Hamadoni's sagacious wisdom and the power that emanates
from his grave. Hamadoni's brother-in-law's burial place outside Kulob
on the road to Danghara similarly evokes strong feelings of reverence
in many of Tajikistan's Muslims. As a figure of transnational historical
importance, Hamadoni's face and an etching of his shrine even grace
Tajikistan's ten-somoni banknote.

On a winter shrine day, I traveled to Kulob while snow flurried. The
shrine's grounds were empty that crisp morning save for several salaried
caretakers in the employ of the Ministry of Culture. No rue was for sale.

Figure 3. Hamadoni's shrine (photograph by the author)

No beggars stood at the gates in anticipation of pilgrims' charity. No religious literature was available for purchase, stacked neatly on wooden carts. A photographer stood nearby, ready to take any willing pilgrim's souvenir picture, a banknote in his hand to use as a prop. I sat on a bench perpendicular to the mausoleum's entrance on a wide terrace covered with interlocked, geometric paver stones. A family—two women, two men, and two small children—walked past, removed their shoes, and entered the sepulcher. Raising their palms, one man silently mouthed a prayer. Over the course of the morning and early afternoon, only a few additional pilgrims arrived and repeated the actions of the family before them.

"Can I take your photograph?" the photographer said. He approached me holding his camera and mimed taking a photograph.

"Where is the rue?"

"They don't allow it," he said.

"Who doesn't?"

"The Ministry of Culture," he answered, already walking back to the main road to wait for potential customers.

The Spartan shrine grounds, obviously tended with great care, included several archaeological excavations, a medieval kiln for baking

clay pottery, and placards highlighting their significance. The grounds
also contained a small, four-room museum, one room highlighting the
recent restoration of the shrine and the construction of the archaeological park on the occasion of the 68oth anniversary of Hamadoni's birth
(1994), only completed recently with the financial support of the Iranian
government. Another room displayed the saint's written works and secondary literature about him published in Iran and Pakistan. The third
room included poster-sized descriptions of the lives of local figures of
historical importance, poets, and others. The president's smiling visage
greeted visitors to the final room with a framed quote underneath (figure 4): "Mir Saiid Alii Hamadoni is without a doubt among those famous
figures in Tajikistan, Pakistan, India, Iran, Afghanistan, Uzbekistan, and
Arab countries whose fame and popularity evoke positive feelings."

Hamadoni's shrine has an almost antiseptic feel, a religious site wiped
clean of piety, offering visitors a vision of Muslim history without living Muslims, Sufi heritage without Sufis, and a celebration of the Muslim past without active veneration. That is the vision of Sufi history that

Figure 4. Rahmon's quote at Hamadoni's shrine (photograph by the author)

governing elites put forward. Like the billboard on Dushanbe's streets, the shrine's rhetoric appropriates the religious heritage of Central Asian Sufism but oriented away from the referents of its symbols. Of course, a shrine as a tourist trap is not unique to Tajikistan, nor does it inherently represent the curtailing of religious expression.[20] Yet still, Hamadoni's shrine works as a carefully curated artifact of historical Sufism, of which organs of the Tajik state act as conservator. Sufism at the shrine exists only as cultural heritage, a historical legacy, and something to be parceled off to a museum visit and experienced later through souvenir kitsch, a photo of a smiling would-be pilgrim holding a ten-somoni note, whereas the Ministry of Culture almost completely proscribes the activities that would ordinarily exist on shrine day, for example, bringing wild rue and water for blessing, reciting the Qur'an, or seeking the saint's intercession.

The rhetoric of the billboard and at Hamadoni's shrine adopts Sufi idioms and imagery without any treatment of the signs' contingent meanings for living practitioners. Tellingly, Rahmon's vacuous quote, displayed prominently in the museum, offers a tepid recognition of Hamadoni's fame and historical influence on the people of Central and South Asia while simultaneously obscuring the theological precepts and saintly power that animates visits to his shrine. In this regard, Rahmon has perpetuated Soviet era legacies of the co-optation of religious sites (Louw 2007, 57; Saroyan 1997, 69). Rahmon's state operates on the same symbolic level, often with symbolism "spectacular" in scale (Adams 2010). Elites use billboards, political speeches, museum exhibits, parades, and even celebrations on the occasion of the six-hundred and eightieth anniversary of a saint's birth as vital ways to communicate with their citizenry and legitimate their conceptions of Muslim history.

Governing elites can only assert continuity between history and their domestic religious policies by suggesting the ways in which other temporal continuities remain troublesome. As such, official rhetoric isolates Sufis and ambivalently renders them as heritage. Heritage marks them as obsolete, nonmodern survivals and their devotional activities and historical imaginations as anachronisms. What is especially significant here is not just that governing elites mobilize religious rhetoric, appropriate Sufi imagery, and anachronistically relegate both to the domain of heritage, but rather that state discourse has the power to fix the possibilities of historical imagination and organize Muslim social reality (Heathershaw 2014, 39). Heritage provides a politically expedient tool of power and culture becomes a resource ripe for manipulation. The point here is not that organs of the Tajik state hold the power to "determine subjectivities" (Rasanayagam 2011, 121), but rather that the state attempts and often succeeds in fixing the terms of debate, in "framing the possibilities of being Muslim" (Rasanayagam 2014).[21] Officially sanctioned notions about history and the demerits of contemporary devotion come into being precisely through their projection into space in places like the billboard and shrine.

The state religious bureaucracy does not have to turn a shrine into a museum or resort to heritage discourses for this to occur. At Haz-rati Mavlono in the suburbs of Dushanbe, the burial place of Yaqubi Charkhi (1358–1447), another early and influential figure in the history of the Central Asian Naqshbandiya, symbolism similarly trumps devotion even as, unlike Hamadoni's shrine, it functions as a congregational mosque and hundreds visit its grounds each shrine day. At Hazrati Mavlono, Sufis demand vigilance. The mosque's imomi told me during one of my regular visits, "There aren't any Sufis here." He added that he wouldn't allow Sufis to practice zikr at the shrine or engage in any other kind of public ritual. As an added flourish, he even critiqued Sufi pious dress and the recitation of ethical poetry. Such practices, he added, were *shirk*, the sin of attributing some power or quality reserved for God alone to another. An alternative to turning problematic nonmodern survivals into heritage is zombification (Noyes 2016, 371–409). When heritage offers governing elites no recourse, Sufis and other Muslims become zombies, the problematic still-living dead of the contemporary religious landscape. Zombies cannot be allowed to roam free.

Assaults on Public Islam

"We haven't been meeting for two weeks," one Sufi told me in the spring of 2014 after an alleged terrorist gang had been arrested for attempting to bomb the Tajik Aluminum Company (TALCO) plant in Tursunzoda, an industrial juggernaut estimated to have been responsible for as much as 40 percent of Tajikistan's industrial output (Olcott 2012, 177). "The KGB came to see the pir and told him the teaching circle had to settle down for a while after those Hizb ut-Tahrir folks came," the man said.[22]

I often heard Sufis describe similar incidents of government interference in their practices of devotion. In recent years, governing elites have more broadly worked to circumscribe and securitize any form of religiosity that exists outside their spheres of immediate control, not just Sufi groups (Lemon 2016, 139–77). Since 2010 the authorities have shuttered unofficial places of worship, an act particularly unsettling in that as a result of Soviet legacies prayer houses (*masjidi panj vaqta*), smaller mosques in which Friday sermons are not offered, have been a key feature of both rural and urban life. Imomi khatibs, the office of prayer leaders in congregational mosques (*masjidi jomeh*), have also seen their teaching privileges curtailed and the requirements of their office quicken. Previously selected and supported by local communities, all imoms now work at the pleasure of the State Committee for Religious Affairs (Komitai Oid ba Korhoi Din)—the government organ responsible for regulating religious life along with the High Council of Ulamo—which chooses the mosques in which they serve and, ideally, pays their meager salaries. Even more, since 2011 the committee has exclusively dictated the topics of Friday sermons, and imoms face sanction if they deviate from them. On my last visit, I heard sermons on patriotism and respect for the nation's leader. As of 2014, imoms must also wear a common garb, intended to mark them explicitly as in the employ of the state.

At the same time, only one institution of Islamic higher learning is allowed to operate, the erstwhile Islamic University of Imom Termizi in Dushanbe, demoted in status to an institute under the authority of the Ministry of Education in 2010. Additionally, each imom now must hold an official credential from the committee, which is only given to those who have studied in Tajikistan at the institute, not to those who learned their craft informally, as most did during the Soviet period, nor to those who studied abroad in the Middle East or South Asia. In the first decade after independence, informal madrasas proliferated as individuals sent their children to learn rudimentary Arabic grammar and Qur'anic recitation. By the fall of 2016, the Ministry of Education had shuttered all the madrasas. In 2010 legislation with the Orwellian title Law on Parental Responsibility even went so far as to forbid youths under the age of majority to attend congregational prayers. Although it was applied unevenly, if at all, the law had a chilling rhetorical effect on pious Tajiks, making it a crime to offer children religious instruction outside nonexistent official frameworks.

The regime's anti-Islam campaigns have also had a gendered focus (Nozimova 2016). Women have been strongly encouraged to wear so-called national dress, the long shirt and baggy pants common in the region, as opposed to pious dress imported from abroad. In 2016 the committee circulated a list of approved "Tajik" names for children, with the result that so-called Islamic names are now de facto forbidden. Police have at times removed men with beards from city and village streets and required barbers to shave their beards. Continuing governing elites' fixation on national dress, in 2011 the committee even distributed matching uniforms for pilgrims, differentiating them from the millions of other pilgrims to Mecca, who wear the standard white pilgrim's robe.

Recent state interference in the free exercise of religion doesn't even approach the most egregious aspect of governing elites' recent efforts to regulate the mechanisms of Islamic knowledge production and actions in the political sphere. Taking many observers by surprise, the regime ramped up the arrest and likely torture of its religiously motivated political opponents in the summer of 2015. To that point, Tajikistan had distinguished itself among its Central Asian neighbors by boasting the region's only legally registered religious political party, the Islamic Renaissance Party (Ḥizbi Naḥzati Islomī), which had been allotted power as part of the power-sharing agreements that concluded the civil war. The courts forcibly disbanded the party, and many of its leaders, along with their lawyers, were arrested. Some were ultimately sentenced to long prison terms for their previously legal political activities.

Muslims routinely face the prospect of open criticism or arrest if they do not openly tow the official line. They become pariahs, denounced variously as Salafi, Wahhabi, or, worse, sympathizers of the Islamic State in Syria (ISIS). All this is not to suggest that self-identified Salafis and would-be ISIS foot soldiers do not exist within Tajikistan, yet their drastically inflated official numbers belie the magnitude of their support within the country. Even as a steady, small stream of disaffected Tajik labor migrants from Russia have traveled to Syria, including several high-profile defectors such as Gulmurod Halimov, the former head of a Ministry of Interior special forces unit, government elites have used ISIS as a euphemism and smokescreen for any form of religious expression external to that controlled by the state religious bureaucracy.

Strikingly, many of my Sufi friends and acquaintances did not fear the state's aspirational panopticon per se. They viewed government surveillance as inevitable and its effects negligible in light of their pirs' mystical insight. One disciple told me about a covert KGB officer who had acted as a member of his group for more than six years. Disappointed at the lack of actionable intelligence the agent had gathered, his superiors ultimately deemed his work unsuccessful due to the fact that "all of it was just zikr and mystical tasks." Many Sufis remain quietist, the exact opposite of the alleged ISIS sympathizers who face venom from state mouthpieces and agree with the agent's assessment, maintaining that Sufism is primarily "zikr and mystical tasks" and as such need not concern the state.

In 2014 a glossy billboard depicting Rahmon standing in a bed of red poppies towered between two recently pruned mulberry trees beside the M41 highway linking Tajikistan's capital to Uzbekistan. Its caption, a line of poetry, read:

> Long live [Rahmon], [and] our people under his leadership.
> Tajikistan is our Kaaba, and he is the nation's imom.

The lyrics, drawn from a song by Afzalshohi Shodi in praise of the president, deploy a particularly apt metaphor for understanding the governing elites' ideal. Rahmon is the leader who guides the congregation in prayer. The axis mundi of religious life, Rahmon sits on the pulpit of state secularism. If Tajiks are to worship anything, it is that. Rahmon's spectacular performance state celebrates Muslim history and imagery under a veneer of prosperity and peace, even as it simultaneously denies the devotional precepts adhered to by many of the country's Muslims, and deviance potentially provokes sanction, arrest, or exile.

In the midst of state displays of national belonging and monolithic constructions of apolitical Islam, fissures open up, which suggest alternative histories and modes of being (Bhabha 1994, 199–244). While Rahmon feigns having eaten of Luqmani Hakim's bread, Sufis dialogically tread the same discursive ground put forward by governing elites with their grand, symbolic constructions of Central Asia's Muslim golden age. Faced with the prospect of heritage or zombification, nostalgia offers a potent alternative (Hafstein 2012, 503–5). The next chapter discusses how Ibrohim's "There's no Sufism here" accomplishes real social work by exploring the contours of Sufi memory and the forms of nostalgic longing it supports.

chapter 2

⌘⌘⌘⌘⌘⌘⌘⌘⌘⌘⌘⌘⌘⌘⌘⌘⌘⌘⌘⌘⌘⌘⌘⌘⌘⌘⌘⌘

Nostalgia and Muslimness

"There aren't any pirs in Tajikistan anymore," Firuz told me one after-noon as we sat, sipping lukewarm tea on his veranda. The fan turned idly in the oppressive early summer heat. As Firuz talked, I adjusted the set-tings on my recorder. Firuz was always conscious of it and tempered his comments accordingly, his body signaling its awareness. I remember that the first time I met him he seemed more like a bodybuilder than the musician he was, years ago having trained at the state philharmonic in the capital. He had only returned the previous summer from Krasnodar in southern Russia, where he had worked as an unskilled laborer on a construction site. Unemployed now and recently pious, Firuz occasion-ally performed classical melodies for drunken guests in Dushanbe's wedding halls, although the intermittent work deeply battered his con-science. His hands, now calloused not from playing his lute but rather from loading bricks in the Russian Caucasus, reached to turn off the recorder.

"Really?" I replied, somewhat incredulously, thinking to myself, "What about your pir or the eshon we talked to last week in Hisor?" I sometimes missed what Firuz was trying to tell me. It wasn't so much that I couldn't follow his conversation. Firuz was patient with my Afghan-inflected Per-sian, and he was always willing to talk. Rather, he punctuated his speech with baffling, mystical interpretations of mundane reality. I regularly puzzled over whether I should interpret his comments literally or meta-phorically. After describing some seemingly inexplicable mystical con-cept, his ever-frequent refrain was "The mind (*aql*) can't truly grasp it." Sometimes the comment seemed more like an indictment than a state-ment of wonder.

Almost in answer to the unspoken dialogue in my head, Firuz began, "Sultan Mahmud sent his slave across the realm to pay tribute in gold to the pirs living in his land. The slave returned to Mahmud with all of the gold with which he had originally set out. Mahmud asked him, 'What happened? Why didn't you give away the gold?' The slave replied that all who wanted the gold weren't real pirs, and real pirs wouldn't take any gold."[1]

Seemingly satisfied with his explanation, Firuz began to sip his tea. I remained somewhat less convinced. Although he had warned me that the mind can't grasp mystical realities, I still tried to reason through his comments. "Was this a story he had heard from the pir?" I wondered. Still unsure how Firuz could say there weren't any real pirs in Tajikistan after we had spent so much time over the past few months talking about them, I did what I often did. I asked him to clarify. "What does your story mean?"

Firuz explained, "The pirs in Tajikistan are no longer true Sufis, and the real Sufi pirs remain hidden."

In Firuz's telling, the real Sufis, if any still existed, now only lurked in the shadows unwilling to accept patronage from Tajikistan's Sultan Mahmud. In the past, Sufis living within the boundaries of contemporary Tajikistan may have enjoyed the patronage of kings and emirs, controlled vast properties through religious endowments, and garnered easy respect from those they passed in the street. However, contemporary Sufi memory stresses that present devotees remain only a small remnant of their past numbers and those left now possess only a small shadow of their past renown. Much more recently, powerful pirs still lived in the Tajik SSR, and contemporary devotees even relate how Soviet era pirs received high Communist Party officials in audience and worshipped unencumbered by state interference. For many Sufis, the religious present holds few virtues. Recent years have seen ever tighter state control, and state-sanctioned narratives about Muslim religiosity preclude any discussion of individual religious agency apart from official frameworks. The mutually exclusive categories of "good Muslim" and "bad Muslim" to which governing elites standardly classify Tajikistan's Muslims leave little room for the complexities and negotiations of everyday religious life.

In this chapter, I focus explicitly on how Sufis speak nostalgically about the past and how such talk contributes to what it means to be Muslim in Tajikistan today. Significantly, Sufi nostalgia does not focus

linearly on an ideal before and a devalued after. Rather, as Carolyn Dinshaw has aptly noted, "Everyday life is profoundly asynchronous." Individuals inhabit multiple temporal worlds, living simultaneously in both
the present and the past. It's all the more the case with Sufi nostalgia. For
Tajikistan's Sufis, different times and temporal systems nostalgically
"[collide] in a single moment of now" (2012, 5). The fundamental paradox of the present is this: on the one hand, there exists a cultural narrative about Islamic revival, detailed in the last chapter, a time of discovery
and newfound opportunities for public piety, yet on the other hand Sufis
engage in lament about the way things used to be, sentiments like Ibrohim's "There's no Sufism here." Even more troublesome, Sultan Mahmud's
slave may have been right; there might not be any real pirs left at all. As
Sufis wait in anticipation for eventual vindication on the Day of Judgment, they simultaneously celebrate the glories of the past.

Because of these seeming paradoxes, it is more analytically productive
to think in terms of the discursive entanglements of contemporary Sufi
life rather than of simple binaries like past and present (Whitesel and
Shuman 2016). Among other features, entanglements, in Karen Barad's
(2007, 74) formation, are temporal configurations that change with each
"intra-action" and relationally bridge seemingly disparate moments in
time. Barad's concept of entanglement foregrounds the way multiple
temporal regimes intersect in the present Sufi moment.[2] In total, Sufi
nostalgic talk functions as a discursive formation that mediates between
the sacred past and the paradoxes of the religious present. A focus on
alternative temporalities draws attention to the ways Sufis enact the past
in the present, the ways the present evaluates the past, and the ways
paradoxical presents are actively constructed and exchanged for hopeful
futures. Pasts, presents, and futures exist alongside each other as entangled, juxtaposed communicative resources, allowing Tajikistan's Muslims
a sort of temporal agency over their religious lives that they are routinely
denied in the wider public sphere.

Sufi conceptions of nostalgia also do not operate exclusively in terms
of affect, that is, a simple pathos-filled longing to return to a time or
place that no longer exists; rather I understand nostalgia as a conscious
making of the past in the present via expressions of memory. In this
frame, Sufi nostalgia is poesis, as nostalgic talk provides Sufis with space
in which to imagine the past such that acts of expressive communication "[bring] the past into the present as a natal event" (Seremetakis

1994, 7).[3] There is a temptation to understand poesis as merely artifice, as an assertion that narrative pasts are nothing but social constructs. For the ethnographer, attention to the now and its entangled web of multiple temporalities becomes especially important in that many of the communities in which we work may vehemently oppose social scientistic ideas about how traditions are "invented" and communities "imagined" (Hobsbawm 1983; Anderson 1991). Indeed, many Sufis would likely chafe at the notion that their memories are constructed and their direct historical connections to the sacred past remain only tenuous at best. Thinking in terms of asynchrony and entanglements circumvents these challenges by allowing us to interrogate distinct, and sometimes conflicting, modalities for living historically (Freeman 2010, xvi).

THE PARADOXICAL PRESENT

One late spring morning, I traveled to Rudaki district, just south of Dushanbe, to meet with an influential pir and a former deputy (*khalifa*) of Eshoni Abdurahmonjon. Ibrohim and I entered his village compound not long after early morning prayers had ended. Uncharacteristically wearing a robe over his neatly pressed black slacks, Ibrohim went in first. The pir, white bearded and thin, sat on the floor at the far end of a cavernous guest room, listening intently as two young boys recited from the Qur'an. Looking up, he gestured for the boys to leave. Although Ibrohim had earlier told me, "When I was younger, I would go to pirs, kiss their hands, act all respectful. I can't do those things anymore," he clasped the pir's right hand and kissed it. Later, in the car on the way back to Dushanbe, perhaps aware of this inconsistency, Ibrohim repeatedly said, "He is different from other pirs. He's a good man."

We exchanged greetings, and Ibrohim introduced me and described the outlines of my project. Upon hearing of my interest in Soviet era Islam, the pir began straightaway, "Now the number of Sufis is very small compared to the number of disciples during the Soviet period." Pausing, he continued, "During Soviet times, there were more devotees."

"More devotees?" I said, skeptical that this could be true.

"Now the people of Tajikistan don't have any inclination toward the Sufi path." He followed this statement with a long and circuitous story whose intricacies I struggled to grasp. He began in medias res in Faizobod during the early 1970s when a large group of disciples had gathered for a ritual meal at Abdurahmonjon's home. The pir's wizened voice and missing teeth, reflecting the village life he had led, magnified my interpretative difficulties. The story focused on a recurrent motif about the vast number of followers of the Sufi path during the height of Soviet era religious oppression. The pir's memories of the not so distant past were tinged with longing as he repeatedly signaled the relative paucity of present-day adherents.

The pir's nostalgia mirrored that of many other Sufis I encountered in Tajikistan. Many imagined that the past included times of religious effervescence and that the spiritual future promises a return to past renown and a vindication of present injustice. In the future, the problems of the present will be remedied and the true nature of Sufi spiritual reality will be ultimately revealed. Almost as often as I heard Sufis invoke the glories of the sacred past, I heard them in anticipation discuss their eventual triumph at the end of time, an idea they shared with Sufis beyond Tajikistan. Such hopeful longing for a future of vindication may in some ways be just as nostalgic as Sufi memories of the past (Piot 2010; Lagerkvist 2013). Firuz once told me:

> On the day of judgment (*rūzi mahshar*), the things that haven't been tasted will be tasted. The things that we don't have will be made available to the followers (*ummat*) of the Messenger, the followers of the Prophet, the followers of Muhammad, peace be upon him. Then, after the world passes, the prophet Iso will come and reign as king for forty years. He'll become the king of the entire world, Iso. Do you understand? All these people of the book, those that have turned away from professing the faith, will all at once become followers of the Messenger due to Iso. Do you understand?

It is this attitude of vindication and the conversion of all those who had previously failed to offer their profession of faith that bookends Sufi ideas of time, both for Sufis inside and outside Tajikistan. What remains between past glory and confidence in future revelation is an inauthentic and paradoxical religious present. Put simply, the way things currently are is not the way they should be; present religious devotion does not approximate the true reality, and the practices in which people are presently engaged are fundamentally inauthentic. There remain only a few living pirs, yet their works and teachings still ring true. Few of them perform miracles, and their instruction often doesn't inspire confidence in their mystical knowledge. Even more troublesome, there may not be any real pirs left at all. Sultan Mahmud's slave may have been right. Those claiming spiritual authority might merely be frauds, tricksters, and moneygrubbers.

The present becomes even more paradoxical in light of the fact that Sufis today are allegedly living in a time of renewal, as the name of Tajikistan's Islamic Renaissance Party aspiringly suggests. To casual observers, nostalgia for the past and hope for the future seem, at least on the surface, to run counter to scholarly and journalistic assessments of the religious present (see Balzer 2006, 79). How can we talk of nostalgia in the midst of a revival of public religiosity? The short answer is that most of the Sufis I met did not share experts' opinions about Islam's new role in public life. Rather than celebrating the relatively recent return of practices of public piety long proscribed under the Soviet regime, many Sufis instead offered a pessimistic competing narrative of continuity and then devolution and decline. They admitted that some facets of a so-called revival might have been realized, at least shortly after the end of the civil war. But at the same time, many maintained, like the pir I visited with Ibrohim, that in recent decades the number of adherents to the Sufi path has decreased and openly bemoaned the alleged fact that the younger generation now shuns the mystical practice of their more pious forebears. Sufis despondently imagined present circumstance to be a dim reflection of historical Islam in Central Asia, especially in light of increased state oversight over the religious sphere during the span of the past decade.

To a certain extent, discourses of decline, nostalgia for spiritual ages past, and a belief in the spiritual fecklessness of current pious exemplars are common across wider post-Socialist religious sphere and even more broadly the Sufi milieu at large.[4] For Sufis, there is an inherent devolutionary concept always at work in which each subsequent pir is understood to be less mystically accomplished than his master. Each pir, going all the way back to the Prophet Muhammad, is an ideal type to which his disciples can only aspire.[5] The millenarian impulse of Muslim spirituality, waiting in expectation for distant perfection while simultaneously attributing spiritual perfection to past masters, prefigures the kind of discourse in which Tajik Sufis engage.[6] Cyclical temporal logics, such as the Muslim millenarian, exist amid the asynchrony of other Sufi temporal regimes. Each is "recessed and seized on" (Stoler 2016, 33) simultaneously. It is precisely this juxtaposition of millenarianism and sequential logics with various nostalgic future-present-pasts that makes entanglements and asynchrony apt explanatory paradigms for thinking through the contours of Sufi memory.

Additionally, as the previous chapter illustrated, the recent present has indeed been a time of intense religious repression. After a relatively short period of freedom that followed the end of Soviet strictures on religious practice, the more recent past is littered with examples of tighter state control. State efforts intended to limit the unrestricted practice of Muslim devotion have all severely curtailed the public practices of Tajikistan's Sufi groups. As such, whatever public renaissance of Sufi practice that may have occurred at the end of the Soviet period and during the first years of Tajikistan's independence is currently under greater pressure from state security organs than since at least before the time of Gorbachev's glasnost and perestroika.

Pessimistic assessments regarding the current number of adherents to the Sufi path might also reflect simple demographic realities. When I was first working in Tajikistan, estimates suggested between six hundred thousand and one million of Tajikistan's citizens worked as migrant laborers abroad, totaling somewhere between 8 and 13 percent of Tajikistan's total population (Marat 2009, 10). Similarly, at that time Tajikistan ranked as the most remittance-dependent economy in the world with as much as 50 percent of the country's gross domestic product (GDP) coming from labor remittances (Danzer and Ivaschenko 2010). Around 95 percent of labor migrants are men between the ages of twenty and forty (Kumo 2012), the very demographic that would ostensibly fill the ranks of Tajik Sufi groups. In contrast, prior to the precipitous economic decline that followed the dissolution of the Soviet Union and the civil war, labor migration to other parts of the Soviet Union for education, participation in mass development projects, or military service occurred but not nearly to the same degree as in the present period. Most able-bodied young Tajik men work abroad and thus cannot actively participate in the life of Sufi groups as they might have before. Although many Sufi labor migrants still maintain connections to pirs, for most of the year migrants are absent from group teaching, ritual observances, and the related life-cycle events. Pirs regularly offer blessings for members of their groups working abroad. Like Firuz, many of the adepts I encountered had spent time working in Russia, and I witnessed a number of migrant workers visiting their pirs upon their return to Tajikistan.

Sufis' memories of the distant and not so distant past confirm the insufficiencies and paradoxes of the religious present. Indeed, as Firuz said, "There aren't any pirs in Tajikistan anymore," and few pay homage to those that might remain. If the story of Sultan Mahmud and his slave holds true, then whatever mystics have survived the perils of the present religious environment remain hidden in the shadows unwilling (or unable) to receive the honor that is rightly theirs. More troublesome, the pirs that remain may only be morally corrupt imposters. What Sufis imagine as the Edenic social order no longer remains (Herzfeld 2005, 147), and by necessity they must invest both the near and distant religious pasts with an aura of religious authenticity that the present lacks (Stewart 1993, 23). In order to bridge the seemingly disparate orientations of an Edenic past and an inauthentic present, Sufis engage nostalgic memory. Nostalgia is the rhetorical glue holding together memories of past greatness and the promises of future glory and mediating the paradoxes in between.

Nostalgia as Mediation

"I'm sorry that there wasn't any poetry singing (*ghazalkhonī*) tonight," the middle-aged man said, looking at me over his shoulder as we crossed a rickety wooden footbridge spanning a dry Soviet era irrigation canal.

"That's okay. We can come another time," I replied. I had traveled one Thursday evening to a village near Dushanbe to visit a pir during his weekly audience with his disciples. Friends in Dushanbe had praised the pir for his knowledge of mystical poetry. I had been especially eager to observe the poetry singing.

My host continued, "The eshon used to recite a number of stanzas of poetry (*baït*), four or five, and then give us his interpretation (*shahr*) of them, normally poetry from Jununi, Hofiz, Rumi's *Masnavi*, or Iqbal. We don't do that anymore because of the bad situation."

"I understand," I said. "Does [the eshon] just recite poetry and give his interpretation of it or do you also do zikr?"

Continuing with his earlier thought, he recalled, "I learned a lot of poetry as a child from my father. We used to do zikr, but it's not that way anymore. The gatherings were strongest during Soviet times. The *hus* could be heard as far away as the *sovkhoz*.[7] Most of the Sufis were killed during the civil war, and since then the gatherings have been less."

In my talks with Sufis, I often encountered similar nostalgic accounts of the Soviet past, stories of when the Sufi path was strong and the "hus"

from zikr echoed across the mountain valleys. At first I was skeptical
of these nostalgia-tinged accounts. They seemed to diverge sharply
from the narratives of Soviet-era religious history I had learned during
my university studies. It was only after the fall of the Soviet Union that
Muslim life was supposed to have flourished in the Central Asian republics, I thought. Later, as I spent more time with individuals persecuted
for their piety and marginalized by a self-interested elite, such accounts
began to resonate deeply with me and increasingly provided fodder for
my field notebooks. I, too, found myself imagining a past in which
Sufis met without interference and religious literature circulated freely.[8]
In the midst of the paradoxical present, there is an accompanying nostalgia for these times, a time when influential pirs like those described
in the last chapter were still alive, a time when the adherents to the Sufi
path were allegedly legion, and a time when religious fervor allegedly
remained strong.

Sufis' nostalgic sentiments approximated a discursive formation in
which nostalgic talk linked a set of complex ideologies about the nature
of the past and the vicissitudes of the religious present. Nostalgic talk
evoked ideas about an entire social order (Briggs 1988; Hill 1998), now
seen as irrecoverably lost. Additionally, it allowed for a ready explanation of the religious present by using constructed memories of the past
social order to evaluate present circumstances. In this way, nostalgia
became a bridge between these two moments in imagined time, allowing for the creation of a remembered past that holds explanatory power
to mediate temporal disjuncture.[9] Nostalgia melds these two disparate
epochs into a kind of "past future" or "future past" (Boym 2001, 351;
Stewart 1993, 23), establishing continuity between Sufis' imagined past
and present selves (Nadkarni and Shevchenko 2004, 500).

Sufis imagined both the near and more distant pasts to be times when
Islam was more firmly enmeshed in the social fabric of everyday life and
in which pious individuals received the respect they were rightly due.
During one of my visits to small village shrine, I asked the impoverished
elderly caretaker about the time when the shrine was built. He replied:

> In the 1950s, there wasn't a shrine here. It was just a burial place. That
> was a time of hunger. Believe me, there weren't potatoes, onions, but my
> people respected the saint, not like now when people have everything in
> the world and ignore him. The men of the village decided they needed to

build a better tomb (*maqbara*) for the saint, so they took sand and rock on their horses and donkeys and began to construct the place. There wasn't much water there, but one bucket of water was enough because of a miracle. Eventually the police came to see what was going on. They took the saint's son to the station. When the head of the department came to see him, the cell door had been unlocked and the saint's son was sitting in the cell reciting the Qur'an. The department head let the saint's son go because of the miracle.

He said he could tell the saint's son possessed the saint's power (viloïat). People used to see miracles, not anymore.

This respect frame dominates much Sufi talk about the past social order. The shrine caretaker's brief history of the saint's burial place privileged the notion that villagers in the past rightly honored religious figures, even when they themselves had very little in the way of material possessions. Even when times were difficult and food scarce, villagers honored their saintly forebears and were justifiably rewarded for their acts of devotion. Indeed, as the story attests, the saint used his power and intervened with a miracle when his son faced possible legal redress for his display of what was then unlawful religious devotion. Paradoxically for the caretaker, now, when the material conditions of life were much more comfortable and shrine veneration was no longer subject to potential prosecution, respect for religious figures from the past had gone by the wayside.

The shrine caretaker's nostalgic appeals valorized particular values of the past social order, for example, respect and devotion for the graves of religious figures, naturalizing those ideals as the way things should still be. As such his nostalgia worked not so much as a wistful commentary on the past, longingly remembering episodes from the 1950s during his childhood in the village, as instead a potent rhetorical claim on the present (Hill 1998, 78; Bayart 2005, 77–78), demarcating the boundaries of proper behavior while imagining a past that still holds some explanatory power for interpreting the paradoxes of the present moment. His claims about how villagers, even in the midst of material want and religious repression, managed to respect a saint buried in their midst functioned as a commentary on the way things should still rightly be. His narrative construction of the past provided him with a powerful communicative resource through which to understand his present circumstances, mediating between his personal memories of the Soviet era past and what he saw as the inauthenticity of the present social order.

His memories also conveniently worked as a gloss on his own present economic situation. Just as with the protagonists of his story, he remains in dire economic circumstances, feeding his family with difficulty even as he continues to give the saint's burial place the care it is properly due. A past in which respect for religious figures was standard renders his present circumstances more intelligible. He can attribute his lack of economic stability to the fact that his neighbors no longer honor the saint. If they did, the shrine caretaker would also seemingly receive some greater pecuniary benefit for the effort he daily expends. As one prominent Sufi also told me, "People used to respect the ulamo, not anymore." Sufi talk about respect and honor provides one of the means whereby Tajikistan's Sufis mediate between the sacred past and the inauthentic present.

An additional way in which Sufis use nostalgic sentiment, mediating the past and the present and marking the real from the inauthentic, is through the use of popular hagiographies (*zindaginoma* and *tazkira*), cataloging the lives and pedigrees of Sufi pirs and other important Central Asian religious figures. For example, in recent years two biographies have been published about the life of Eshoni Abdurahmonjon (Darvozī and Badalipur 2003; Hokiroh 2010), the well-known Soviet era pir discussed in the last chapter. The earliest text (2003) lists only four individuals alleged to have received teaching authorizations (*khati irshod*) from the pir. In contrast the later biography, issued seven years after the first, lists forty-three. My interviews with several of the pir's still living Soviet era disciples would seem to confirm that the pir did only give out four authorizations during the course of his lifetime: to Makhsumi Burhoniddin Kuktoshi, Domullo Hikmatulloi Tojikobodi, Eshoni Muhtadii Kolkhozobodi, and Domullo Muhammadii Qumsangiri.

The forty-three individuals in the later edition represent a veritable Who's Who of contemporary Tajik Islam, including Qozidomullo Abdurashid (1883–1978)—perhaps the most prominent member of the official ulamo during the Soviet period and chief of the state Islamic establishment during the last two years of Stalin's rule—sons from important Sufi families, and a geographically diverse assortment of well-known figures within late Soviet and early independence era Tajik Islam. These more recent editorial additions, which have created new silsila directly linking contemporary figures to Abdurahmonjon, act as a bridge, mediating between nostalgic reminiscences of the saint's life and the contemporary religious milieu in which figures who have only more recently gained prominence and wider renown need real authorization. The hagiographic imagination of Abdurahmonjon's biographers lends authenticity to the paradoxical present via such fictive silsila constructions. Fictive silsila nostalgically mediate between the past and present, substituting authoritative textual evidence for real personal memory. If the supposed revival of Islam has enabled frauds and tricksters to abound, as some critics allege, then one key way to stave off allegations of fraud is to link oneself and the teaching lineage one represents directly to an authentic sacred past, even better if it is meticulously documented in print.

A well-known critic of the present hagiographic process sarcastically noted to me, "The next addition of Abdurahmonjon's biography will list a hundred teaching authorizations instead of the current forty." The nostalgic past of Abdurahmonjon's hagiographers is a Soviet past in which Abdurahmonjon's teaching lineage flourished. During the Soviet era, Abdurahmonjon easily established religious connections across the mountains and valleys of the republic, conveniently ignoring Soviet era religious repression. Indeed, the volume lists few instances of Abdurahmonjon's sainthood being subject to the political demands of his time or of when he faced limitations on the open practice of public ritual. Several of Abdurahmonjon's still living disciples even recounted how Jabbor Rasulov (1913–82), the first secretary of the Communist Party of the Tajik SSR, who served from 1961 until his death in 1982, regularly performed pilgrimage to the shaikh and consulted him on religious matters in the republic. As such, stories about Abdurahmonjon's power and authority represent a nostalgia imbued with both a "remembering" and a "forgetting" capacity (Berdahl 1999, 198), as purveyors of such stories forget Soviet era repression and instead remember religious renown.

The editors of Abdurahmonjon's hagiography included a story narrated by Amir Qaroqulov (1942–2014), a Soviet era minister and later candidate for president of independent Tajikistan (Hokiroh 2010, 210–11). Qaroqulov recounts an occasion in which he wanted to visit Abdurahmonjon but couldn't due to his high position within the Communist Party. Qaroqulov recounts how he had to seek special permission from Rahmon Nabiev (1930–93), the first secretary of the Communist Party of the Tajik SSR (1982–85), to make his pilgrimage to the pir. Qaroqulov says:

Because I was the leader [of the Communist Party] in the Faizobod district, I asked permission from Nabiev, the leader of the Communist Party
in the republic. [Nabiev] sent me along with his dear friend Sohibnazar
Odinaev. At that time, it was very difficult for government leaders to visit
with religious people. In a word, I worked well. Despite the fact that I was
awarded the all-union flag two times, I couldn't perform pilgrimage to see
Hazrati Pir or any other of the ulamo without permission.

Having secured permission, Qaroqulov goes on to tell of his eventual
audience with the pir and how it changed his life. He says that after his
audience, "Love of religion and faith grew stronger inside my heart and
breast. . . . God's strength purified my soul." Qaroqulov's story offers a
nostalgia-tinged portrait of how Abdurahmonjon was able to surmount
Soviet era restrictions on public religious practice. According to Qaroqulov, Abdurahmonjon's power was such that even First Secretary Nabiev
permitted his subordinates to freely offer their obeisance to the pir.

Beyond the ways in which the purported mystical inheritance embodied in oral and written hagiographies instantiate religious authenticity,
genealogies (*shajara*) also render the paradoxical present more authentic. For example, Hoji Saiid Abdujalilkhoja's *From the Genealogies of the
Descendants of the Prophet in Transoxiana* (2009) includes brief historical glosses on the histories of a number Central Asian families alleged to
descend from the Prophet Muhammad. The book begins with a description of the Prophet's immediate descendants and then moves quickly to
offer lists of their progeny who settled in medieval Central Asia. The
majority of the text describes the Dahbedi pirs of Samarkand and lists
their descendants who still live within the territory of contemporary
Tajikistan. At the end of the volume, the author curiously catalogs various well-known pirs along with their silsila. These are pirs not directly
linked by genealogy or silsila, nor can they claim any direct descent from
the Prophet. The result of this amalgamation of genres linking genealogical tables to contemporary silsila is a kind of genealogical pastiche,
the direct effect of which is to substantiate and authenticate the present
by linking it to the perceived genealogical authenticity of the past. The
author takes pains to substantiate his version of Central Asian sacred
history using photographs of aging manuscript sources, tombstones, and
shrines containing the remains of those he includes. He explains such
material traces and artifacts of historical Central Asian Islam by locating

them within the wider arc of Muslim history, situating the local vis-à-vis broader currents of what Tajiks would consider to be transcendent Islamic tradition. In this regard, recently published genealogies have an important linking function, explaining the present by offering a nostalgic portrait of the sacred past.

"There are three kinds of ulamo," a well-known figure within Tajikistan's religious circles told me, "the real (*aslī*), the specialists (*ikhtisosī*), and the imposters (*taqallubī*). The imposters have taken someone else's shajara or forged one. Many of the eshons in Tajikistan are imposters," he continued. "One time, I went to the home of a very popular pir, one who has many followers. I asked if I could see his genealogy. He initially refused, but after a while he finally obliged. When he unrolled it, it must have been sixteen meters long. I could tell almost immediately that it was a fake. When I told the shaikh that his genealogy was forged, he said that he knew it was, but not to say anything."

I said, "What do you think would happen if his followers found out?"

"I don't think it would make any difference. The shaikh is still well versed in the Islamic sciences (*ilm*), and that's why his disciples come," he said.

The shaikh's allegedly forged genealogical table directly connects the circumstances and personages of present religious devotion with figures from the past, mediating between the two and establishing a claim for an authentic present by linking the inauthentic present to an authentic past. Purported filial and mystical relationships between present figures and well-known figures of the past also serve as substitutes for real personal memories of the recent past. As such, Sufi nostalgia mediates between the past and the present because of the way it fills in the gaps in present-day understandings of recent history. Indeed, many of those who currently participate in the Sufi path, individuals like Firuz, were not actively involved in mystical practice prior to the independence of Tajikistan. The flowering of public religiosity after the fall of the Soviet Union, that is, the stuff of the so-called Islamic revival in Central Asia, enabled many to cultivate direct relationships with pirs for the first time and even enabled the creation of new silsila with pirs from Afghanistan and Pakistan who were not known to those living in the Tajik SSR. Newer initiates retain little real connection to the more recent Soviet era past and have no personal memories of religious practice prior to the past few decades. The story about the forged genealogy similarly works as a

critique of the perceived religious inauthenticity of the present. Its implicit nostalgia is an act of discrediting the religious present (Stewart
1993, 139) by "othering it" (Stewart 1988, 228).

"I want to show you something," Khurshed said as we were returning
from one of our visits to a small local shrine. Like Ibrohim and Firuz,
Khurshed was a Sufi who I came to know well during my time in Tajikistan. The first time I saw him he was sitting alone in his immaculately
detailed car, parked along a side street near Dushanbe's central mosque.
He sported a short, tidy black beard, and a turban rested on his head. The
windows of his car were open, and he was looking down at his phone.
I asked him straightaway if he was Sufi. My uncharacteristic boldness
that day still surprises me. The look on his face suggested not so much
surprise at an unexpected question as a wry, knowing recognition, as
though my question confirmed for him his special attention to outward
piety. Khurshed was a businessman. His older brother had been successful working in Moscow and financed his younger brother's small-time
business efforts at home: a taxi, energy drinks, and a stall in the bazaar.

On the way back to my apartment, Khurshed told me about various
members of his family. When we arrived in the courtyard outside the
apartment block, he went to the trunk of the car and pulled out a plastic
grocery bag filled with aging photographs. He flipped through them until
he found the one he was looking for, a faded, small black and white photograph of a bearded man in a turban and robe sitting beside a number of
others, all beardless and wearing white dress shirts and dark trousers.[10]

"This is my grandfather," he said, pointing at the man with the beard.

"When was it taken?"

Khurshed replied, "It must be from about twenty-five years ago. He
was a Sufi (*ahli tariqat*), a follower of the Great Master.[11] He often went
up the mountain to see the pir."

Khurshed later recounted that that one of his uncles, also deceased,
had been a disciple of the pir, but because he was a schoolteacher he
did not grow a beard and wear a turban like Khurshed's grandfather had.
Khurshed further lamented the fact that he did not realize any of this
about them when they were still alive. It was only after he finally gave his
allegiance to the pir and told him about his family that he learned about
his grandfather's and uncle's devotion.

Khurshed had no direct memories of his grandfather's and uncle's
Soviet era Sufi affiliations. The faded photograph of his grandfather,

dressed in the traditional garb of the faithful, and the pir's word were the only testaments to their piety. Khurshed expressed regret that he did not know the truth about any of this when was a child, when his grandfather and uncle were still alive. His nostalgia for the connections he shared with the not so distant religious past became a substitute for any real, personal memories of the past. His nostalgia both mediated between the present and the reality of a past that he has only now recently discovered and a seeming void that my questions about the past had opened and thus necessitated he bridge in his answers.

Nostalgic sentiments instantiate powerful notions about the past social order, a time when respect for pirs was the norm and mystical practice flourished. In total, Sufi nostalgia celebrated the past social order and connected present adherents to the Sufi path to that irrecoverable past today. In this way, narratives about the past social order approximated a kind of allegory on present circumstances (Shuman 2005). In their mediation between the sacred past and paradoxical present, they operated as narrative claims on the larger social universe of the stories' tellers. They acted as commentaries on and rhetorical claims for the more than personal relevance of the tellers' memories' meanings. The paradoxical nature of the present makes these meanings all the more problematic. Amy Shuman (2005, 68) terms the relationship between "the constructed present and the lost past" the "problem of the relation between the personal and allegorical." She argues that this is a necessary relationship. If the two were divorced, "the personal would lose its relevance to others, and the allegorical would lose its relevance to the self." So if nostalgic discourses serve as mediatory agents over disjuncture, then Tajik Sufi nostalgia also in a sense mediated between the individual adherents to the Sufi path, that is, figures like Khurshed, and the larger social worlds that they inhabited. As Hannah Arendt (1958) has argued, storytelling works more broadly as a strategy for transforming private into public meanings.

In early 2015, Eshoni Temur, the popular Naqshbandi pir introduced in the last chapter, was arrested and accused of polygyny, stealing his followers' possessions, and other offenses against official state notions of traditional religiosity. On February 6, 2015, state television broadcast a thirty-minute exposé under the ominous title *The Story of Shaikh Temur* (*Rivoĩati Shaikh Temur*) in which a nameless interrogator presses Temur to answer questions regarding his family life. A local imom even accuses him of defying Hanafi jurisprudence.[12] Other religious officials offer their own commentary regarding what they see as Temur and his adherents' general lack of intellectual rigor. In between repetitive video montages of Temur receiving his disciples' respect, Temur sits despondently, never looking at the camera, and answers his faceless interrogator only with monotone, single-word replies. The report repeatedly mocks Temur's disciples for their devotion, for example, the way they kiss his hands and bow in his presence. The most provocative of the clips shows Temur's disciples laying a red carpet before his car before he drives by. Following the report, posts on social media severely criticized Temur's trickster (*firebgari*) nature, a potent criticism in the present religious context, and his supposed deviation from the norms of Tajik Islam (Shafiev 2015).

The television report's outright discrediting of Temur sets out to accomplish a different sort of discursive work than Sufis' nostalgic appeals about the past. Nonetheless, for many Sufis *The Story of Shaikh Temur* embodied the lack of respect Tajikistan's Sufis imagine the present order to entail. The film confirmed their deepest fear—authorities' disdain for the Sufi path—even though many Sufis might also have criticized the excesses of Temur's practices. For many the television special also vindicated their nostalgic discourses about the past, a time when the social order remained legitimate and religious figures received the respect they were rightly due. On state television, Sufi ideas about the past were openly mocked. Perhaps unsurprisingly, many of those most conversant in nostalgic talk about the past social order are those most marginalized by current discourse, and those most vocal about the virtues of the past social order were those most relegated to the social margins. In this regard, the nostalgia I often heard indexed the lack of respect Sufis now receive in relation to how they imagine they should be honored. For them nostalgic talk did not just mediate between the past and the present, but it also provided them some agency over the exigencies of religious present.

NOSTALGIA AND AGENCY

Recent folkloristic takes on nostalgia have foregrounded its agentive capacities (Abrahams 2003; Cashman 2006; Green 2007; Saltzman 2012). Nostalgic memory is not a social disease, nor is it an inherently politically suspect endeavor. Instead, nostalgic memory as embodied in particular expressive forms carries with it agency over the present and works as a productive vehicle for coming to terms with social change. Nostalgia offers the possibility for reasserting community and group identity, providing individuals with the ability to reclaim some power over their present circumstances and critique the perceived limits of their presents and to realign their asynchronous "cubist portrayals of the past" (Beiner 2007, 134). Narrative provides a cogent vehicle for reassembling their paradoxical, broken pasts and presents into a coherent new whole (Stewart 1988, 236).

In 2014, on a return visit to Tajikistan, I was reminiscing with friends about how things had changed since the last time I had seen them. Somehow I broached the issue of how people initially were often scared to talk with me when I first arrived in country. One man, who had first introduced me to his pir, began to tell what had happened when I visited his pir's home for the first time.

"A lot of people asked me things like 'Why did you bring him? What does he want? Why would he want to come?'" he said. "I told them that everybody should mind their own business. Nobody but God knows who might become a follower of the Sufi path. I might want one thing, but God wants another. It's all in his hands. If God didn't do it, I couldn't have done it. I have one plan. He has another. There are my wishes, but another thing is written down."

The point he seemed to be making was that who would visit the gathering or express an interest in joining was beyond his control. God has fated, that is, "another thing is written down," who will become a Sufi. If I had an interest in coming, who was my friend to deny that my visit might be due to God's deterministic will? To further emphasize his point, he quickly followed his series of rhetorical questions with a brief gloss of how the archangel Jibril places a grain of sand in a mother's womb before birth. It is that action that determines one's fate. "From this," he added, "There is no remedy."

For Sufis, time is similarly deterministic. God's will dictates action, and determinism allows little space for individual agency. If God has determined one's life from the time of one's time in the womb, as the story of Jibril's placement of a grain of sand would suggest, then it leaves little opportunity for making a place in the world apart from one's fated destiny. It is precisely here that nostalgic talk enters as an expression of individual agency over the vicissitudes of contemporary life, counteracting social marginality and the effects of religious repression. For fate there indeed may be "no remedy," as my friend asserted, but memories about the nearer and distant sacred pasts open up space for agency amid the determinism of Sufi time.

Perhaps somewhat unsurprisingly, those most in need of agency in their own religious lives are those most conversant in nostalgic talk (see Hill 1998). Rural village pirs, impoverished followers of particular eshons, and/or those whose ritual practices somehow make them liminal to mainstream understandings of proper Muslim comportment and fealty to the state seem to express nostalgic ideas about the past social order to a greater degree than those more central to the contemporary religious hierarchy do. The shrine caretaker discussed in the previous section is a case in point. The result is that those who already possess some degree of real agency in their everyday religious lives have perhaps less reason to engage in nostalgic talk about the past than do the more marginal adherents to the Sufi path. While the less nostalgic likely owe more of their current financial and religious positions to the realities of the contemporary moment, those on the margins have to trade instead in nostalgic visions of the pre-Soviet and Soviet era pasts (Abramson 2000).

In all of the time I spent with religious figures in Tajikistan, Hoji Akbar Turajonzoda and his younger brother Mahmudjon were perhaps the least nostalgic of all the people I encountered. When I asked them to share stories about Islam in the Tajik SSR, they instead preferred to celebrate the triumphs of the 1990s and 2000s. They concentrated on the gains their family had experienced since the end of the civil war rather than looking longingly back to aspects of the past social order. When they did engage the past in our talks together, it did not emerge in the form of wistful memories or ideals yet to be realized, that is, as a potent rhetorical claim on the present. Instead, the religious past they narrated was one of tragedy and destruction in which the pious were denied the opportunity to fulfill their religious obligations and the transmission of Islamic knowledge was severely curtailed.

The Turajonzodas might also be distinct due to the fact that they hold actual personal memories of the past and need not trade in nostalgic talk to the same degree as those more marginal to the contemporary religious sphere. Unlike Khurshed, who retains no personal memories of his ancestors' piety and whose piety exists only in the present, the Turajonzodas still possess potent memories of the past as sons of Soviet-sanctioned ulamo and graduates of Soviet era madrasas. They were central to the religious circles of late Soviet era Islam and acted as integral parts of the Islam-inspired political movements of the civil war era. Whereas Khurshed and others like him can only engage the past in the form of past-tense narratives, the Turajonzodas actually remember.

Many Sufis I knew rarely used words such as *remember* or *memory* in talking about the past. However, in interviews Hoji Akbar and Mahmud-jon repeatedly used phrases such as "I remember that . . ." or "I remember when . . ." Their expressions were not nostalgic even when they engaged topics about the religious past they have only recently encountered. Instead, their discussions of the past suggested discovery and newness as virtues unto themselves. If nostalgia operates as a substitute for real memories of the past, then those who still hold real memories of the past need not express nostalgic sentiments to the same degree. Nostalgia here represents both loss and attachment as they fill in for the perceived loss of memories even as it also represents the longing for and attachment to an authentic past (Stewart 1993). Because the Turajonzodas have real memories of the past and retain agency over their own religious lives, nostalgic talk perhaps proved less necessary as a rhetorical strategy.[13]

One evening early in my time in Tajikistan, I went to visit a pir who lived not far from Dushanbe. The pir lived in quite humble circumstances, farming a small patch of land with his sons and receiving little if any financial benefit from his religious position. He regularly gathered with a small group of disciples, teaching them the recitations (*vazifa*) of the Naqshbandi path and receiving villagers who came requesting prayers for such things as illness, the birth of a child, or difficulties emigrating to Russia. The pir spent most of our time together instructing me in the basic tenets of Sufism, evidently imagining that I needed significant instruction after hearing my questions. Early during our talk together, he related to me a story about the life of Bahouddini Naqshband (1319–89), the eponymous founder of the Naqshbandi path. In the story, Naqshband discovers the internationally famous mystical Persian poet Hofiz (1325/26–1389/90). The pir began his story thus.

One day Bahouddini Balogardoni Naqshband was compelled to pass through the city of Shiraz on his way back from the hajj.[14] There an Uvaisi had been born.[15] Then, ah, this is the way that Uvaisi become disciples, grasp a pir's hand. After an Uvaisi has truly gone along this path, he reaches the level (*maqom*) of sainthood (*avliëgī*).[16] Uvaisi have been blessed by God so that they don't need a pir to explain the litanies of the faith to them, to train their heart.[17] Then, Bahouddini Balogardon, the great saint, arrives in Shiraz. He goes and knocks on a door, and Shaikh Hofiz's father opens it. Do you understand my story?

BG: Yes.

Then he asks, "How many children do you have?" He responds, "Six or seven. There's myself, my wife, and my kids. I have one that's gone mad," he said. "He's locked in the cellar." The cellar, the cellar [in Russian the second time].

BG: Yes.

The basement [again in Russian]. Then, Bahouddini Balogardon says, "He's not crazy, you're the crazy one. He's the sensible one." Then he says, "Show him to me." Then Shaikh Hofiz's father replies, "It'll make him go mad. I can't open the door." When he opened it, Bahouddini Balogardon, he noticed a hat made of mud. When Hofiz looked at it, it turned into gold, the kind of crown that a king buys.

Oh, there are a lot of these stories.

Then, now, I'll get back to the story of Shaikh Hofiz. Then Bahouddini Balogardon put his attention (*tavajjūh*) on his heart and gave him the vazifa of the heart, so that Shaikh Hofiz would reach the level of Imomi Siddiq.[18] Then one day there was a gathering. Some years had probably passed, and a young boy comes in. He was carrying water in his hands to wash everyone's hands.[19] The ulamo were there. There were mullahs. Many non-Sufis (*ahli zohir*) were all there.[20] The imomi khatib was there. The *mufti* was there.[21] They were all sitting there.

Shaikh Hofiz was sitting at the feet of the imom.[22] At this point, they weren't aware that he was a saint. As the boy washed Shaikh Hofiz's hands, he was sitting in contemplation, reading from the book of fate (*lavhal mahfuz*).[23] He saw the boy's name in the book and that in six days the boy would die. He saw that the boy was charming and lovely, good-looking, and Shaikh Hofiz had mercy on him. He went again into contemplation as the water was running over his hands into the basin.

BG: Yes, yes, yes.

The water was running over his hands, but the water in the pitcher never ran out. The basin never filled. Shaikh Hofiz's hands were being washed, but he was still in contemplation. He said to God, "Oh God, lengthen the boy's life. Write down his fate. Write down a new day and hour. If you don't, I'll keep my hands under the water as long as the water remains under the ground of Shiraz. I won't let the boy stop pouring water."

BG: Yes, yes.

Because Shaikh Hofiz was God's friend, God couldn't refuse what he had said. Then Shaikh Hofiz saw in his contemplation, he found the boy's name in the book of fate, and it was written that the boy had twenty-six or twenty-one years of life left. Then Shaikh Hofiz took back his hands from the water. Those there in the gathering said, "See. Didn't you see the way he looked at the boy? He must be a pederast." They all gossiped and said he was a pederast. Shaikh Hofiz was sitting there listening to all of it. He stopped his contemplation so that he could get permission to reveal to them that he was a saint, so that they would all know.

After that, he got up, he said, "Listen." He said, "I'm not a pederast. I'm not an adulterer or any other thing," he said. "I looked down at the boy with mercy," he said. "I heard from the book of fate that he only had six days left of life. I asked God to give him twenty-six or twenty-one years, so that he would die on such and such a day and at such and such an hour." They laughed and said, "Who are you? You think that you're some kind of saint that can read from the book of fate? What kind of business is this? You're a pederast, one that looks at boys without mercy." Shaikh Hofiz said, "Me?" They said, "Yes!" Right then, he told them about all their sins, and they all got up and bowed down before Shaikh Hofiz. They said, "We now believe that you're a saint."

The pir ended his story by saying, "There are many, many stories like this. These things are secrets (*sir*) and mysteries (*asror*). There are some secrets that can be uttered and some that cannot, that remain hidden, closed."

In the terms used by Katharine Galloway Young (1987), the "taleworld" of the pir's story shared some affinities with the "storyrealm" of our conversation. For Young, the taleworld is the world of the characters of the story, in this case the events unfolding for Hofiz and Naqshband in medieval Shiraz. In contrast, the storyrealm of my conversation with the pir is the situation of Sufis in contemporary Tajikistan. In the story, the pir brings the two realms into dialogue as the concerns of the taleworld are mapped onto the storyrealm. In the taleworld of the story, Hofiz's father locks him away despite his Uvaisi initiation and his ability to perform miracles such as turning mud into gold. Still, later the key religious minds of his city slander him and accuse him of pederasty, even as he sits in quiet contemplation, miraculously reading from the book of fate and mercifully advocating on behalf of a young boy about to face premature death. Even as Hofiz engages in astonishing feats of mystical prowess, the reality of his spiritual initiation and status as a friend of God remain hidden from non-Sufis. In the taleworld, the real and authentic remain hidden and closed, and what seems ordinary is actually extraordinary.[24]

Simultaneously in the storyrealm, the pir more broadly suggested how he saw the entire mystical enterprise. What seems on the outside to be madness in reality is communion with the divine. The pir's story operated as an assertion of the real over what he saw as the inauthenticity of the paradoxical present. Just as nostalgic memories mediate the perceived disjuncture between the pre-Soviet and Soviet era pasts and the present, nostalgia also asserts a notion of the real, creating narrative space for agency denied to their tellers in the public sphere. Like Hofiz, the pir's vision of mystical reality provided him with some agency over the ignominy he regularly felt in the presence of contemporary Tajikistan's noninitiates, that is, the religious functionaries within the state's religious bureaucracy. There is an interesting dialectic at work between the hidden, "secret" mystical reality, which nostalgic appeals make manifest, and what is apparent on the outside. Put in dialogue with the Turajonzodas' memories and agency, the pir's "secrets and mysteries" ran coterminous with his nostalgia. "Secrets" and their stories seem to have all the more potency when coupled with a lack of agency.

I often found similar sentiments expressed by Sufis from various groups and with varying degrees of proximity to the current religious establishment. They all told stories in which the protagonist at first appears ordinary but is only later revealed to be a pir or another Sufi in disguise. The story about Iskandar's cook related in the previous chapter is one example. Another is a story I often heard told about Hasan al-Basri (642–728), a prominent figure in many Sufi silsila, in which Hasan at first seems ordinary to his companions but through a dream is eventually shown to be a pir. In such stories, the protagonists seem ordinary at the outset but in the end become saints. In actuality, pirs, eshons, shaikhs, and their followers may be marginalized or even outright persecuted by organs of the security apparatus, but within the taleworlds of narrative the ultimate, true reality can be revealed. Through such tales, narrators can gain some narrative agency over their current socially marginal positions. Nostalgic talk provides Sufis with space for the defeat of injustice, for example, the accusations of pederasty Shaikh Hofiz faced in the pir's story, by displaying a mystical reality not apparent on the surface to the uninitiated.

The rhetorical claims found within nostalgic stories about the past social order and agentive allegories that explained the paradoxical present operated akin to a coherent language ideology (Woolard 1998). Sufi nostalgic talk, with its set of common discursive frames and linguistic resources, in total put forward a consistent notion of how Sufis should rightly talk and think about the past. This Sufi talk did more than simply narrativize the nearer and distant pasts. It also identified the speakers and the taleworlds of their stories vis-à-vis the broader communicative situations in which their speech acts were situated (254). It is in this way that nostalgic talk became constitutive of social action and moved beyond a mere statement or even a commentary on the present state of religious affairs in Tajikistan. If in the last chapter the rhetoric at Hamandoni's shrine helped constitute state-sanctioned ways of being Muslim, then Sufi nostalgic talk operated similarly. It also worked as a public performative projection that powerfully organized Sufi social reality.

Nostalgic talk, including assertions about the nature of the religious reality behind the stories I have discussed, made a pragmatic claim on the present,[25] allowing Sufis rhetorical space for commenting and acting on the uncertainties of their wider social and political worlds. As a pragmatic language ideology, Sufi nostalgia was necessarily political because it functioned as a site for collective reflexivity and public interaction in which Sufis sought to shape the conditions of their collective religious lives (Hirschkind 2006, 8). Sufi politics were not simple interventions in the political process such as electoral participation or policy advocacy. Rather, their nostalgia was oriented toward discursively shaping group conceptions of what a Sufi life ought necessarily to entail. This shaping happens through asynchrony, nostalgia-tinged reconfigurations of the present. It is temporal reconfiguration that holds agentive capacities (Whitesel and Shuman 2016, 38). The production of the present is always political.

THE POLITICS OF NOSTALGIA

Sufi nostalgic talk was a longing for the past, but a longing for a particular past, a past imbued with special qualities, many of them directly in contrast to notions of Muslim piety put forward by organs of the Tajik state. Scholars working in various post-Soviet contexts have emphasized that nostalgia's mediatory power is never ideologically neutral.[26] Of course, as a social practice, nostalgia has no one political orientation. It is neither singularly politically innocuous, operating exclusively at the level of individual memory, nor actively politically meddlesome, working in opposition to the mandates of the state. In its polysemy or indexicality (Boyer 2012), nostalgia works as a powerful symbol co-opted into various ideological agendas. Still, nostalgia necessarily engages the political due to the fact that it is a discourse about cultural value and authenticity through which citizens debate the national subject itself (Nadkarni 2010). In particular, citizens of many post-Soviet states have engaged religious nostalgia to both support and reject their countries' nationalist projects (Simons and Westerlund 2015).

The memories and narratives about the sacred past I heard from my friends implicitly countermanded the almost hegemonic force of state discourses related to both the religious past and present, that is, the sorts of official conceptions about recent Muslim history discussed in the previous chapter. Indeed, elites' ideas about history were one means to subjugate ideologically public religiosity. Manipulating time and the past routinized their ideological projections, imposing upon Tajik Muslims a kind of "chrononormativity" (Freeman 2010, 3). In pointing to the positive features of the past social order, drawing comparisons between the topics of saintly narrative and contemporary religious figures, constructing fictive genealogies and silsila, and accusing the present of religious inauthenticity, Sufis put forward other times and histories, creating an alternative picture of what it meant to live as a Sufi in contemporary Tajikistan yet still in dialogue with the symbolically performed visions of Muslim religiosity proffered by governing elites. This Sufi nostalgia implicitly operated as an oppositional, countermemory in relation to the subjects and concerns of official state discourse (Bunzl 1998); as a discursive formation it directly contravened official notions of what a pious Muslim life should properly entail.

Sufi nostalgia's political work came in its agentive capacity, the way that it asserted countermemories of the past. This is what Debbora Battaglia calls an "active nostalgia," a nostalgia that "abides in a convergence of mimesis and poesis—in acts of replicating the social conditions of and for feeling, such that one's experience of social life is supplemented and qualitatively altered" (1995, 93). Indeed, nostalgic talk held the possibility that Sufis could resituate themselves among national narratives to which they do not give their assent and to which they are routinely denied access. Their nostalgic talk became political in the way it held the discursive power to reposition its actors in the present.[27] Its creative possibilities, that is, the acts of poesis inherent in its every deployment, may not have allowed its tellers to transform their social existence concretely, but it did allow them to become its critics (Cashman 2006, 146). The political work of their nostalgia was in its agentive capacity to change one's subjective experience of disempowering circumstances and thus "qualitatively alter" one's existence (Jackson 2013).

I would argue that there is little distinction here to be made between the social functions of nostalgic rhetoric and the enactment of real social change (see Green 2007, 65). The power of nostalgia lies not in the way it alters the concrete social and political situations of its tellers but rather in the way it allows Sufis the possibility of actively engineering their experience vis-à-vis the disempowering circumstances in which they now live. In ideological terms, this nostalgia is an inward move that does not directly critique the political status quo (Battaglia 1995, 92). Instead, it operates as an insulated form of social critique to which the political authorities cannot as easily offer censure. Beyond the ways in which Sufi nostalgia opens up a space for political agency in the face of a generally disempowering political landscape, mediatory nostalgia also works as a form of strategic identification. Through nostalgia, Sufis are able to disentangle the events of history from the paradoxical present. By separating the present from a genuine past, they open up the possibility of asserting counternotions of national belonging and put forward a particular sense of what it means to be Muslim in the present context.

NOSTALGIA AND MUSLIMNESS

"To reconstitute events in a story is no longer to live those events in passivity, but to actively rework them, both in dialogue with others and within one's own imagination" (Jackson 2013, 34). For Tajikistan's Sufis, this active reworking of historical memory helped connect the individual purveyors of nostalgic talk to the larger social worlds they inhabited, as storytelling is one of many activities that make sociality even possible. The telling of nostalgic stories itself even makes it possible for groups to coalesce around networks of narrative performance. More broadly, facets of Sufi expressive culture open up the opportunity for groups to delimit intragroup distinctions and enable facets of commonality (Magliocco 2004, 58). Nostalgic narratives linked Sufi groups through the performance of common memories and stories about the past. Nostalgic talk was an important signpost of what it means to be Sufi in contemporary Tajikistan.

One of the clearest examples of this in my fieldwork came one day when I was chatting with a number of adepts at a teahouse outside Dushanbe. As was my custom when I met with Sufis, I asked them to tell me stories about pirs, eshons, saints, and so on. On this one particular afternoon, we passed our time together sharing stories we remembered about saints from Persian mystical literature and still living Tajik pirs. Curiously, each teller made some reference to the fact that "this doesn't happen anymore" at the end of his anecdote chronicling some miracle or act of devotion. It was almost uncanny how each individual echoed a similar "no longer" sentiment after narrating a unique story or referencing some singular event from mystical history. Many of the Sufis with whom I interacted also spoke in similar terms. They in some ways defined contemporary Muslimness in Tajikistan in the way that they imagined and talked about the past.

Nostalgia's work as a marker of commonality and an active practice of identification is not unique to Tajikistan. Similarly, scholars working in post-Socialist contexts have emphasized the ways in which nostalgia for the Soviet era past has contributed to aspects of intergenerational unity (Nadkarni and Shevchenko 2004, 508; Schwartz 2013) and even how particular social practices have enabled social networks to exist among Central Asian Muslims that otherwise would not (Schwab 2015). Nostalgic narratives about Central Asian Muslim life are in this way also about the production of a Sufi *communitas* in which countermemories of the past function as an implicit critique of the political status quo (Bunzl 1998, 175). Rather than showing how Tajik Muslim identity exists independent of the individuals who express it, nostalgic talk illustrates how stories about the past are instead strategic, political moves of identification (Bayart 2005, 92), marking group membership and delimiting the boundaries of proper piety. In a sense, Sufi identity becomes rationalized through nostalgia in the sense that ideas of commonality concern the maintenance of connections to their common past (Abrahams 2003, 213).

For Tajikistan's Sufis, nostalgic talk, along with a host of other routinized expressive forms, are critical to maintaining the cohesiveness of their groups (Mendoza-Denton 2008, 177). In the next chapter, I still engage the issue of memory, but I explore it as it is further elaborated and formalized within one specific narrative genre, stories that I term historical narratives.

chapter 3

▣▣▣▣▣▣▣▣▣▣▣▣▣▣▣▣▣▣▣▣▣▣▣▣▣

Narrating the Past

Not long after I arrived in Dushanbe, a devout acquaintance lent me a slim chapbook titled, *The Biography of Eshoni Abdurahmonjon.*[1] The booklet immediately piqued my interest. In it the authors offer a broad introduction to Naqshbandi spirituality interspersed among lines of mystical Persian verse and stories about the life of Abdurahmonjon, the Soviet era pir discussed in the first chapter. One day I brought the text with me to one of my chats with Firuz. Since our earliest nostalgia-tinged conversations, he had become a tireless interpreter for me of Sufi life in Tajikistan. He loved sorting out peculiar episodes in my field notes, stories I had read in a book, or the meanings of mystical poetry. Always patient and ever eager to explain something I had observed or read, Firuz flipped through the chapbook that day, eventually stumbling onto a tale about a medieval Persian mystic who the book's authors listed as a favorite of Abdurahmonjon. Firuz read the story aloud, annunciating each word clearly, ensuring I would understand.

Akhi Faraji Zanjoni once had a cat.[2] Whenever guests visited the shaikh's home, the cat would meow the exact number of times as the number of guests. In this way, the kitchen caretaker would know how much rice to prepare for the guests. One day the cat meowed once more than the number of guests, causing everyone in the shaikh's audience to become confused. The cat then walked into the middle of the gathering and sniffed each one in attendance. Finally, he urinated in front of one man. When they inquired as to the man's situation, they found that he was an unbeliever.

They say that one day the kitchen caretaker was pouring milk into a pot in preparation to make milk rice. When he wasn't looking, a black snake fell from the stovepipe into the vessel. The cat saw the snake fall and purred excitedly while walking around the fire. Yet the caretaker, oblivious to what had happened, pushed the cat away. When the caretaker wasn't looking, the cat jumped into the pot and died.

When the milk rice was finally prepared, they discovered the snake. The shaikh exclaimed, "The cat has sacrificed itself for the sake of the dervishes. Dig it a grave and build a shrine." They say that to this day the grave is still a site of pilgrimage. (Darvozī and Badalipur 2003, 52–53)[3]

Firuz looked up, squinting his eyes with the look he saved for especially important insights, and said, "The pir also had a cat." Looking away again, he said, almost as an aside, "Of course, there's no shrine dedicated to it." He picked up his pacing. "Even so, the cat knew who was an unbeliever. One day a mouse fell from the ceiling into the middle of a gathering of disciples. The cat was there, but it didn't try to harm the mouse. Hazrati Pir explained the cat's hesitation to chase the mouse by saying, 'This cat knows which creatures are under the protection of my house.'"

It is a curious tale. It isn't often one hears a story about urinating cats who martyr themselves to save the pious.[4] Firuz suggested as much, his tone skeptical, hinting at the seeming absurdity of dedicating a shrine to a cat. Even so, he envisaged a strong commonality between the substance of contemporary devotion and hagiographic models from ages past. Just as the mystic's selfless pet possessed the capacity for supernatural discernment, Firuz's pir's cat enjoyed a miraculous ability to distinguish the faithful from those outside the shaikh's protection. My focus in this chapter is similar in that I consider how Sufis make narrative comparisons between the sacred past and the religious present. Specifically, I discuss the primary discursive form the Sufi nostalgia discussed in the previous chapter takes: stories I call historical narratives.[5]

Sufis like Firuz tell stories about the lives and spiritual exploits of religious figures that draw on key intertextual relationships with traditional paradigms of saintly and political power. Relationships of intertextuality lend vital authenticity to contemporary devotion and allow for unique configurations of cultural continuity in the way they establish discursive connections between the pre-Soviet and present religious environments. My attention to cultural continuity is not discordant with the temporal asynchronies of the previous chapter. Indeed, it is precisely the paradoxes of the present that engender Sufi aspirations for maintaining (temporal) continuity. In that frame, I am redeploying Dipesh Chakrabarty's (2008, 97–116) notion of "affective histories" to understand Sufi historical narratives, especially in the way the historical "now" intersects with pasts, presents, and futures. The term, then, is doubly apt, not only because of the way it connotes the creativity inherent in Sufi invocations of the past but also because stories told about saintly exemplars evaluate asynchronous Sufi presents and futures by narrativizing what it means to be a Muslim.

Memories of a New Saint

By the time the eshon told me the story, I had already been his guest for several hours. That Saturday winter morning, I had come to the village of a hundred or so mud-walled, tin-roofed homes not far from Tajikistan's capital to learn about Mavlavi Jununi, a nineteenth-century pir and poet, from his great-grandson, the eshon. The village looked almost identical to other small hamlets spread between the Soviet-built irrigation canals and ridgelines surrounding the Tajik capital—a small maze of narrow lanes framed by fading white-painted mud walls holding back cows and chickens. The nondescript village contrasted sharply with the newfound reputation of the saint, the village's best-known former resident. Apart from the hollow shells of a few half-constructed concrete homes on its outskirts, funded by remittances from relatives working in Russia, tin roofs with their satellite dishes, and poles set askew, which brought electricity for several hours each day, I could almost imagine the village as it might have looked in Jununi's day, then populated much like the village of Dushanbe before its transformation into the Tajik SSR's model, modern capital.

When I arrived, expecting to drink tea and engage in leisurely talk about family history with Jununi's descendant, his young son relayed a message from the eshon: I should meet him at a *chilla*, a ceremony marking the fortieth day after someone's death. The boy took me there, up a winding, muddy village lane to a house clinging near a ravine farther up the mountain, where the eshon was already sitting with a twenty or so village men in a circle around a feast of fragrant rice cooked with carrots and hunks of fatty mutton. His shoulders back, he carried himself with the grace of an aristocrat, the village men turning toward him with rapt attention each time he spoke. I had barely filled my mouth with an oily fistful of rice, when the eshon apologized to our elderly host, saying he was expected at a wedding in the next village over.

Cutting through a side alley, we sidestepped murky puddles left from melting snow and evidence left by grazing sheep or goats. On our walk to the wedding, the eshon began to talk about his ancestor, narrating the details of his biography: birth in Kandahar, Afghanistan, early life as the eleventh son of an itinerant Sufi mystic, his establishment of a Sufi lodge in the Hisor Valley, not far from where we were walking, and finally the prolific author of didactic, mystical poetry. Two young men greeted us at a gate and directed us to a scene almost identical to the last: a large guest room where twenty or thirty mostly bearded, elderly men were chatting happily over loaded plates of rice. The eshon poked at his second meal of the morning, pretending to eat more than he actually consumed.

"Our guest is here to learn about Mavlavi Jununi," the eshon announced, gesturing toward me, not long after we had arrived, evidently accustomed to the attention of a willing audience. He picked up where he had left off in the saint's biography as the men, mouths still filled with rice, nodded in affirmation, pleased at either the eshon's story or the fact that a guest had come to hear it.

"During the reign of Emir Muzaffar Khan,[6] now our, our president of Tajikistan, at that time the president was in Bukhara," the eshon said. "You've heard of Bukhara?" he said, looking at me, and then turned back to the still affirming looks of the village men.

Emir Muzaffar Khan was the grandfather of Olim Khan, his grandfather. Emir Muzaffar was in holy Bukhara. These mullahs wrote a complaint against Hazrati Mavlavi Jununi, that there's a poet that's come. Then, Hazrati Mav— . . . Emir Muzaffar himself invited Hazrati Jununi. He came from Bukhara. There the ulamo were in the court of the emir. They looked through Jununi's book to see that all of it was consistent with God, that there wasn't any error in the book. Muzaffar Khan became a disciple of Hazrati Mavlavi. That is to say he took him as a spiritual guide (*murshid*). And those ulamo also took him as a guide. And, Hazrati Mav— . . .

"Muzaffar, what did he say to him?" the eshon said rhetorically, again scanning the still receptive faces of the wedding guests.

He told Hazrati Mavlavi that he should stay here in Bukhara, work right here in the court. But Hazrati Mavlavi didn't want to. He, when he had

become a guide, he compelled them. He became irate. He came to Rohati.[7]
He preferred to stay here. And here they also gave him a little bit of trouble. For example, in one of his lines of poetry, he says:

> You wrote that my abode would fall among the apostates,
> That for shame, the foot of Jununi would fall in this land.

> During his life, Jununi consumed the stone of blame,
> After his death, the power of this witness will be made manifest to
>   people.[8]

"When I am dead," Jununi says, "then my worth will reach you." It's like
this a lot, after his death it reached people.

Among the Sufis I knew, some of the popular stories about pre-Soviet
pirs concerned Mavlavi Saiid Nasimkhon Qalandar ibni Shohsohib Qan-
dahori (1810–87).[9] He was a Qodiri shaikh and prolific poet, better known
as Mavlavi Jununi.[10] Though purportedly the author of at least seven
extant works of mystical prose and poetry (Nodiri 2004), during his own
lifetime his literary output was likely unknown save to his own disciples
and those within his village and kinship networks. Similarly, during the
Soviet period even fewer persons were aware of the details of his life or
familiar with the nature of his extensive literary output.[11] It was not until
after the dissolution of the Soviet Union and the independence of the
Central Asian republics that any of his works were published or made
available to the reading public at large.[12]

Narratives of Jununi's nineteenth-century fame abound among Tajikistan's Muslims, even among those who do not claim direct spiritual descent from the saint or hold an initiation into a Sufi group. These accounts
work to resituate the spiritual memories of Soviet era Tajiks and resur-
rect Jununi's spiritual legacy. The chief discursive move of these narratives' telling is to locate Jununi within the power structures of both the
pre-Soviet and Soviet eras. These newly narrativized temporal assemblages support the possibility of Sufi recursive histories and work to lend
spiritual legitimacy and authority to the pre-Soviet social order by connecting contemporary devotion to national historical antecedents. My
point isn't so much to explain how Sufis invoked the various pasts that
stories about Jununi and others referenced but rather to interrogate the
possibilities and foreclosures of positioning oneself in and out of these
times (Stoler 2016, 35). Such positioning is particularly necessary in the

case of Jununi where the vast majority of his present-day devotees were ignorant of his historical legacy prior to the collapse of the Soviet Union. Specifically, these stories offer potential accounts of how Jununi was received by the authorities of his day and, by extension, why this reception is not recorded in any extant textual artifact.

The eshon's narrative similarly worked to contextualize Jununi's life historically, foregrounding the dialectic between the religious past and present. He framed the contemporary political situation as potentially analogous to nineteenth-century political realities. Like today, there is a president, the emir, who ruled from Bukhara. Similarly, just as present-day Tajiks must judge the religious merits of Jununi's recently published writings, so, too, the Bukharan religious elites evaluate Jununi's writings. The narrative seemed to hinge on the derivation of authority with two such loci posited—Emir Muzaffar and the ulamo serving in the emir's court—both political and spiritual authority.

The eshon's narrative holds some historicity. The potential for quarrels breaking out between the Bukharan religious elite and the rural mullah, Jununi, as well as the need for adjudication by the emir in Bukhara, shares some affinity with the historical climate of late-nineteenth-century Bukhara (Dudoignon 2004). Often one key cleavage within the emirate was between those hailing from within the central areas of the emir's realm and those from the more recently annexed regions at the far eastern edges of the emirate, areas contiguous to Jununi's likely sphere of influence. Theological controversy, dogmatic rivalry, and jockeying for political favor and patronage within and among the Bukharan elite of both urban and rural extraction were also characteristic of the interaction between the ulamo and emir. Even more, the image of the pious emir supporting traditional Central Asian Muslim life similarly resonates with the impression the emir attempted to cultivate in the face of ever-growing Russian political and economic dominance in the region during the latter half of the nineteenth century (Khalid 2000, 370). It is in this way that the rivalry between the Bukharan ulamo and the rural mullah, Jununi, shares some affinity with the historical climate of late-nineteenth-century Bukhara, and the texture of the narrative performance holds a historicity that would prevent its summary dismissal by contemporary Tajiks.

During the New Year's holiday break, the schoolyard was empty. The middle-aged schoolteacher waited for me that evening beside a rusty

metal gate on a paved road leading to the village. Behind him stood a
Soviet-built two-story school building with decorated eaves, distinct
from the surrounding mud walls and maze of narrow lanes. The schoolteacher was a devout man. After studying literature in Dushanbe, he had
uncharacteristically attained a graduate degree from the International
Islamic University in Islamabad when it was still possible to study abroad.
He now taught literature in the district high school and supplemented
his meager government salary by giving informal lessons in Arabic and
Qur'anic recitation to village children. As a contemporary devotee of
Jununi, he had been recommended as someone who had studied Jununi's
poetry. I had even heard that he had integrated the poet into his state-
mandated teaching rubrics. It could sometimes be difficult to arrange
meetings with powerful men such as pirs, well-off disciples, imomi khatibs, and state bureaucrats. The schoolteacher had agreed to meet with
me the same evening I first called.

We left the neat grid of paved lanes along the main road and walked
along a dirt path to the mosque to sit and talk. A few other men were
resting in the mosque waiting for evening prayers to begin. The schoolteacher told me about growing up in the village and what he taught in
school. The other men chatted with us, adding their own observations.
The schoolteacher's excitement quickened when he told me about
Jununi's books and the status of the poet's still unpublished manuscripts.
At first the schoolteacher had been was wary of my recorder, preferring
that it remain turned off, but when we talked about Jununi he gestured
for me to turn it on.

"I've heard that someone from the Academy of Sciences came to con-
fiscate manuscripts that included Jununi's poetry. Is that true?"

"I think I was a child. It was the beginning of the sixties that Mirzo
Tursunzoda came," he said.

"Mirzo Tursunzoda?" I said, not expecting him to mention the famous
Soviet era poet.

"Yes, this poet, when he had heard about this thing of Jununi's, wanted
to publish it."

"Good, good," I offered quietly, hoping he would continue with his
story.

"But at that time when they were publishing, they were throwing out
religious things. There were censors."

"Yes, yes," I said, encouraging him.

"The books of Attor, Hofiz, Jomi, and the like that were published in the time of the Soviets, wherever there was the name of God, they would strike it out. The Soviets were heretics. That is to say, they were atheists. They didn't like these things. For this reason, not telling them and not giving them the books was a good deed. If Jununi's poetry had been published at that time, they would have censored the religious parts, and it would have seemed worthless to people, the book. Its value would have been lost."

In addition to asserting political and spiritual legitimacy, Sufis like the schoolteacher also told stories about Jununi's literary prowess. Moreover, the theme of legitimating authority was not limited to events that occurred prior to the October Revolution and the forceful integration of the mountains of eastern Bukhara into the new Union of Soviet Socialist Republics (USSR). Other historical narratives also relate to the ways Jununi and his works were received during the Soviet period. Like the previous story, the schoolteacher's short anecdote contains features that have some historical resonances. Soviet era scholars did search across the Tajik SSR for poetry and other emblematic artifacts of national culture to add to a series of catalogs and anthologies of Tajik literature (Alimardonov 2009; Gatling 2015). The narrator did not mention these specific cataloging efforts. Rather, in this narrator's telling, the scholar who came looking to read Jununi's poetry was Mirzo Tursunzoda (1911– 77), the national poet of Tajikistan, not a nameless Soviet ethnographer.

Tursunzoda was an important figure in both the political and literary life of the Tajik SSR. A prolific poet, novelist, librettist, and scholar, Tursunzoda was the chair of the Union of Tajik Writers, held a prominent position in the Tajik Academy of Sciences, and was a member of the Supreme Soviet of the Tajik SSR (Bečka 1968, 577–79). In his death, he still enjoys the reputation of a Tajik state hero, and even the Tajik one-somoni currency note bears his photograph. Then, as the story attests, Jununi was not only an important religious and literary figure in the nineteenth century. His reputation also carried over into the period of state secularism and atheistic literary sensibilities in the century following his death. Even the well-regarded Soviet poet Tursunzoda recognized Jununi's literary mastery and hoped to share Jununi's verse with the Soviet public at large.[13] In narrative, Jununi again was not an unknown entity. Instead, even during the height of religious oppression, he was well regarded by the elites of the day.

Beyond the fame of Tursunzoda, the story's historical resonance comes in that Tursunzoda treasured the folk poetry of Tajikistan, and his poetry reflects this influence, a fact not lost on the schoolteacher and the products of Tajikistan's educational system, the other men listening to his story. Although Tursunzoda valorized a folk aesthetic, he vilified the religious content of much of its expression (Saĭfulloev 1983, 116–31). His militant atheism extended to much of his work in creating a new Soviet national literature (Saĭfulloev 1956). The schoolteacher's historical anxiety about how someone like Tursunzoda and the establishment he represented would treat the legacy of their mystical forebear is of course well rooted in the historical circumstances of Soviet era religious politics. Simultaneously, it is curious that the godless Tursunzoda would seek out a village pir's religious verse and, if such a figure did indeed come demanding manuscripts, that humble villagers could have refused. Even so, the schoolteacher's story legitimated memories of the saint and contributed to his contemporary canonization. What allowed this to happen was the way both the eshon and the schoolteacher connected their stories to wider bodies of folk literature within their performance frames.

Historical Narratives and Intertextuality

Legitimating authority for both the eshon and the schoolteacher was an aesthetic communicative practice. The authenticity of the saint, Jununi, came about as a result of a "system of interconnected authorizing acts" (Kuipers 2013, 404), stories that built on already authoritative discourse, borrowing its forms and rhetorical power (Bauman 2004, 153). Both the eshon and the schoolteacher's narratives were somewhat amorphous and deeply embedded within their conversational matrixes. A rich scholarship exists related to the variable ways in which performers move in and out of performance frames within conversation.[14] What makes the narratives I discuss here aesthetic performances is the way their structures oriented them to the past and how the narrators utilized differential speech effects, such as literary attributions.[15]

In each story, the narrator begins by using a past time frame. In the first narrative, the narrator says, "During the reign of Emir Muzaffar Khan," and the second narrative begins, "I think I was a child. It was the beginning of the sixties." This "replaying" frame (Goffman 1974, 504) sets the texts apart from their wider conversational contexts. Additionally, the first narrative exhibits characteristics of speech prestige that heighten its aesthetic qualities. For example, the eshon recites four half lines of Jununi's verse, "You wrote that my abode would fall among the apostates . . ." A replaying frame and the inclusion of poetry elevate the narrative texts above and beyond their more mundane speech contexts and into performance frames. The narrators' explicit concerns with didacticism also suggest how each story should be interpreted specially in performance terms. These were not occasions of idle talk or merely instances of legend report (Hymes 1981, 84). Instead, these were pedagogical performances of a heightened register. The wider purpose of each conversation was to educate the audience and me about Jununi's life and historical legacy. It is also worth emphasizing that, to some degree, didacticism may be an inherent generic quality of historical narrative performance, as historical narrative itself uses past events in order to evaluate the present performance context.

In both stories, the past, the historical core of the storytellers' performances, acts as a communicative resource "providing a setting and an expressive pattern for discussions that transform both past and present" (Briggs 1988, 99), as the past and present are put in dialogue vis-à-vis each narrative rendering. As Ray Cashman (2008, 117) has argued, "It is precisely the comparison of past and present in order to evaluate the status quo that gives rise to historical discourse." In this case, such comparison works in the first narrative through the explicit identification of traditional paradigms of political and spiritual power, for example, Jununi's relationship with Emir Muzaffar. And in the second narrative the comparison centers on literary prowess, for example, Tursunzoda's affection for Jununi's poetry. In both cases, the narrators introduce legitimizing paradigms and then relate Jununi to the model. In this way, Jununi's valorization works as a kind of expressive pattern that enables contemporary Tajik Sufis to incorporate the saint's canonization into the boundaries of their present religious practice. Discourse itself works to transform contemporary religious understandings. By comparing the pattern with the status quo, contemporary devotees can then properly venerate and utilize Jununi's poetical works.

Ignominy may be appropriate for classical Persian poetical rhetoric and the attainment of spiritual gnosis that is the goal of the wandering mendicant, yet it holds some difficulty for linking pre-Soviet spirituality to the present epoch. The archetypal figure of Persian mystical literature,

Ibrohim ibni Adham, a king who forswears earthly power and wealth and commits himself to God alone, seems not to be the type to which contemporary Tajik Sufis aspire. Instead, after the disjuncture of the Soviet period and the political upheaval of the first few decades of independence, contemporary Sufis consider the emirs of Bukhara and their ulamo to be prime examples of pre-Soviet devotion and spirituality.

One can interpret the valorization of pre-Soviet Muslim exemplars inside historical narrative as evidence of an intertextual iteration of traditional Persianate oral narrative. To a certain extent, intertextuality is a key feature of all folk narrative performances (Briggs and Bauman 1992, 147–48), as narratives must be inscribed with a degree of conventionality in order to be read as generically related to the wider bodies of folk literature from which they derive. Inside a performance frame, performers make use of a body of motifs, character types, and so on, enacting and enabling new discursive formations generically related to bodies of conventional oral narrative. Attributing spiritual legitimacy and authority to the emir is not unique to the eshon's telling. In other Tajik narrative contexts, narrators also substantiate other varieties of legitimacy on the basis of creating discursive connections between present circumstances and the emirs of Bukhara (Mills and Rahmoni 2015).[16] Narratives in which a person of political power becomes the disciple of the pious are also well represented in folk literature, specifically in bodies of lore operating in the Persianate cultural sphere.[17] Such intertextual relationships between new historical narratives and wider bodies of folk literature allow the narrator to lend legitimacy to his devotional project, the lionization of the "new" saint Jununi.

My emphasis on the intertextual connections between the eshon's story and common folk motifs and historical understandings is not meant to argue for the "inventedness" of his tale. Rather, commonalities between historical legends and other bodies of folk literature attest to the narrator's hermeneutical deftness and the weight of cogent interpretative schemas active among members of his audience. What distinguishes narratives about Jununi's life and exploits told in contemporary Tajikistan from conventionalized iterations of standard generic intertextuality (i.e., the appropriation and deployment of conventional forms, structures, motifs, etc.) is the importance of discursive reflexivity in the tropes' narrative deployment. That is, narrating historical narratives about the recently canonized Jununi requires a kind of intertextual maintenance that is not always necessary in other performance contexts. As Walter Benjamin famously noted, "Allegories are, in the realm of thoughts, what ruins are in the realm of things" (1977, 178). Just as ruins require piecing together if they are to be made interpretable, so stories about Jununi, with their attendant allegories of contemporary religious life, necessitate constant (re)evaluation.[18] This, of course, is not to suggest that discursive reflexivity is not a feature of narrative performance more generally or that narrators of stories about better-known Sufi figures do not exhibit an awareness of their wider performance contexts.

After the eshon and I left the wedding, he took me to see Jununi's mausoleum (figure 5). Along the way, he offered further clarification and "augmentation" (Haring 1988, 370) regarding Jununi's interaction with Emir Muzaffar. This time, the eshon told me, "Emir Muzaffar became the chief disciple of the saint." Now, not only did the emir submit himself to Jununi's guidance and spiritual authority, as the first narrative attests, but Emir Muzaffar also became Jununi's most devoted disciple, in effect the spiritual descendant and mantle carrier of Jununi's mystical legacy. This added flourish to the earlier narrative even more firmly emphasizes the recursive nature of Tajik Muslim narrators' intertextual maintenance. Additionally, the narrative detail evinces even more cogent commonalities with the devotional models of ages past and folk motifs I discussed previously. Additionally, one could read the eshon's narrative elaboration as more directly undermining the political status quo than his earlier story did. The first tale limits itself to simple political respect for Sufi saints, whereas in the second the eshon elevated religious authority over that of the state. Irrespective of the eshon's political intentions, implicit or explicit, discursive reflexivity requires Tajik narrators to continually work to validate their intertextual connections.

Both narrators of stories about Jununi in effect minimize gaps between paradigms of spiritual, political, and literary authority and their stories (Briggs and Bauman 1992). This minimization of intertextual gaps allows for the creation of a kind of discursive equality between the pre-Soviet and Soviet eras and contemporary devotion. These discursive moves allow narrators to make direct parallels between narrated history and the vicissitudes of contemporary religious life (e.g., rooting narratives of Jununi's life and mystical exploits within common saintly paradigms and amplifying the degree to which the figures of pre-Soviet, Soviet era, and contemporary Islam are linked). The minimization of gaps thus

Figure 5. Jununi's mausoleum (photograph by the author)

offers contemporary Sufis the possibility of sacred equality with pre-Soviet devotional models to which they might not have been compared previously. Hearkening back to the pre-Soviet era—an age uncontaminated by Soviet state atheism and one in which the political and spiritual were more closely intertwined—offers a source to which contemporary devotion can aspire. A pre-Soviet provenance for religious practice today likely helps to render the Soviet disjuncture less jarring and the reintroduction of religion into the public sphere more interpretable.

I often heard critics of the Bahodiriya, the Tajik followers of the Afghan Qodiri pir, Khoja Abdulvakil Bahodir, whom I discussed in the first chapter, charge its newly authorized Tajik shaikh with charlatanry, calling him a trickster or even more seriously alleging that Bahodir's Tajik representatives were engaged in sorcery. Similarly, at the end of the Soviet period some ulamo considered groups of so-called innovators as "Wahhabists" and deniers of traditional Central Asian Islamic spirituality (Babadjanov and Kamilov 2001; Babadjanov 2004). As such, in the religious marketplace religious novelty often is potentially suspect, while clear genealogies linking contemporary practice back to pre-Soviet exemplars make contemporary Islam more palatable to generations that perceive themselves as bereft of religious heritage.[19]

In this respect, it is not so much that narrators conventionally render contemporary stories, as is the case with (all) folk narrative, but rather that the degree of topical conventionality often indexes the extent of contemporary religious authenticity. As such, the "filiation" (Bauman 2004, 2) of new narratives with conventional motifs helps legitimate contemporary devotion. That is, stories about Jununi are authoritative precisely because narrators establish features of Jununi's sainthood using models of political and spiritual authority that resonate with contemporary citizens of Tajikistan. Conventionality is what makes Jununi's contemporary lionization possible. Because the narrator "is perceived as conforming to the rules" (Haring 1988, 366) of traditional Central Asian political, spiritual, and literary legitimacy, historical narratives about Jununi become traditional. By extension, the narrator's traditionalization moves also worked as acts of authentication themselves (Bauman 2004, 27). The minimization of intertextual gaps creates the possibility for more recent figures' saintly canonization and legitimates devotional projects associated with them.

One Soviet-trained scholar of Tajik Persian literature, reflecting on the creation of Jununi's legacy and his works' newfound popularity, told me, "Jununi's descendants explain the fact that [Jununi's] name wasn't in literary compendia (tazkira) by telling a story." Next the scholar began to tell a historical narrative describing Jununi's life and mystical prowess. Literati in late-nineteenth and early-twentieth-century Bukhara authored copious poetry anthologies cataloging poets and other key figures of Bukhara's literary and religious spheres. Inclusion in these collections signaled one's literary renown and popularity. Instead, as this scholar said, Jununi's legacy is supported by a story.

In the case of narratives told about Jununi, establishing intertextual relationships between the seat of pre-Soviet, Persian-speaking Central Asian Muslim authority and contemporary religious practitioners is one means of legitimating the status of a new group. Folklore can be central to the maintenance of group identities as well as contributing to aspects of a group's social differentiation (Noyes 2003). As I suggested with nostalgia in the preceding chapter, the telling of stories enabled facets of Sufi commonality. Likewise, it was the performance of historical narratives that also contributed to the formation of new self-understandings among Sufis. Narrative created imagined boundaries around legitimate group practice; in this case, historical narratives suggested the pre-Soviet saints that Tajik Muslims should venerate, a standard feature of hagiography.

Historical Narratives as Oral Hagiography

Tajik Sufi historical narratives approximate other hagiographic genres found in Central and South Asia, for example, *malfuzot, maqomot, munaqib*, and tazkira. The story Firuz read to me also comes from book that is similar to these genres. The chapbook hagiography's format, including a record of the teachings of a Sufi pir, a small compendium of key figures of Naqshbandi spirituality, a short manual of proper devotional practice, and a brief survey of the history of the Naqshbandi path, firmly emphasizes its affinities with other historical forms of Central Asian religious literature. One might also argue that the historical narrative about Jununi is similar to other hagiographic genres in the way it ascribes honor to religious exemplars and roots their valorization within preexisting saintly paradigms.

Additionally, the eshon's later "augmentation" of his story, in which Emir Muzaffar becomes Jununi's chief disciple, is similarly consonant with standard processes of saintly valorization. Hagiographic genres often function through a kind of accretion, that is, the addition of spurious texts to a preexisting body of texts (Ernst 1992, 77–84) or other forms of retrospective biographical maintenance and/or authorial pragmatism (Lawrence 1982, 1993). Subsequent iterations of a devotional canon evince new structures and stories. Later additions often include new miracles and attribute new features of saintly prowess to the object of veneration. Interestingly, iterations of Abdurahmonjon's biography, the text from which the opening anecdote comes, exhibit similar processes of accretion. As I argued in the preceding chapter, with each publication new adepts are said to have received teaching authorizations from the pir and the authors include additional stories of his saintly prowess.

Just because a particular text, such as a historical narrative about Jununi's life and exploits or the published teachings of Abdurahmonjon, contains features a literary critic might term spurious does not suggest its lack of canonical authority or centrality to religious tradition. Carl W. Ernst (1992, 83–84) has rightly pointed out that creating taxonomies of authentic and inauthentic biography in light of critical standards obscures how communities interpret and use such texts. The historicity of these texts in any kind of absolutist rendering is irrelevant.[20] Both the eshon's and the schoolteacher's stories offer an authoritative "truthiness," in the words of noted American philosopher Stephen Colbert, that resonates with their respective audiences. The facticity of stories matters less than to what extent the narrative rings true for its tellers (Taneja 2012, 561–62). What makes the stories true representations of the historical past is the truth of the ideals they communicate (Alver 1989), in this case the importance and reputation of the individual Sufis now venerate, not some journalistic standard of factual accuracy. Tim O'Brien (1998) even argues that when tellers adopt this orientation to the truth, their stories become more believable to their audiences because "true" stories, in the absolutist sense, often do not as clearly communicate the transcendent "truth" their narrators intend.[21]

In some regard, it is the generic possibilities of historical narrative itself that enables narrators to vary the content of their narrations maximally according to each unique context (Cashman 2008, 109), unlike other forms of discourse more dependent on quoted speech and more rigid morphological constructs. In this sense, historical narratives hold

a kind of minimized textuality since there is no narrative script from
which a storyteller reads or an ur-version of the tale. Instead, stories are
maximally variable toward each narrator's performance end. Historical
recollection is always in this way a dialogical enterprise (Briggs 1988, 81).
This is not to diminish the eshon's or the schoolteacher's historical reality, but rather to emphasize how both narratives can discursively enact a
unique oral commentary on the nature and history of contemporary
Islam in Central Asia. What stands out in this reading is how both narrators firmly enmesh the particularities of saintly typology within larger
logics of community and local praxis (Green 2004b). Or, as Tony K.
Stewart puts it with regard to South Asian hagiography, "Life history
becomes indexical to the tradition's history" (2010, 229). A particular
shaikh's biography becomes merely the "ostensible subject" of said work,
while the "real subject" is the transcendent truth the text contains (237).

The move to locate saintly relevance and biographical complexity
in their relationship to the religious ideal they attempt to inculcate and
not in the specifics of a particular pir's life is also extremely relevant for
thinking through the particularities of Sufi historical narratives. In the
case of stories told about Jununi, creativity in the construction of the
"ostensible subject," i.e. Jununi, contributes more broadly to the legitimation of the religious ideals of Sufis in Central Asia. The "real subject"
of the narratives could be read as the legitimation of the Sufi devotional
project and not as the specifics of Jununi's saintly biography.

Rian Thum (2012) has likewise argued that genres of religious literature in Uyghur Central Asia have been especially oriented toward the
construction of what he terms "local histories" irrespective of their earlier generic purposes. Thum means that such texts serve most often as
a sort of emic history and textual mechanism to tie religious exemplars
of supranational reputation to a particular local religious milieu, local-
izing religious tradition and firmly subordinating transcendent truth to
the needs of local religious communities. In other words, the real subject
of Uyghur hagiography may not be the biographical details of a particular saint's life but rather the localization of a transcendent ideal.

What distinguishes the case of historical narratives told among Sufis
from other genres of religious literature operational in greater Central
and South Asia is not the fact that the Tajik narratives are structurally
similar and contain common folk motifs and character types or that a
kind post facto attribution occurs in which the forces of time work like

a stalagmite on the cave floor where each subsequent iteration of a shaikh's biography adds another narrative layer to legends surrounding the historical life of the pir. Nor is Tajik hagiography unique in how Sufis mobilize the particulars of saintly biography in the service of substantiating group religious tradition or localize transcendent ideals. What distinguishes Tajik historical narratives from other regional processes of saintly valorization is the purpose to which the hagiographic impulse is marshaled. In short, Sufis in Tajikistan need historical exemplars with clear genealogical relationships to contemporary practice. Stories about Jununi and others like him provided particularly robust vehicles for accomplishing this task. Jununi's reintroduction was not some Weberian charismatic breakthrough into the present (Weber 1963). Instead, historical narratives stress an uninterrupted progression of religious sensibilities framed as continuous with the arc of Central Asian history. For Tajik Sufis, forms have remained constant and meanings transcendent, irrespective of temporal breaks in public consciousness and performance. Historical narratives allow for temporal continuity.

NARRATIVE AND CULTURAL CONTINUITY

Hagiographical genres, such as historical narratives told about Jununi, necessarily minimize intertextual gaps between a performed text and a more temporally distant historical text. However, with respect to the present Sufi moment, historical narratives and their accompanying intertextualities seem especially oriented toward the establishment of continuity for ironing out the uneven temporal sedimentations of Sufi life.[22] Scholars of folklore have long recognized the importance of folkloristic practice in establishing cultural continuity and the ways in which cultural continuity is implicated within nationalistic projects (Wilson 1976; Herzfeld 1982; Handler 1988). Historical narratives told by Sufis similarly function within particular kinds of nationalistic frameworks and historical projects in support of the Tajik nation. Hagiography becomes "nationography" (Paul 2002; Louw 2007, 60). Michael Herzfeld has shown how social actors can reformulate and recast official state narratives both in opposition to and in support of nationalistic projects. "Cultural form" becomes "a cover for social action" (Herzfeld 2005, 2). By extension, even when expressive culture works in opposition to dominant state narratives, it still often operates within the same cultural logic as state nation-building projects. Tajikistan is particularly instructive in this regard.

The continuity Sufis posit in their historical narratives most importantly enables religious dispositions, yet it is still firmly enmeshed in the
Soviet-created idea of the Tajik nation and what it means to be "Tajik."
During the early years of the Soviet Union, the area encompassed by
contemporary Tajikistan was still in its infancy as a discrete political
entity. The Tajik SSR did not become a republic within the Soviet Union
until the end of 1929 and beginning of 1930 (Bergne 2007, 100–118), and
Tajik didn't yet exist as a language separate from other Persian and Turkic dialects spoken in the region. The Soviet experience helped fashion
a Tajik nation and a self-understanding distinct from that of its Central
Asian neighbors and historical Persianate cultural heritage. By extension,
Soviet efforts created a conception of what it meant to be a Tajik and
what kinds of expressive forms sanctioned such an orientation. The Sufis
I knew similarly integrated newly performed narratives within a Sovietized cultural logic, the result being that they conflated Soviet-created
notions about the Tajik nation with Muslim frames of reference in a
kind of uniquely post-Soviet historical "bricolage" (Lévi-Strauss 1966). In
short, purported cultural continuity within historical narrative allowed
the Tajik Sufi "bricoleur" to connect "Tajikness," as created by Soviet era
formulations, to what it meant to be a Muslim today.

In Tajikistan, with its contentious twentieth-century history characterized by upheaval and conflict, the power of hegemonic narratives and
their constituent counterpositioning has been extremely strong. It is in
this climate, in the midst of one of the last stanzas of Tajikistan's civil
war, that narratives of Jununi's fame began to circulate and, simultaneously, his works were first published. Issues of provenance and historical
relevance were particularly relevant at the time of their printing. Up to
this point, I have considered historical narratives told about Jununi's life
and exploits, yet newly published editions of Jununi's writings similarly
contextualize Jununi's life and mystical exploits for a Tajik readership
unfamiliar with the poet and his extensive literary oeuvre. In some ways,
these introductions operate as published historical narratives by offering another venue in support of the saint's new canonization. Specifically, the text editors focus on the origins of the poetry and the poet's
place within the pantheon of Tajik Persian spiritual and literary masters.

The impetus for and editing and publication costs of these texts were
borne completely by the Turajonzodas, the Sufi family discussed in both
preceding chapters. Eshoni Turajon, was a Qodiri pir in Jununi's lineage,

linked through his father, Sufi Abdukarim, who was the successor of Jununi's closest disciple, Sufi Pechifi (Junūnī 2004, 39). Not long after assuming the mantle of the brotherhood, Eshoni Turajon took possession of Jununi's surviving original manuscripts, which then were hidden from the Soviet authorities by one of Jununi's granddaughters (figure 6). Eshoni Turajon was known to have memorized large portions and frequently quoted verses in his Friday sermons when he served as imomi khatib of Rohati's mosque. Older men in the village still remember select couplets of the work as taught to them by their imom in the 1960s and 1970s.

Recognizing the novelty and new potential for access to this sort of previously proscribed literature, the editors of Jununi's first published work in 1997, Abdulnabi Sitorzoda and Eshoni Turajon's son Mahmudjon, write in the first sentence of the book's introduction, "The heads of government during the time of the Soviets not only intentionally kept us far away from our rich past heritage, but they also asked that we

Figure 6. Manuscript of the *Devoni Jununi* (photograph by the author)

would relinquish parts of it and gradually we would hand it over to for-getful hands" (Junūnī 1997, j). Thus, the publication itself is heralded as a salvo in a new Kulturkampf, in which Tajiks can now remember a past not long ago relegated to the dustbins of their supposed new progressive history. It is important to note that memory projects necessarily include forgetting just as much as remembering (Beiner 2007, 31–33). That is, it is not just relevant what Tajik Sufis remember about the pre-Soviet and Soviet eras but also what they forget and what pasts they remain unable to express. While Soviet era politics contributed to Tajiks' igno-rance of the weight of their own religious history, the editors claim that there has been a willful relinquishment of the Tajik literary religious heritage, which their publication rightfully remedies. Tajiks have forgot-ten Jununi and his contemporaries. His lack of notoriety is due not only to overt Soviet machinations aimed at wiping him and his ilk from Tajiks' memories but also to the fact that the Tajik volk has willfully forgotten its cultural heritage. In Islam forgetfulness/heedlessness (*ghaflat*) is a basic human sin. As such the editors' accusations have all the more reso-nance as a culturalist echo of an Islamic principle. In this frame, the editors conflate Soviet ideas of Tajik nationhood with a static, essential-ized concept rooted in new notions of the Tajik Islamic heritage. Now that Soviet strictures have been released, this history must be remem-bered, recovered, and revived. Jununi's new publication is a not a novel act or a new imposition. Rather, it is a return to past practice and a resur-rection of past literary renown, just as the narratives discussed in the previous sections attest. Here Sufi aphasia has found its cure (Stoler 2016, 122–23).

   The editors argue that their publication is positioned within this point of opportunity as a correction and reorientation of the Tajik national her-itage, yet their discussion still occurs within Soviet interpretative frames. That is, they take Soviet conceptions of Tajik nationhood for granted. Except in their revisionist accounting, Islam is a vital component of that enterprise, what Tim Epkenhans refers to as a new "normative Islamic hegemony" (2011, 87). This conception of groupness is firmly an opposi-tional one. By adopting a self-understanding distinct from that of Soviet era Tajiks, contemporary Sufis are able to differentiate themselves from the era of more problematic religious devotion and state socialism. The editors' rhetorical force here is oriented toward an essentialist rendering of "national culture." In the same vein, Mahmudjon Turajonzoda's older brother, Hoji Akbar Turajonzoda, echoes this sentiment in one of his later published works, *Sharia and Society*. Turajonzoda writes, "One of the important and fateful processes that our society has begun is to rediscover and become acquainted again with the original national culture. . . . One of the key examples of the movement to rediscover national culture in Tajik society is the reacknowledgment of the plan and place of the true religion of Islam and the value of Islam in the composition of the Tajiks' national culture" (2007, 9).[23]

Here Turajonzoda further contextualizes the cultural reclamation movement in which editors have previously situated Jununi's work—the same movement to which the narrators of historical narratives subscribe. There indeed is an "original" Tajik national culture, as engineered during the Soviet era. In addition to Soviet conceptualizations, however, Islam is a core component of that culture. Interestingly, in a later, Cyrillic-script edition of Jununi's work, this introduction has been modified. One key reason for the revision might be that the earlier turns of phrase need no longer be offered. By 2009 the editors believed that their readers knew only too well why key religious figures of the pre-Soviet period were unknown to their Tajik readers.[24] Indeed, using Jununi's own phrasing as way of introduction, they instead write, "Thanks and unending gratitude to great God that in past years favorable conditions have come together for some of the writings of the men of the path of God, that for clear reasons have been resting under a hidden veil, to be newly resurrected, revived, and offered to keen readers and the culture-loving and God-praising Tajik nation" (Jununī 2009, 3).

Their project, this time the Cyrillic-script publication of Jununi's work, is even more explicitly a return to the pre-Soviet era, a fortuitous "unveiling" for the Tajik nation. The editors take for granted their readers' notions of the reasons behind his "hiddenness" and no longer need be chided for their "forgetfulness" as they did twelve years previously. Interestingly, the editors have also resurrected Jununi's own poetic phrasing in this regard. Quoting him, they write:

The men of God have passed to a hidden veil,
The dear ones have passed with pain, destitution, and want. (2009, 3)

In the context of his verse, one can imagine that Jununi is explicitly referring to past Sufi masters.[25] The "hidden veil" in that context connotes an important mystical theme, annihilation into the ultimate reality. That is, past masters have passed into the gnosis lying beyond the current mortal sphere. In the context of the text as a whole, in which Jununi discusses key religious figures and the feats of spirituality associated with them, the half lines of poetry offer a poetic gloss on the poverty that often accompanies devotion to the divine while utilizing the standard poetical trope of the poet as a beggar in need of the sovereign's patronage. Now, after Jununi's death and his own imagined passing beyond the veil and absorption into the divine, the text's editors perceive the hidden veil as an apt metaphor for the spiritual situation in Tajikistan. Jununi has become the object of his verse. He is now one of the men of God passed on, as opposed to one of the perpetuators of godlessness during the Soviet period. The borrowed metaphor of the hidden veil is a symbol of the kind of recovery project in which Tajik Sufis have been engaged. All that is missing from a full Tajik Muslim history is a recovered history— that which was hidden behind a veil by a hostile Soviet regime. Now that the veil has been removed, Tajik Sufis are able again to see the "true" nature of Tajik Muslimness and to perform previously abrogated devotional practices.

In total both historical narratives and the introductions to Jununi's published works posit specific continuities among pre-Soviet, Soviet era, and contemporary Muslim devotion. Thus, contemporary veneration of religious exemplars like Jununi is not a novel practice, a Weberian charismatic breakthrough rupturing through into the Tajik Muslim present, despite its novelty to many contemporary Sufis. Rather, as historical narratives and printed introductions to Jununi's works attest, his spiritual and political contemporaries held Jununi in high regard. Even during the height of Soviet era repression and militant atheism, Soviet literary and cultural giants recognized Jununi's literary merit. However, what distinguishes such narrativized cultural continuity from other sorts of instantiations of folkloric history making are the notions of group membership that the historical narratives in this case study support—along with the discursive routines through which group membership is articulated.

What binds together pre-Soviet, Soviet era, and present culture is an essentialized notion of the Tajik nation that endured Sovietization and then became firmly enmeshed in a new sort of "sacralized identity" (Mol 1977), by which I mean a conception of group and self that regulates varieties of social change and operates within a religious framework.[26]

This conception of the group differs from some folkloristic interpretations of the nature of individual and group commonality in which identity is often taken as a synonym for a common set of cultural practices or expressive forms whereby group membership is marked (see, e.g., Dundes 1989, 1–39). Other folkloristic treatments of identity have welcomingly emphasized the fluidity inherent in acts of identification and the negotiations in which individuals and groups engage in order to construct and critique contingent selfhoods (Abrahams 2003, 217; McDonald 2013; Shutika 2011). Despite the problematic essentialisms and constructed nature of the term *identity*, and its use in ethnographic practice, it retains some value as a designator for some common features of individual and group practice. In the case of Tajik Muslims, the secular, Sovietized frame of group reference—and the identity politics that result from it—become subsumed into a new religious idiom, which in turn helps Muslims adapt to the exigencies of the their religious environment. Governing elites share the same frames of cultural reference, yet their notion of what religiosity properly entails is sharply distinct from that of Sufis, even as each camp shares a similar, Soviet-inflected vision of "Tajikness" and attempts to create continuity between the sacred past and contemporary religiosity via narrative.

(Counter)Narratives and Religious Politics

Independent Tajikistan's only president, Emomali Rahmon, stood erect behind the oversized wooden dais, embossed with the golden seal of the Tajik state. Behind him, a flagpole, on which the Tajik flag rested, finished the framed television shot. "Dear countrymen, respected conference participants," he began that February morning. On television the auditorium seemed filled to capacity. Middle-aged men wearing dark suits, clean-shaven or sporting trimmed mustaches, sartorially mirroring Rahmon, occupied most seats. The auditorium could have been any of the venues in the capital, which variously hosted presidential addresses, buildings such as the appropriately named Palace of Unity (Kokhi Vaḣdat). The occasion could have been any anniversary or state holiday, to which Tajikistan's citizens have now grown accustomed, a time when Rahmon delivers platitudes while standing in front of the symbols of state.

The audience clapped in unison, as if some invisible force compelled them to match the enthusiasm of their seatmates. The highly choreographed affair—lush bouquets of white and yellow flowers decorated the

stage, and variegated green lighting created a mood of showmanship—
demanded their attention, even as the bored looks on their faces suggested that they did not anticipate the announcement of new initiatives
of state.

Rahmon was there to deliver a keynote address to participants of an
international conference devoted to Abuhanifa (699?–767?), the eponymous founder of the Hanafi school of Islamic jurisprudence, one of four
main legal schools within Sunni Islam and the school most prevalent
in Central Asia. Tajik authorities had proclaimed 2009 the "Year of the
Great Imom," the ostensible aim of which was to promote the relatively
"tolerant" Hanafi school of jurisprudence over the more rigid and politically active schools of Islamic thought Tajik officialdom feared were
gaining traction in the region. In addition to the conference, organized
at the behest of the Islamic University, state efforts to promote Abuhanifa's historical legacy also included television specials, banners on
Dushanbe's streets, and local celebrations held throughout the country.
In short, governing elites leveraged the full performative weight of the
state's "spectacular" politics, discussed in chapter 1, in support of novel
historical constructions of Abuhanifa's life.

Rahmon's audience that day was much larger than just the government bureaucrats assembled in the auditorium. In addition to the television broadcast, the speech was later compiled with other writings
credited to Rahmon and published in Tajik, Russian, English, and Persian under the title *The Heritage of the Great Imom and the Dialogue
of Civilizations* (Rahmon 2009a, 3–26). Similar state-sanctioned books
celebrating the jurisconsult's life and his apparent apoliticism filled Tajik
bookstalls.

Immediately following the speech as it is reproduced in his book, Rahmon writes about "The Great Imom and the Dialogue of Civilizations."

There's a story that Abuyusuf, a disciple of Abuhanifa, relates: On one
occasion, we were sitting next to Abuhanifa when two members of the
ulamo were brought in. They describe to him a situation in which one
guy believes in the existence of the Qur'an and another does not. They
ask Abuhanifa for a decision concerning each of the two individuals.
Abuhanifa gives his answer, "Don't allow the prayers of either of them."
They replied, "Surely you are correct concerning the first, but why would
you decide thusly concerning the second?" Abuhanifa said, "Because they

brought discord into religion, and dissension is a form of heresy." Abuhanifa's verdict is rooted in the Qur'an. Its purpose is to protect the unity
of Muslims and the stability and security of society. (Rahmon 2009a,
41–42)

Rahmon explicitly interpreted Abuhanifa's jurisprudence as intended
to protect "unity," "stability," and "security," the precise aims of his own
domestic religious policies (Lemon 2016). At other points in both the
speech and the larger book, Rahmon presented Abuhanifa anachronistically as a Tajik, as an enemy of "fanaticism," as an advocate of "har-
mony" and "tolerance," and finally as a promoter of "state-systems" and
the Tajik "nation." Rahmon summed up his purpose when he argued, "To
prevent such undesirable phenomena [the threat of religious extrem-
ism], we must use the theory and life experience of the Great Imom"
(Rahmon 2009a, 178). In a longer and more detailed biographical treatment of Abuhanifa's life (Rahmon 2009b), which Rahmon is dubiously
credited with authoring,[27] Rahmon similarly glosses several narratives
about Abuhanifa's relationship with the ruling authorities in eighth-
century Basra and Kufa and chronicles several times in which Abuhanifa
goes before the caliph in Baghdad, mirroring the way Emir Muzaffar
summons Jununi to court.

Rahmon's valorization of Abuhanifa's religious politics are particularly curious in that Abuhanifa likely died while imprisoned for refusing
Caliph al-Mansur's offer to assume the post of head judge in Baghdad
or possibly due to critical remarks the saint made about the caliph's policies (Yanagihashi 2014). Rather than highlighting Abuhanifa's failure to
lend his full support to the caliph, Rahmon merely hints at some ambi-
guity in what might have happened during Abuhanifa's audiences. Rahmon goes so far as to describe two times when Abuhanifa ostensibly
did give the caliph his allegiance. When summoned and demanded to
provide his oath to the caliph, Abulabbos, Rahmon writes that Abuhanifa replied, "In this godly work, I pledge my loyalty to you, and I will
be faithful to you throughout your reign until the day of resurrection"
(2009b, 161). And later, Rahmon writes what Abuhanifa similarly pledges
to Abulabbos' successor, al-Mansur, "As God as my witness, I pledge my
allegiance to you until the day of resurrection" (2009b, 164).

Just as Sufis use historical narratives, so, too, Rahmon utilizes stories
from sacred Central Asian religious history to provide a historical basis

for the contemporary political environment. Narratives such as the ones Rahmon referenced about Abuhanifa and his interactions with the ruling elites of his day provide discursive support for political stability, religious tolerance, and national unity. Rahmon's historical narratives confirm his hope for how Tajik Muslim scholars will properly relate to the Tajik state. For Rahmon the ruler is justified in demanding political obeisance with the goal of promoting stability and state security irrespective of the particulars of an individual Muslim's moral compass.

Sufi narratives, stories like the eshon's and the schoolteacher's, operate as potent counternarratives to Rahmon's tales about Abuhanifa by offering contrasting hopes for the religious present. In Sufis' telling, religious exemplars are honored by ruling elites, not subservient to them. Jununi's devotees may assert a narrative vision in which the political and literary establishments celebrate Tajik Muslims and in which the products of pre-Soviet and contemporary Islam are closely linked, but in contrast Rahmon envisions an environment in which Tajik Muslims submit to the state's guidance and subsume their individual moral compasses to the broader imperatives of security and stability. The notions of cultural continuity highlighted by Sufi historical narratives and their printed analogues mirror the way Rahmon uses historical narratives in substantiating repressive religious policies, the same policies discussed in chapter 1. Yet, taken together, each group's narratives assert a notion of Tajik religious history that is "differentially performed, differentially perceived, and differentially understood" (Bauman 1972, 38). It is this implicitly differential understanding of Tajik religious history that makes Tajik Muslims' historical narratives a counterdiscourse to the state's prevailing analytical categories about Muslim practice in Central Asia.[28]

What it means to be a Sufi is based on these narrativized assemblages of pre-Soviet and Soviet era Muslim life, Soviet era notions of Tajik nationhood, and, finally, a new religious imagination in which Islam becomes coterminous with an imagined Central Asian Islamic past and functions in opposition to narratives crafted by governing elites. The new, sacralized identity of many Sufis should not simply be seen as a legacy of the Soviet past—a stubborn holdover from a previous epoch. Instead, contemporary Sufi practice should be recognized as a new adaptation and response to the present (Burawoy and Verdery 1999, 1–5). Indeed, Sufis' narrativized pasts, though coupled with Soviet ideas of Tajik nationhood, still functioned as creative responses to contemporary religious experience rather than as a state-sanctioned, cultural carryover from the Soviet period. Their asynchronies were especially attuned to the paradoxes of the present. The present milieu, with its refashioning of ethnic, national, and political self-understandings, as well as the reintroduction of religion into the public sphere, has allowed Tajik Sufi groups to utilize cultural building blocks and expressive culture in the formation of what it means to be Muslim.

Historical narratives told about Jununi are not anomalies in the religious landscape of the present moment in Tajikistan. The works and newly historicized memories of other mystical poets and newly prominent religious figures who lived during the pre-Soviet era and whose literary creations have similarly recently entered the Tajik religious marketplace (Gatling 2015) also illustrate how new, narrativized conceptions about the grand Muslim past have helped to legitimate Sufi practices of saintly veneration. The establishment of a historical basis and a perceived static locus of spiritual authority for Sufism in Tajikistan has been vitally important. Sufis needed both local and recent historical legitimation for their nascent religious projects because of the ways the Soviet regime forcibly divorced Soviet era Tajiks from their religious and family heritages.

Figures like Jununi have filled the lacuna left by Soviet redaction and cultural destruction. Simultaneously, Sufis have adopted a notion of Tajik nationhood inherited from the Soviet period, an adapted Soviet primordialism (Hirsch 2005, 442–51) in which the Tajik nation is naturalized and further coupled with historical memories of pre-Soviet and Soviet era religious devotion. Historical narratives about the lives and exploits of pre-Soviet religious figures have helped to fashion a new Tajik Islam in which the "forgetfulness" of the Soviet period has been remedied by lionizing the ignominy of the rural backwaters of the nineteenth-century Bukharan Emirate. Importantly, such narratives do not only circulate orally among Sufis; they also exist in published form.

One day Firuz told me a bewilderingly detailed tale about a pir and a lion. "Where did you hear the story?" I asked.

He looked at me and wrinkled his brow, seemingly taken aback by the question. He replied, "All these stories are in books, Ben." That is the focus of the next chapter.

chapter 4

🔲🔲🔲🔲🔲🔲🔲🔲🔲🔲🔲🔲🔲🔲🔲🔲🔲🔲🔲🔲🔲🔲

Material Sainthood

"Who's going to the city?" the pir said, taking me by surprise. The ceremony had just ended, and I wasn't expecting to leave so quickly. Five or six murids straightway raised their hands. The pir gestured at one man sitting in the back of the room. "You can take him," he said.

When I had arrived in Tajikistan almost two months before, I naively thought that it would be easy to fill flash drives with recordings of rituals and teaching. If my experience with Sufis in Afghanistan was any measure, it should not have been difficult to attend Sufi gatherings. Over the past two months, I had slowly made contact with pirs and their murids, but I still had not been able to attend zikr, the collective remembrance of the name of God, a standard ritual for many global Sufis and one in which I was especially eager to participate. The political climate had put everyone on edge. Usually cautious pirs were even more reticent to welcome outsiders to their teaching circles. Eventually, I got the phone call for which I had been waiting; I could participate in a ceremony that night after night prayers.

Later, still reeling from having attended my first zikr in Tajikistan, I got into the car to ride back over bumpy village roads to the district center and eventually take a late-night taxi back to Dushanbe. Rustam, the evening's poetry singer (*hofiz*), also got into the car, holding a small stack of well-worn pages in his hands. Rustam was another Sufi I would come know well during my time in Tajikistan. He was the kind of person it was impossible to refuse. The next time I met him he handed me two CDs, one a video of him crooning Iranian pop covers and the other a collection of zikrs he had compiled from YouTube.

"I sell them for ten somoni [about two dollars] each," he said, not objecting when I took money from my pocket and handed it to him. I liked him instantly.

Rustam was entrepreneurial and a tireless self-promoter. During one of my subsequent visits to Tajikistan, he announced that he had started making cheese to sell in supermarkets in Dushanbe. "Do you want to try it?" he said, proudly handing me a piece. Another time, breathless, he called and told me to meet him right away. When I got there, not sure what to expect, he was sitting outside a concert venue where Sami Yusuf, the popular British Muslim singer, was to perform that evening. "Can you write a letter for me?" he said, hoping to give Yusuf a CD with my note attached, in English.

"Are those the booklets you sang from tonight?" I said that first night in the car.

"Here, you can see them," Rustam replied, handing me the stack.

The mass-produced chapbooks with frayed covers were full of *ghazals*, the short lyric poems favored by poetry singers. Many of the already browning pages had Rustam's penciled notations on them, hash marks indicating the end of a recitation, "2x" scribbled after certain lines, and other portions elided or crossed out and new words inserted in the margins above. Quickly flipping through the cheaply produced pages, I did not recognize their author.

"What's this?" I held up a booklet with the title *A Collection from Mavlavi Jununi's "The Mine of Mystical States."*

"It's Jununi. You can get ones like it in the bazaar."

He was right. I found similar books everywhere books were sold: on a book cart in Dushanbe's central Shoh Mansur bazaar, in shops adjacent to the city's Hoji Yaqub mosque, on the shelves of a bookstore on Rudaki Prospekt, and even on a scarf holding items for sale during a rural village's market day. Despite the booklets' ubiquity, at this point during my time in Tajikistan I did not yet know about their author. I had not yet heard the stories about his fame and exploits, discussed in the previous chapter. When I looked for information about him in some of the standard English-language reference works of Persian literature, for example, Edward G. Browne's magisterial four-volume *Literary History of Persia*, Jan Rypka's always helpful *History of Iranian Literature*, and the *Encyclopædia Iranica*, Jununi wasn't anywhere to be found. "Maybe he was specific to the literary history of Persian-speaking Central Asia, not the wider Persianate literary sphere," I thought. I looked in Tajik-language reference works: *The Encyclopedia of Tajik Literature and Art*, a Soviet-era book series on the history of Tajik literature—*Tajik Literature in the Seventeenth Century*, *Tajik Literature in the Eighteenth Century*, and so on. I still couldn't locate any mention of him.[1]

It was only later that I discovered Jununi was simply a village pir and poet who lived in the rural eastern regions of the Bukharan Emirate during the nineteenth century. It wasn't until the end of the country's civil war that any of his works saw publication or distribution beyond his immediate descendants and successors in the Qodiri silsila. His literary and historical marginality is further attested in the fact that he doesn't figure in the copious anthologies of pre-Soviet Bukhara or in Soviet era collections of Tajik poetry.[2] His noninclusion and the dearth of his works in manuscript collections in Tashkent, Saint Petersburg, and Dushanbe suggest he did not enjoy wide circulation during the span of his lifetime or afterward.[3] Even so, by 2010 Jununi's poetry could be found everywhere books were sold. It is this move, from anonymity to relevance, obscurity to importance, and family heirloom to best seller that is indicative of the contemporary Sufi project.

In addition to nostalgic memories and historical narratives, a key feature of the effervescence of public Islam in post-Soviet Tajikistan has been the publication of religious literature.[4] In recent decades, publishers have released numerous Sufi books, works for the most part previously unavailable to pious Tajik readers. By Sufi books, I mean collections of mystical poetry, including both classical and newer Tajik verse, prose texts intended as instruction for adepts, hagiographies, sermons, prayer manuals, commentaries, government-sanctioned religious histories, touristic shrine literature, and other works that defy neat taxonomies. Some individuals have even begun to make their family heritage available to the Tajik nation at large by publishing and disseminating the manuscripts and writings of their ancestors, manuscripts they have held since the pre-Soviet era, turning their family heritage into national heritage.

In this chapter, I discuss the publication and circulation of Sufi texts.[5] Sufi texts are not merely the by-products or instruments of Tajik Islam, nor are books simply the means whereby Sufis graphically communicate. Instead, the material textual artifacts themselves engender social action as living embodiments of and agents for what it means to be

Muslim in the contemporary context. Like nostalgic memories and historical narratives before, books also bridge moments in time, simultaneously acting both as preserved transmissions from the sacred Persian past and as objects that find relevance in their present use. What distinguishes Sufi textual practices from the forms of expressive culture I have already discussed are their material dimensions. As folklorists have long recognized, language and materiality are intricately related (Jackson 2016).[6] Tajik Sufi texts similarly operate as forms of materialized communication, materializing sainthood itself and carrying with them traces of saintly power and authenticity.

MATERIAL COMMUNICATION

"When I was in school, we didn't read any of this, *any*," Shavkat said, emphasizing the last word, while he perused the titles displayed on the rickety book cart in front of him, the mass-produced books arranged in rows with their covers exposed to potential buyers (figure 7). It was a cold winter shrine day at Hazrati Mavlono, the tomb of Mavlono Yaqubi Charkhi, an important fifteenth-century Naqshbandi saint whose grave sits just on the edge of Dushanbe proper on the eastern side of the international airport's runway.

I met Shavkat by chance. Raised in the Faizobod region, he had come to Dushanbe to work as a bureaucrat in a government ministry. One night, long after buses had stopped running through the city, he flashed the lights of his car and held up three fingers as my family and I were standing on a downtown intersection hoping for a ride. Three was the number of the unofficial shared taxi route that ran through the center of the city. Like many underpaid government workers, he sometimes supplemented his commute by taking passengers aboard. The next week I recognized him shopping in the small bazaar near my apartment. It turned out that he lived in an apartment block nearby. Sometimes I called him when I needed a ride to a place not easily accessible by public transport. That day we had come back from a village east of Dushanbe, where I had hoped to visit a shrine and meet with a pir. On the way into the city, we decided to stop at Hazrati Mavlono.

"My daughter brings home all sorts of books from school, but I don't know any of the poets in them," Shavkat added as a Soviet-built, four-engine Antonov cargo plane rumbled overhead. "We didn't read any of this kind of literature when I was in school," he repeated. "Literature was

Figure 7. Book cart at Hazrati Mavlono (photograph by the author)

something else entirely. We read all about wine, Khaiyam. She reads Attor, Shohin."[7]

Shavkat's statement about the novelty of the texts available for sale at Hazrati Mavlono neatly summed up the broad changes that have occurred in the textual marketplace in recent decades. The quantity and variety of Islamic literature available for purchase have dramatically expanded. Texts, including Cyrillic and Persian-script printings of classical works, chapbook prayer guides, manuals outlining proper Muslim comportment, and hagiographies describing the lives and exploits of both pre-Soviet and Soviet era religious figures are all newly available. Somewhat paradoxically, this more extensive body of religious literature exists within a context of tight state control over the practices of public religiosity, the situation described in the first chapter. All religious books, especially those imported from abroad, ostensibly faced censorship constraints imposed by the State Committee for Religious Affairs. Still, the financial barriers to book ownership were not insignificant. Luxuries like books were beyond the means of many middle-income Tajiks, whose monthly salaries might not have exceeded seventy dollars. As such, books held considerable social capital among many of the Sufis with whom I regularly interacted.

Scanning the book carts at Hazrati Mavlono, one would find a wide variety of religious and tangentially religious texts. Yet, in spite of the works' topical diversity, or even in fact because of it, taken together they speak to something larger than the individual sum of their parts as they function similarly in communicative terms. By communicative, I do not simply mean to emphasize that writing is a mode of communication but rather to foreground how Sufis' use of religious texts mediates the contours of Tajik Islam. As the word *media* implies, texts do not just transmit discourse; they also mediate the social relationships of their producers, writers, publishers, buyers, readers, and listeners (Hull 2012, 1–33). Bruno Latour (2005, 39) has usefully stressed the distinction between what he calls "intermediaries," which convey meaning without engaging in any act of transformation, and "mediators," which transform, translate, distort, and modify the meaning of the elements they transmit. The textual artifacts of Tajik Islam are mediators in the sense that they help give shape to how Sufis understand their project.

Moving from the book carts and vegetable sellers in the bazaar, seated on their makeshift boxes, Shavkat and I walked through the gates of Hazrati Mavlono, past women in tattered kurtas holding small children and limbless men resting in wheelchairs. The contrast between the scene outside the gates and that inside the shrine complex was striking. The cries of vegetable hawkers and the jostling of beggars gave way to a mood of somber reflection and prayer, an environment quiet enough that I could hear water flowing in a reflecting pool. Inside the shrine's courtyard (figure 8), people strolled down stone sidewalks with their children in tow, sharing tea from Chinese-made thermoses. A boy unrolled a prayer mat, took off his shoes, and prayed under the portico of the shrine's mosque. A family inspected the tiled minaret at the far corner of the yard, the father pointing out its intricate tile work to his son.

At the far end of the courtyard, an imom sat with his assistant on a raised platform in front of the saint's grave. "Oh God, accept her pilgrimage," he intoned as he bowed his head and raised his hands, his palms joined and turned toward the sky.

"Grant every hope and desire she's brought with her to this place. Have mercy and forgive her every sin, oh Lord," he continued.

"May her children's every misfortune, pain, and calamity be under your protection. Bless her work and life. Bestow on her every success. She that seeks good fortune, heal her every ache. In the name of his greatness, have mercy on her."

Two women with their young children, one an infant wrapped tightly against the cold, got up from where they had been seated on a long wooden bench and walked to the carved platform, where the imom rested with his legs crossed. She dropped money into a clear plastic box already filled with folded bills and coins.

"Amen," the imom said, bringing his cupped hands to his face.

Four books rested on the platform beside him: a faded booklet entitled *Who Is Mavlono Yaqubi Charkhi?*; a green hardback text, *Mavlono Yaqubi Charkhi: His Life, Writings, and Ideas*; a paperback copy of *Mavlono Yaqubi Charkhi and His Treatise "The Reed Flutes"*; and a hardbound copy of Yaqubi Charkhi's commentary on the Qur'an. It is precisely this varied constellation of printed texts that indexes the larger social worlds of Tajikistan Muslims.[8] All four texts directly or indirectly related to the concerns of those visiting Hazrati Mavlono, yet at the same time they were written and published for disparate purposes and with different audiences in mind, variously oriented toward tourist kitsch, government-sanctioned history, mass-produced devotional import, or serious-minded Muslim scholarship.

Figure 8. Shrine day at Hazrati Mavlono (photograph by the author)

In toto the books draw together different historical epochs and social relationships to the extent that together they put forward a coherent notion of what textual authority entails in contemporary Tajikistan.[9] On one level, the works are icons, representative of the saint buried at the shrine and the organs of government that administer his shrine complex. On another they gesture at the significance of the figure buried beneath the ornately carved stone sarcophagus in the shrine's inner courtyard. They operate as tokens of the saint's wisdom and international reputation and simultaneously give him voice from beyond the grave, allowing him to speak to the significance of the pilgrim's prayers and, perhaps, even provide implicit sanction to the devotion of those gathered on shrine day. In that regard, the books on the platform hold an agentive capacity (Latour 1999, 113–44; Jones and Boivin 2010). That is, the books are more than simply representatives of the saint. Rather, they are forms of materialized communication (Tilley 1999), able to transform, translate, distort, and modify what it means to be Muslim and by extension Sufi, in Tajikistan.[10] They become tools for the reconfiguration of the Sufi present.

For the most part, this agentive power does not derive from the content graphically printed inside them. Instead it comes from the contexts in which the works themselves circulate. Once printed, Sufis can take the books from their original contexts of use and redeploy them in new contexts (Bauman and Briggs 1990; Urban 1996). Folklorists have most often discussed entextualization and re/decontextualization in terms of spoken or graphic discourse. Those insights can easily be applied to the social work of Sufi texts. For example, repeated de/recontextualizations have allowed Tajik Muslims to use Jununi's poetry in diverse and unrelated situations. Jununi's poetry has variously supported general Islamic ethics and eschatological fervor when it has been read within the context of a Sufi teaching circle, and in the context of state television broadcasts, it is simply lauded for its verbal artistry (e.g., Rashtī 2005, 198–214; Zubaïdulloh, n.d.).

Beyond this, entextualization and re/decontextualization also provide a productive framework for understanding how textual artifacts can also work as forms of material communication. The books on the imom's platform at Hazrati Mavlono gain new efficacy to affect the social worlds of Tajikistan's Muslims when they move from their original contexts of writing and publication, whatever they might have been, and are put into new contexts of use like the platform at Hazrati Mavlono. In this case, their communicative potential doesn't come only from the discourse the books graphically communicate, but also from their existence as material artifacts, which "perdure" (Silverstein and Urban 1996). Because of their perdurance, they can "render tangible" facets of Sufi social life, sacred history, and contemporary religious politics in ways that words alone cannot (Lemonnier 2012, 14).

What brings together the diverse textual artifacts of Tajik Islam is that there is little change in the larger functions of the communicative acts in which they are embedded, even across repeated entextualizations and recontextualizations. Disparate texts, originally written for distinct purposes and audiences, become similarly representative of the social worlds of Tajik Muslims because of the way each new recontextualization materially embodies sainthood.

THE MATERIALITY OF SAINTHOOD

Not long after I had stumbled upon Jununi's significance to Tajikistan's Sufis, I took public transport to Rohati, not far from the eshon's village described in the preceding chapter where Jununi had lived during his adulthood. I hoped to talk to anyone I could about the saint's newfound importance. The aging minibus turned off a newly tarmacked road about twenty-five kilometers to the east of the capital onto a potholed, winding lane that headed north into the hills with snow-capped mountain peaks towering off in the distance. When it stopped in the middle of the village, I got off and walked into a shop to ask for directions to the town's mosque. The shopkeeper pointed to a gray-haired man squatting on the street corner, saying he was the mosque's groundskeeper. I introduced myself. Smiling as if reunited with a long lost friend, he welcomed me and insisted that I accompany him directly to his house. As much as I tried, he wouldn't let me refuse.

We walked up the muddy lane together and into his yard. It had only been four days since Idi Qurbon, and the man's guest room, paint chipping from the walls, a worn carpet on the floor, was still filled with fruits, nuts, and candies, ready to welcome a tardy holiday guest like me.[11] I sat on the floor. Just as the man filled the plate in front of me with holiday goodies, his middle-aged son-in-law and teenage grandson entered the room. When they heard about my project, the boy hustled out in the time it took to take one sip of tea and returned holding two books in his hands: a worn copy of Jununi's *Mine of Mystical States* and a green hardback version of Jununi's *Devon*. Encouraged by the boy's enthusiasm, I asked him to recite a ghazal. His shoulders back and head held high, he recited one from memory, as my host and his son-in-law beamed with obvious pride. As I nibbled on candied almonds and sipped tea, our conversation circled around topics such as the history of the village, Jununi's life and works, and the saint's importance to villagers. My host, almost summarizing our conversation together, pointed at the two books his grandson still held in his hands and said, "There are only two Mavlavis: Mavlavi Jununi and Mavlavi Rumi."

For the mosque caretaker and his family, there was a direct connection among textual artifacts, materiality, and saintly authority. When I asked them about Jununi, the caretaker's grandson immediately brought out Jununi's books. Before I left, the caretaker linked those books with the claim that the saint's mystical authority exists on the same plane as that of the most famous of Persian Sufis, the thirteenth-century Anatolian mystic and author of the best-known mystical treatise in Islamic history, Rumi. My host, his son-in-law, and his grandson could have narrated stories about Jununi's life or pointed out landmarks of his life in the village. Instead, they presented the two books, material representations of his sainthood and importance. It is also worth emphasizing that they did not read from the books, but rather the caretaker's grandson recited a ghazal from memory. As such, the power of the books they held did not necessarily derive from the material contained within them, but rather the textual artifacts themselves served as material representations of it, so much so that the caretaker even called Jununi one of only two Mavlavis, further emphasizing the centrality of the saint in the life worlds of Rohati's villagers.

That spring Khurshed and I had begun to spend more time together. Still, our relationship was an uneasy one. Many of the other Sufis with whom I regularly interacted had become comfortable with my outsider status. Whereas Firuz was content to share stories and Rustam enjoyed talking about poetry and singing ghazals, it bothered Khurshed that I didn't seem to be making any progress in my spiritual journey. The intensity of our conversations sometimes left me unsettled. Khurshed understood that I was a sympathetic researcher, not a seeker. But despite my repeated assurances, he still held out hope that I would eventually submit to the pir. My questions sometimes frustrated him as they might a parent faced with the incessant requests from a wayward child.

"You need to read it. The book has all of Sufism (tasavvuf) in it." Khurshed said, pulling the book from the bag. "If you want to know about the secrets of the path, you need to read the *Rashahot.*"

The *Rashahoti Ain-ul Hayot* (Drops from the source of life), a sixteenth-century Naqshbandi hagiography by Fakhr al-Din Kashifi (d. 1532/33), discusses the mystical exploits and teachings of Khoja Ahror (1404–90/91), an early figure in the Naqshbandi silsila, and other illustrious personages from the Khojagon lineage of the Naqshbandiya. In 2011 a Tajik publisher had released the book's first Cyrillic-script printing. We got out of Khurshed's car and walked together across the lane to one of the open bookshops adjacent to Tajikistan's Islamic University. The smiling bookseller, dressed in a crisp white robe and skullcap, greeted us as we walked inside the shop.

"Do you have the new *Rashahot* book?" Khurshed said.

The bookseller walked to the back of the shop and shuffled through a small stack of books. "Here," he said, handing us a crisp, never-opened copy.

"I'll take two," Khurshed responded. He paid without bargaining, and we walked together out of the shop. Back in the car, Khurshed scanned the text for the passage he had in mind.

"This is Sufism," he said, looking at me with an intensity that I had come to both loathe and recognize as his signal for me to pay special attention. He found the page he was looking for and read the poem aloud.

Oh God, how sweet it is to laugh without smiling,
To gaze at the world without using one's eyes.
How good it is to sit and travel,
To walk around the world without owing anything to one's foot.

"This book has stories about 530 saints," Khurshed said. "This book is Sufism," he said again for emphasis.

The relationship between a Sufi master and his disciples centrally animates what it means to be a follower of the mystical path for most global Sufis, though what this means in the context of a specific Sufi group can vary tremendously. Most of those who claim an affinity with Sufism in Tajikistan have submitted themselves to the guidance of a pir by giving him their pledge (*baiat*). In return pirs offer their murids spiritual guidance by teaching them the recitations of the path of which they are a part and advocating on their behalf to God. In short a pir provides his murids with the spiritual tools necessary to become closer to the divine. As one of my most pious Sufi acquaintances routinely noted, "If one really wants to know God, he has to enter the tariqat." In other words, in order to experience the divine one has to submit to the guidance of a pir and partake of his overflowing spiritual wisdom. Since at least the end of the civil war, one need not exclusively interact with a pir in order to access spiritual wisdom. Khurshed's comments suggested that an aspiring adept could simply read about it in a book. For Khurshed, the *Rashahot* encapsulated the ideas we had been discussing over our past few months together. Indeed, as he noted twice, "This book is Sufism." Khurshed made a direct connection between the textual artifact, that is, the physical text of the *Rashahot*, and the power of the saints whose stories it chronicles. In this frame, spiritual authority and mystical truth were attainable merely through the act of reading.

Khurshed's sentiment was echoed by a number of other aspiring Sufis. One claimed, "All of Sufism is in [the book]. It has everything you need to know" (Gatling 2015, 226). This time, the murid was referring to the poetry of yet another pre-Soviet Tajik poet only recently introduced to Tajikistan's pious reading public, Abdulhai Mujakharfi (1867–1931). Again the murid stressed that one can experience transcendent truth merely through the disciplines of individual reading. Yet another Sufi told me that every few days he picks up a mystical poetry collection, turns to a random page, and reads a few ghazals. He stressed that he doesn't always exactly understand what he reads, but just by reading it he encounters the author's grace (*faiz*). Commenting on his seemingly random choice in reading, he said, "They're all about love. It doesn't matter which one you read." That is, what was important wasn't that he grasped the referential particulars of a single line of verse but rather that reading the text, any part of it, enabled him to experience the transcendence he so earnestly sought. It was the textual artifact itself that held transforming power.

Some of this transforming power comes in the way that the texts of Tajik Islam provide their readers with some distance between the immediacy of the reading event and the context(s) of the books' original writing or publication (Stewart 1993, 22–23). This distance, "transcendence" (Green 2004a), or "externality" (Shryock 1997) allows texts to stand simultaneously outside both the present and the past, lending them a resonance of truth that they might not otherwise contain. Texts, like memories and narratives before, thus move between different times. Richard Firth Green has noted that there is an "almost universal association between writing and authority" (1999, 257–63). In this respect it's not insignificant that even the earliest English-language etymologies of authority render it as a synonym for a written text. It is important to note that the authority of the textual artifacts of Tajik Islam is different from the authority inculcated by narrating historical narratives or expressing nostalgic memories. Authority derives not so much from textual artifacts' connections to the past, as it does with nostalgic memories, or applicability to the present, as is often the case with historical narratives, but rather from the ways in which texts seem independent of both. Texts in their externality seem to transcend the asynchronies that Sufis experience.

At the same time, externality is more complicated than simply past, present, or neither. The externality of textual artifacts is shifting and contingent. Texts connect their readers to the past, yet they are only read when relevant to their readers' presents. The copy of the *Rashahot* from which Khurshed read embodied the spiritual power of its author and the mystical protagonists of its stories. At the same time, its importance did not derive exclusively from its referential particulars but rather from its applicability to our ongoing conversations about the basics of the Sufi way. Even more, the *Rashahot* wasn't only relevant to the context of our developing friendship; it was also significant because of its associations with the history of Central Asian Sufism and what the book conveyed about Khurshed's direct relationships to that history, a not insignificant fact due to the financial barriers to book ownership and the social capital it carries among pious Tajiks. In some ways, this shifting and contingent externality is enabled precisely because of the text's materiality. As a material representation of its author and/or subject's spiritual authority, it becomes independent of the contexts (e.g., the particular social milieus, publishing houses, means of transmission, etc.) of which it earlier was a part. At the same time, it still holds some more than personal relevance in its reading (Shuman 2005), denying the singular significance of the present reading event. Reading, that is, another act of entextualization, allows the *Rashahot* to transcend the multiple de/recontextualizations it has already traversed by erasing any entextualizing work that brought it into the present reading context.

There is an interesting conjunction here between the externality and materiality of textual artifacts. Sufi textual artifacts express spiritual wisdom precisely because of their immediate accessibility, that is, their materiality. In the preceding section, I suggested that textual artifacts work as materialized forms of expressive communication, but textual artifacts also materialize sainthood itself in the way they embody the wisdom of past pirs. In effect, texts become material representations of the direct speech of past masters, so that in reading it is almost as if one is encountering a pir's teaching directly. Through their materiality, books themselves become pirs to aspiring adepts, substituting for the intricacies of a master-disciple relationship.

However, just because books materialize spiritual authority, substituting reading for the intimacy of direct face-to-face instruction does not mean that an aspiring Sufi need only read a book to progress along the mystical path. Tajik Sufi conceptions of textual primacy are not akin to more Muslim reformist ones, in which a text can be divorced from embodied tradition to the extent that the work of interpretation becomes graspable for even the most humble seeker. Instead, interpretation never remains self-evident. A book might contain the spiritual wisdom of its author or allow one to experience authentically the mystical exploits of its stories' protagonists, but it can never be a priori more authoritative than the words of one's living master, nor can it entirely replace the requirements that exist within the bounds of an active pir-murid relationship.

Several weeks after our purchase at the bookstore, Khurshed and I were again reading the *Rashahot* together. "If you look here, it says that there are eight stages (*zina*)," I said, pointing out a particular passage in the book. "I thought you said there were seven?"

Khurshed nodded. Not looking up, he skimmed the pages.

Over the past few weeks, Khurshed had described the stages of the mystical path in detail. Since our last time together, I had noticed a number of discrepancies between his descriptions of the path and what was written in the book he had given me. I wasn't trying to be antagonistic. I just wanted to get a clearer picture of how he used the book in conjunction with the teachings of his pir. He had commended the book to me with the statement "This is Sufism," yet it wasn't difficult to notice that the "Sufism" of the *Rashahot* was seemingly distinct from Khurshed's.

Khurshed kept reading.

Maybe I should have waited longer for him to respond, but I pressed him, perhaps emboldened by the increasing acrimony of our conversations. "I think I may have written in my notes that you said the first stage was 'watching over one's steps' (*nazar dar qadam*), but here it says that 'awareness in breathing' (*Hush dar dam*) is first."

After a long pause, Khurshed replied, "I only know the secrets that have been revealed to me by Hazrati Pir. What secrets I know, I learned from him. The book is just so I can study on my own. I can only read what Hazrati Pir tells me to read."

My conversation with Khurshed wasn't the only time I noticed seeming inconsistencies between a particular pir's teachings and the contents of the books their disciples read and recommended. On one occasion, Rustam even told me about the time his pir corrected his reading of one of Jununi's ghazals. He had been reciting from a booklet containing Jununi's poetry in the pir's presence. When the pir heard it, he told Rustam to read a few lines differently, saying he had seen in a vision (*muroqiba*) that the booklet's editors had changed Jununi's originals. Despite the fact that the booklet exists as a material representation of Jununi's lasting mystical prowess, it cannot act as a pure substitute for face-to-face instruction in the context of an ongoing relationship between a Sufi and his master.

Critics of Sufism, including the state-sponsored religious elite, might point to such examples as additional proof of the unlearned nature of traditional Tajik religiosity. Quite to the contrary, they merely highlight how books, as material representations of the speech of past pirs, operate within the context of Tajik Sufism. As these anecdotes indicate, a pir still must guide what his murids read, and a living pir's words always trump the testimony of an ossified textual artifact. Textual artifacts aren't immutable objects. Rather, they are always open to intervention (Thum 2014, 56). In the case of the pir changing Rustam's recitation, the issue isn't that the booklet containing Jununi's poetry lacked spiritual authority. It is merely possible that the printed words on the page are distinct from their original utterances.[12] It is the legitimacy of subsequent entextualizations that potentially remains suspect. As Nile Green puts it with respect to Sufi textual practices in early modern South Asia, "Textual authority—even an author's control over his own text—was subsumed within a wider schema of the authority of the shaykh" (2006, 40).

On the surface, the pir's correction also complicates my earlier argument about the externality of the written sphere. Here the pir has prioritized a kind of originalism, holding up the original utterance as of primary importance. However, his originalism does not privilege the original context of the text's writing but rather the personal authority contained within it. He is calling into question the veracity of intervening entextualizations, not due to some hesitation about the processes of de/recontextualization inherent in the Tajik textual sphere but rather because he is suspicious of editorial practices. Just because editorial practices might complicate the spiritual authority a particular textual artifact holds doesn't mean that it isn't external, transcending the contexts of its writing or publication. Indeed, texts must be readily re-/decontextualizable in order to be used. If a Sufi cannot easily insert a text into a new discursive context, the text can't be authoritative because it cannot speak as directly to the contexts of its immediate use. So, with Jununi's suspect ghazal, it wasn't that the pir called into question the book's externality but rather that he valued only one particular entextualization. A textual artifact might sometimes be pir-like, yet a devotee cannot create his own singular hermeneutic. Texts, specifically those newly introduced to the Tajik Sufi reading public, are authoritative because of their materiality and externality, but Sufis still premise their meanings on their active, ongoing relationships with their pirs.

The Meanings of Books

When Firuz and I walked into the pir's house that afternoon, the pir became visibly unsettled. He obviously hadn't heard that I was coming. Firuz wasn't the pir's disciple, but he knew him well and was a good friend of his youngest brother. I had spent some time with the pir early on during my time in Tajikistan, yet after the authorities ramped up their campaign against public Islam in late 2010 and early 2011, he stopped meeting publicly with his disciples. It soon became apparent that my attendance at group teaching events was a potential danger to the group; the presence of a foreign researcher drew too much unwelcome attention to Sufis who were doing their best to fly under the radar of the state's increasingly attentive security services.

Months had passed. For the moment, political pressures seemed somewhat more relaxed. Firuz suggested that I come with him to offer my pilgrimage to the pir and rekindle our relationship. Before we went,

Firuz assured me that I was welcome and no longer posed any danger to the group, despite what had occurred months earlier. I was still somewhat hesitant, but I had grown to trust Firuz. To smooth over any remaining hard feelings, we brought along a fifty-kilogram bag of rice and a tub of cooking oil as a gift to the men at the lodge.

Our gifts didn't obviously do their work. Remembering my project, the pir straightaway asked me, "What questions do you have today?" Without waiting for my answer, he said, "I don't think you need to ask anything about the *Letters* because their apparent (*zohir*) meaning is clear."

The last time I met with the pir, we had spent the majority of our time talking about the primary text from which he taught his disciples, the *Letters of Imom Rabboni*.[13] Without a doubt, the pir's summary dismissal of a potential discussion topic signaled his displeasure with my visit. I never discovered the exact reason for his discomfort, but I suspect it was due to his general caution in light of the broader political situation. However, his hesitation might just as easily have been because he genuinely disliked me or disapproved of my research. Regardless, the deflection foregrounded a significant distinction between varieties of knowledge the textual artifacts of Tajik Islam contain: apparent (*zohir*) and hidden (*botin*). The apparent, zohir, meaning most closely approximates the explicit, mostly referential, topical focus of a given text, while the hidden, botin, more closely relates to the wider mystical milieu of Tajik Sufism. Apparent meanings are plain and available to the uninitiated, while hidden meanings are esoteric and reserved for initiates alone. In the previous chapters, botin are the "secrets" of Sufi nostalgic discourse and historical narratives.

The distinction between the two types of meaning is not an altogether clear one. There remains a steady, interpretative tension between, on the one hand, each textual artifact's apparent meanings, readily interpretable by those able to grasp the conventions of literary Persian, and, on the other, each piece of mystical literature's inherent esotericism, only accessible to those who are already initiated into the group and have progressed to the requisite stage on the mystical path. Just because there is a difference in the kinds of knowledge a given text communicates does not mean that semantics are unimportant. Apparent and hidden meanings go hand in hand. It is not as if one can divorce a given text's apparent meanings from its mystical ones. At the same time, an emphasis on semantics alone obscures the pragmatic functions of textual artifacts

(Keane 1997, 110). Sufis hold the inner, hidden meanings in higher regard and primarily work to understand the esotericism communicated by the texts they use, not simply letting their apparent meanings suffice. Each mystical text contains both types of meaning, different "voicings" simultaneously speaking to multiple audiences and purposes (Bakhtin 1981).[14] Even ostensibly simple texts still contain esoteric, inner discourse. The result is that every text requires explication, no matter how apparent its meanings really are to its listeners and readers. Within individual or group teaching contexts, explication routinely happens when a pir offers his commentary on the texts he recites or reads from during group gatherings. The pir's commentary often includes everything from simple glosses of mystical terminology to the wholesale reinterpretation of a text.

Despite the pir's unwillingness to engage me in conversation, Firuz insisted we stay and share lunch with other guests at the lodge. I continued to worry that the pir's hesitation to talk marked not his personal feelings but some larger threat to those gathered that day. I followed Firuz's lead. He knew better than I did what was appropriate.

We were still sitting in the pir's guest room when one of his business partners arrived to discuss a shipment of goods they had recently imported from Afghanistan. Like many religious figures in Tajikistan, the pir didn't derive his income exclusively from the generosity of his followers; he also imported goods he could sell in the bazaar. After deliberating about some of the particulars of his business arrangement and customs procedures, the pir took out two books that were resting behind him on a cushion, both printed in ornate Persian script with bookmarks throughout. One was a slender lithographed volume and the other a newer, thicker book with the title *Holy Fruits from the Saints' Genealogical Trees*.[15] He handed the newer volume to his partner.

"Here, look at this. I just bought it in Kabul," he said, turning to a bookmarked page about one-third of the way through the book. "Read this part about Khizr," he continued.[16]

"What saintly power (viloīat)!" the man exclaimed after reading the short paragraph on the page.

Later, after his business partner had left, the pir looked at us and, obviously for my benefit as I was the only one in attendance not an initiate, said to Firuz, "See how the power of the saints brings people to the path!"

The contrast between the pir's comment when I first arrived and his statement at the end was striking. Earlier the pir had emphasized the fact that the apparent meanings of Imom Rabboni's letters should be readily accessible to anyone with the patience and determination to read the Persian text, yet his subtext still suggested that there was much more I could learn from the letters. Taking our conversations in previous months into account, the pir's abrupt dismissal of my project carried with it the implication that I would never grasp the wisdom the letters held unless I submitted myself to his guidance. Later he explicitly celebrated the apparent aspects of Khizr's story. It is its apparent meanings that "bring people to the path." This will be impossible unless the uninitiated, people like me and the pir's business partner, can grasp the referential particulars of Sufi texts. The textual artifacts of Tajik Sufism might contain mystical insights reserved only for the initiated, but they still must communicate mystical wisdom plainly.

"Why do you think poets like Jununi have become so popular recently?" I said to Ibrohim one day in his office at the institute.

"When people read Mavlono's *Masnavi*, you know, the *Masnavi*, it can sometimes be difficult to understand what it is he's saying," he said with a scholarly air, as if he were lecturing about Tajik literature to a classroom full of undergraduates. Ibrohim always felt that I needed a better grounding in Persian literary and religious history in order to understand my talks with Sufis.

"When people read Jununi, it isn't that way. One of the main reasons that Jununi is so popular is because he wrote his works in an extremely simple style," he continued.

Ibrohim immediately began to recite a few lines of Jununi's poetry

Go and make yourself the servant of the masters.
Live with God in your thoughts.
He won't visit you twice,
Even if you knock on a hundred doors with a granite stone.

"Who doesn't know what it means?" he said. "Everyone knows. It was the same way when Jununi wrote it. Mountain Tajiks couldn't read Bedil, but they knew exactly what Jununi was writing."

He paused. This time drawing a contrast between Jununi's poetry and that of other, more famous poets, he again recited from Jununi, "He was a lamp in his time, a sun for the people."

He continued, "Hofiz, Bedil are difficult to read."

Just like the story of Khizr that the pir's business partner read, Ibrohim argued that Jununi's poetry had become popular because of the simplicity of its apparent meanings. Whereas contemporary Tajiks might
find Rumi's Persian somewhat tedious and the density of metaphor characteristic of well-known Persian poets like Hofiz and Bedil (1642–1720)
impenetrable, Jununi was easy to understand.

Rustam told me something similar. "There are ghazal in here that
no one in the group understands," he said, pointing at the booklets he
used for zikr. "No one understands. No one understands Bedil at all. If
you recite from him, they're all sitting there saying, 'What did he say?'
They just don't know what it means. They can't grasp it." He stopped,
turning back to the movie playing on the television behind him.

"Right, they don't understand." I interjected into the silence, hoping
he would go on.

"Yes, yes. Because of this, I separate out a few simple ghazals, simple
ones so that they'll understand. That way they'll know what they mean,"
he said. "There's one thing here that you should know. Not everybody
loves this stuff, but one type of person does. And, those people, maybe
now, in six months time, maybe in one year, they'll become a part of the
path."

Rustam's statement echoed the pir's; it is the simplicity, the easily
interpretable, apparent meanings of a text, that draws people to the Sufi
path. Precisely what allows this to happen is that the apparent meanings
of a text operate as traces of saintly power.

Books, Traces of Saintly Power

I often heard Sufis reference both stories found in books and stories
orally performed as evidence (*dalel*) of a particular saint's intimacy with
the divine. One pir described it to me like this: "Here there are lots of
stories (*naql*), hours and hours of them. You should come, come and
listen sometime to my recitations. Then there are books that have lots
of stories, great stories, stories with a lot of action, stories all with evidence. Not one of them is without evidence. All of them have come with
evidence. Do you understand?" The pir's "evidence" here is not synonymous with juridical proof, but rather it exists as an index of a saint's
power. This is also the same terminology Sufis use to discuss the physical, material manifestations of sainthood (books, landscape features,
shrines, etc.).

One day I was meeting with the descendants of an important nineteenth-century Sufi pir in a mountain village approximately 150 kilometers northeast of the capital. Some villagers pointed out the grave of the pir, situated in a small graveyard on a bar between the banks of a narrow, rapid-filled river. Beside the small graveyard stood a two-meter-tall boulder. One man told me that the previous summer a flash flood had brought down mud, rocks, and other debris from the mountain above. The boulder became dislodged, pushed by the river current until it stopped directly beside the pir's grave. The boulder was "evidence" of the saint's power, the man said.

Just as with the pir's reference to stories and evidence, the villager's statement about the boulder foregrounds the representational. In Charles S. Peirce's terms, both the evidence of stories and physical evidence such as the boulder are indices of the same object, traces of the same sign (1955, 107–11). Peirce's semiotics has been well developed across a wide variety of global contexts in terms of Muslim shrine visitation practices and iconographic routines. Yet what is just as relevant to the anthropology of Islam as the semiotics of sacred sites and objects of veneration is recognizing that narrative often serves similar symbolic functions (McDowell 1982; Bauman 1986, 5; McDowell 2000, 13–38). Both the material textual artifacts of Tajik Islam and the referential content of the stories they contain are indices of saintly power; Sufi stories and books both index saintly power.[17] A story chronicling the deeds of a saint can reference its saintly sign just as much as the materiality of the books containing them.

It is not just the apparent, for example, stories, books, and boulders, that are indexes of a particular saint's mystical prowess. Hidden (botin) texts also similarly operate as "evidence" of saintly authority. For example, many Tajik devotees of the Afghan pir Khoja Abdulvakil Bahodir displayed a Persian-script list of Bahodir's spiritual names (*ésmai mubo-rak*) in their homes (figure 9). The list states that its recitation brings about God's favor for the pir and by extension for his disciples: "God willing, the Most High will relieve the hidden and apparent difficulties of that condition and bring good." Interestingly, many of these same adepts have little practical literacy in Persian script, which means they often cannot read it. As such it is not recitation, reading, that invokes the potential for God's healing power to work. Rather, its very visual presence in an adept's home reifies the abstract silsila connection between

اظهار اینجانب الحاج غلام فاروق معروف به مرشد قلندر ولد نورالحق
یوم پنج حوت سال ۱۳۸۰ که در خواب دیدم.

در باره یازده اسمای مبارک مرشد الثقلین مجدد ماء ته الف، عبدیت جهان صاحب اسرار بی چونی خواجه عبدالوکیل

المعروف به بهادر آغا که برای شان لطف گردیده قرار ذیل است

الهى به حرمت مرشد الثقلين **بهادر** جمال الله

الهـى بـه حرمت الشيخ **بهادر** اسرار الله

الهـى بـه حرمت اوليا **بهادر** لطف الله

الهـى بـه حرمت مسكين **بهادر** نور الله

الهـى بـه حرمت صديق **بهادر** رحيم الله

الهـى بـه حرمت سلطان **بهادر** كريم الله

الهـى بـه حرمت خواجه **بهادر** (فضل) الله

الهـى بـه حرمت مخدوم **بهادر** صفت الله

الهـى بـه حرمت درويش **بهادر** محب الله

الهـى بـه حرمت پادشاه **بهادر** معشرق الله

الهـى بـه حرمت فقير **بهادر** غوث الله

ناگفته نماند هر کسیکه به اخلاص و محبت اسمای مبارک را بدرگاه حضرت رب العالمین

شفیع آورد انشاء الله وتعالی مشکلات ظاهری وباطنی آن حل وبر آورده خیر میگردد.

با عرض حرمت:

از طرف مخدوم خاکروب وسگ درگاه بهادریه الحاج غلام فاروق المعروف به مرشد قلندر

Figure 9. The names of Shaikh Bahodir

Bahodir in Kabul and his disciples in Tajikistan by constantly reminding them of their link to Bahodir and claiming their physical space as being under his spiritual jurisdiction. The list serves as both a visual mnemonic for a disciple's connection to his pir and as a material sign of the pir's power within his home.

After seeing the list and puzzling over some of its less apparent aspects, one imom, not as well versed in the particulars of piety as others within this group, angrily commented to me, "This is all blasphemy (*kufr*)." Those influenced by Islamic reformist currents indeed might criticize the list's rhetoric as shirk, that is, polytheism or associating something with God, the preeminent sin of Islamic thought. Indeed, the uninitiated, those unfamiliar with the norms of pious comportment within the Sufi lodge, would find the list perplexing at best and outright heretical at worst. In communicative, though not necessarily theological, terms, Bahodir's list does offer an extreme example of association, but it is not the same association condemned by Muslim reformists. Here association is more importantly a semiotic one, as adherents connect the evidential traces contained in the list back to its saintly antecedent.

Attention to the semiotics of textual artifacts also helps to further unpack how apparent and esoteric discourses operate within Sufi groups. As folklorists and anthropologists have long known, genres can either inhibit or confirm regimes of authority (Briggs and Bauman 1992; Messick 1993, 166). In the same way, the semiotics of texts is also suggestive of power relationships within Sufi groups. Sufi talk about the apparent and esoteric is metacommunicative in the way it foregrounds who has access to a particular text's meanings, who doesn't, and what's at stake in not knowing. For example, an initiate needs a pir to demonstrate what Bahodir's list represents and its proper use. For many of Bahodir's disciples, the list's import derives almost exclusively from its esoteric botin indexicality, while botin indexicality simultaneously emphasizes the preeminence of insider discourse.

One result of apparent and hidden indexicality is that all multivoiced indexes, for example, all Sufi stories, books, boulders, and even lists of spiritual names, become intimately connected to ideas about saintly authority.[18] A given text's symbolic communicative functions often become more important than its nonrepresentative ones. The greater the degree of a text's indexicality, the more significant the pir becomes in interpreting its meanings. Those initiated into the path and under the active guidance of a pir can interpret the intricacies of both its apparent and its hidden meanings, while those on the outside are limited to understanding only the apparent. Although Sufis may especially seek out the hidden, it is the apparent meanings that bother members of the state religious bureaucracy.

READING AND THE STATE

Firuz's associate notwithstanding, pirs often actively encouraged my investigation into the texts they used. Early on during my time in Tajikistan, especially when politics made pirs more leery of my attendance at group ritual and teaching events, I frequently encountered statements like "There's no need to go there. You can just read about it in a book." Or, alternatively, after I asked a question about some mystical practice, the reply was often "Here, you can read about it in this book." In both implicit and explicit ways, Sufis suggested that books were politically unproblematic. Texts, in any of their multiple iterations, were safe, devoid of immediate controversy, and an appropriate site of scholarship, as modeled by an earlier generation of Soviet era Orientalists (Kemper and Conermann 2011). That is not to say that Sufis imagined their texts were open to all manner of interpretation but rather that they viewed the textual artifacts themselves to be apolitical, at least in terms of their apparent meanings.

Their apartness from immediate political concerns relates again to their material externality. What is interesting is that this externality from state frameworks is not oppositional. Sufi notions of textuality did not actively work to contravene state religious policy, but rather they sought to operate completely apart from present political concerns. Whereas something like Soviet era samizdat, the reproduction and circulation of (illegal) texts outside the boundaries of state authorized channels, was an overtly confrontational and oppositional stance toward Soviet policy. For many Tajik Sufis, texts' materiality lent them a not-here quality, devoid of the perceived political problems of contemporary Tajik Islam, which allowed them to hold traces of what we might call authentic experience (Stewart 1993, 135).

Even though he was a government bureaucrat, Shavkat had a particular distrust of state-sanctioned imoms. He often told me that they were all upside down. To remedy this, he purchased a Qur'anic commentary translated into Tajik from Arabic. He brought it home and told his wife and his oldest son to read it. The commentary's externality, seemingly independent of the official currents of contemporary Tajik Islam, lent him some confidence in its resonance of truth and authenticity. Despite the fact that all religious books, especially those imported and translated from Arabic into Tajik, must receive approval from the censor board within the State Committee for Religious Affairs, he still had confidence in the text's externality from state notions about what Islam properly entails. It was its material externality that masked its dependence on state structures.

Just because Shavkat felt that texts were external to political immediacies does not mean that functionaries in the state religious bureaucracy saw it the same way. During the summer of 2011, Abdullo Rahnamo, a prominent political scientist employed by a government-funded think tank in Dushanbe, published a book that quickly became popular among religious activists, *Islam and National Security in Tajikistan.* In it Rahnamo attempts to chart a way forward for the coexistence of freedom of conscience and political stability amid the fragile political order of post-civil-war Tajikistan. After its release, I repeatedly heard about debates it had engendered from my pious friends and acquaintances.

"What ever happened with all of that controversy surrounding Rahnamo?" I said to the bookseller when I went to purchase a copy of the book, curious to see what the big deal was.

"There isn't any controversy. It was a misunderstanding. Rahnamo's a good man, and it's a good book," he somewhat defensively replied, perhaps sensitive to the fact that he was selling a book some people thought shouldn't have been published. I thanked him and walked out of the store.

Since I was already on the street of bookstalls, I went into a few other shops to browse. In the next shop, the shopkeeper saw the copy of Rahnamo's book in my hand. "That book is banned," he said. "We had twenty copies of it last week, but they came in and took them all and said we couldn't sell them anymore."

"Did they say why?" I said, especially interested in finding out who "they" were.

"They're afraid of anything Islamic. They just didn't like it because he told the truth."

"It's because of the new draft law in parliament,"[19] the bookseller's assistant added. "After the law passed, they came and collected the book.

Now I can't take my son to prayers." He paused. "They just want a secular government (*davlati dunëvī*)."

It quickly became clear that "they" were members of the state's security services, still often referred to by the Soviet era acronym KGB. The bookseller's and his assistant's comments stressed the relationships between texts and state efforts to limit open discussion and the dissemination of information about religious politics. It is not just public policy prescriptions that cause headaches for the state religious bureaucracy. "They" also fear the widespread circulation of texts imported from abroad. When I was regularly attending Firuz's friend's teaching circle, I wanted to purchase a copy of Imom Rabboni's letters. It was difficult to follow the pir's teaching without a personal copy to read and study at home. None of the booksellers had one in stock. The first few times I looked, booksellers told me to come back in a few weeks' time after they received a new shipment of books. After a few visits, it became clear that no books were coming. One seller told me that the religious committee had banned imports of "Arabic books" from Pakistan and Iran. Newly printed Persian-script versions of Sirhindi's letters came from Pakistan.

In the preceding chapter, I discussed historical narratives surrounding the publication of Jununi's verse. As those narratives also implicitly suggest, whoever controls the textual products of Tajik Sufism affects its history. It is precisely that control that is at stake and what members of the state religious bureaucracy fear losing the most, akin to the dialectic Rahnamo proposed between freedom of conscience and national security in his controversial book. As such, if further state restrictions take effect and the political present is predictive of the political future, Sufi reading dispositions hold the potential to shape Sufi life more dramatically. As severe restrictions continue to be placed on the master-disciple relationship at the historical core of Sufi practice, texts may become even more vital to the transmission of Tajik Sufi learning. While access to one's pir can be limited, reading for the most part still is not.[20]

Members of the state religious bureaucracy and their allies in the security forces are not so much afraid of books themselves as they are of the texts' unauthorized teaching and performance. The alleged threat to state stability comes not so much from books as from their varied and uncontrollable enactments. There still remain certain "hazards" in the dissemination of written texts (Keane 1997), dangers to which the pir commenting on Jununi's allegedly errant ghazal already alluded. Devoid of the contexts of their original writing, the textual artifacts of Tajik Islam potentially roam free of the speech (and times) that engendered them (Messick 1993, 203–30). Readers might readily insert them into contexts that their authors or contemporary interpreters would vehemently oppose. Subsequent entextualizations become potentially destabilizing to the aspirational state monopoly on Muslim life.

Tellingly, the textual artifacts of Tajik Islam do not merely exist in printed form. To the chagrin of the state security forces, they also circulate within the boundaries of oral performance. Tajik poetry singers and storytellers are intimately engaged with recently published books, and their songs and narratives depend on them. In this way, there exists a mutually dependent and recursive relationship between written, textual artifacts and orally performed ones. In the next chapter, I discuss one context in which textual artifacts are enacted and orally performed, halqai zikr, the collective, out-loud remembrance of the names of God.

chapter 5

🔲🔲🔲🔲🔲🔲🔲🔲🔲🔲🔲🔲🔲🔲🔲🔲🔲🔲🔲🔲🔲🔲🔲🔲🔲

Remembering God

"I don't know where I'll find, the two worlds of the dervishes," Rustam chanted.[1] From the back of the room, he sang with a microphone in his hand, *"For me, it would be better than anything, the two worlds of the dervishes."* It is difficult to translate the prosody of Rustam's lyrics into English. Even without instrumental accompaniment, Rustam's poetic meter acted like a drum, a consistent percussive rhythm just as steady as a *tablak*, the small vase-drum Rustam sometimes played.

Since we met that first night, Rustam and I had begun to spend more time together. I had attended his cousin's wedding and a nephew's circumcision ceremony. I had gone with him to buy supplies for his plastics business and on a sales trip to distribute his CDs. Rustam was an energetic entrepreneur for sure, but more than that he aspired to be a well-regarded poet and musician. He had a deep affinity for Persian mystical verse, and in his spare time he composed ghazals, the lyric poems preferred by Sufis, singing them at the lodge. He relished his role as poetry singer (*hofiz*), anticipating his weekly recitations much more than a paid invoice from a colleague in the bazaar.

The lodge that night could just have well as been any other small mosque somewhere in rural Tajikistan. The mostly middle-aged men prayed their night prayers, just as thousands of others were doing at the same moment in mosques across the republic. After prayers the mood changed. The men knelt on the floor, their heads nodding to the percussive rhythm of Rustam's recitations. Rustam once told me that it is only during poetry singing that love (*ishq*) comes, that an intimate connection to the divine becomes possible. As Rustam sang his ghazals, the men echoed him on the refrains, also hoping to partake of that love.

They cried out God's name, *"Olloh," "Hu,"* and other phrases. When overcome, they danced, intoxicated (*mast*) with God's love.

Reading my field notes from that night, I am struck at how sober and detached the men seem compared to the emotional intensity my body still viscerally remembers. The notes' short, declarative sentences with their economy of adjectives mask the group's emotive energy. Staid descriptors like *intense, ecstasy, drunkenness,* and *haunting* belie the pictures in my head of enraptured adepts, eyes closed, aspirating "Hu" with a ferocity that made their bodies shake, sweat dripping from their brows as if they had just dunked their heads in buckets of water. Even years removed from attending zikrs, it is still easy to summon the melisma of their chants and the disharmonic melodies that accompanied them. I can almost feel the guttural aspirations of an *"H"* leaving the back of my throat as body memory guides me to sway each time I exhale.

Rustam completed the first ghazal and immediately moved on to another, each line a crescendo. *"It removes pain from hearts, there's no God but God,"* Rustam sang. *"It makes hearts come alive, there's no God but God."* The other men sang in unison with Rustam on each refrain.

"There's no God but God (lo iloho illolloh)," they sang. Before long, only the refrain remained: *"There's no God but God. There's no God but God."*

Most Sufis find zikr's basis in the Qur'an and the example of the Prophet Muhammad. "Recollect God often" (Schimmel 1975, 167), the Qur'an commands believers. A sign at a shrine in Dushanbe takes it even further: "The greatest speech is this remembrance (zikr) of God and saying blessings for the Prophet Muhammad, peace be upon him."[2] For most Tajik Sufis, zikr encompasses two distinct but related practices: silent (*khufī* or *zikri qalbī*) and loud (*jahrī*) zikr. Silent zikr, which adepts perform as acts of personal piety, encompasses the voiceless repetition of God's name. Loud zikr are gatherings (*halqa*) initiated exclusively at the behest of a pir during which adepts recite the names of God collectively. In Tajikistan, many Sufi groups meet weekly to listen to poetry singing (*ghazalkhonī*), chant the names of God, and comport their bodies so as to achieve the transcendence they seek.[3]

For the men listening to Rustam's recitations, the transcendence they experienced was chiefly a temporal one.[4] Like expressions of nostalgic memory, historical narratives, or the publication of Sufi books, time figures prominently in zikr. Zikr literally means "remembrance,

remembrance of the divine." Perhaps more important, zikr invokes memories from before the Soviet Central Asian experiment and the current repression by Rahmon's regime. In zikr the past emerges as Sufis draw on potent communicative resources from Central Asian Muslim tradition in the context of ritual performance. It remembers bygone masters and a time during which authentic devotion was a common feature of Central Asian life. In this way, like other Sufi memory practices, zikr carries with it a nostalgia as adepts anachronistically perform the rhetoric of "the traditional" in order to alleviate the paradoxes of the present (Mould 2005). Zikr becomes a reflexive space for enacting that change; tradition becomes agency's grammar.

COPYING REMEMBRANCE

One hot summer afternoon, Rustam and I were resting on a raised platform overlooking his garden. When he was not prepping a new business venture, I could often find him at his house reading books of poetry and playing his harmonium. I visited him as often as I could. He was a good conversationalist and extremely generous with his time. We bonded easily over our shared interests in Persian mystical literature. The second time we met he even gave me a slim volume of verse.

That day in the garden I was hoping to piece together the silsila relationship between Rustam's master and another well-known pir, if any existed. To aid my memory of Tajikistan's Sufi lineages, I had brought along a silsila list. Rustam began flipping through the book looking for interesting poetry and eventually stumbled on a short poem praising Abuhanifa, whose legacy the Tajik president also praised in chapter 3.

> Abuhanifa is the sure imom,
> Abuhanifa, the lamp for the people of the faith.
> This reservoir of knowledge would become the imom of the religion,[5]
> Abuhanifa, the defender of the people of the faith.
> The eyes of the age didn't see anyone like him,
> Abuhanifa, associated with virtue.
> Without a doubt, his obedience is honored,
> Abuhanifa, the cure for sinners.
> All the knowledge that is found in jurisprudence (fiqeh),
> The source of it is assuredly Abuhanifa.[6]

Rustam reached for his notebook and scribbled down the poem. His pencil still in hand, he whispered a few lines under his breath. Squinting his eyes, he hummed a melody I had heard at least once during every zikr I attended. Rustam only had four or five melodies that he regularly chanted. He erased one word on the page and added another. This time after the first and fourth half lines, he sang a new refrain: "*The Great Imom is our imom. It's pure religion, it's our religion.*" He looked up and smiled, clearly satisfied with his work.

"I'm going to sing this one at the next halqa. Hazrati Pir will be pleased," he said.

Rustam's notebooks, what he lovingly called in Russian his *tetrad'*, were filled with poems like this one. When he encountered a poem he liked, one that might work for zikr, he wrote it down. Sometimes he adapted it to fit a certain meter, as he did with the poem in praise of Abuhanifa, or excised sections that would not facilitate the correct ritual mood. It did not matter where he found the poem as long as it fit the parameters of zikr. As Rustam once told me, "Really anything can be used as long as it's about God or the Prophet." The poem could be something he copied from another hofiz or read in one of his collections of mystical poetry. Sometimes he modified a ghazal he heard recited on television or found on the Internet. He sometimes even borrowed books from the pir's library, including Persian-script editions, which he could not read without assistance. He asked a neighbor to read them out loud as he copied them into his notebook using Tajik. More interesting to me were Rustam's own poems, the ones he had authored especially for zikr.

I always wanted to photocopy Rustam's notebooks. Filled with the poems he sang in zikr, notations, meters, melodies, zikr formulas, and unique poetry, the notebooks seemed like windows into the wider Tajik Sufi milieu and zikr in particular. Early on during my research, spurred on by what I found in the notebooks, I even considered writing a performer-centered ethnography of Rustam and zikr. Rustam did not mind if I flipped through them and read what I liked. It was not as if they were private. He kept them on a shelf in his guest room along with his other books. It did not bother him if I copied things down in my notebook or asked him questions about their contents. On the contrary, he seemed to become the most animated when I asked about his poems. At the same time, whenever I raised the possibility of borrowing the notebooks or taking them down the street to a shop with a photocopier, he politely demurred. He would apologize, saying he would be remiss if the pir unexpectedly called a zikr. During zikr, he read from them like a script. "I need the notebooks so I don't forget the ghazals," he told me.

Although he never used the term, Rustam's notebooks have historical and cultural analogues in the notebooks (*ṭūmār*) of traditional Persian storytellers (*naqqāl*) or even in the collages or scrapbooks (*majmū'at*), compiled by intellectuals across the Persian- and Turkish-speaking worlds (Page 1979, 198; Sefatgol 2003; Yamamoto 2003, 20–51).[7] As late as the mid-twentieth century, professional prose storytellers in Iran carried notebooks organized episodically with the stories they told. Acquisition of the Persian storytelling tradition included both aural and written components. In addition to hearing their master's stories and committing them to memory, storytellers copied their master's notebooks as part of their apprenticeships (Yamamoto 2003, 23), steadily learning how to tell each story and adapt it orally for each unique performance.

Like the storytellers' notebooks, Rustam's were aide-mémoire of performance even as they were organizationally distinct. Rustam's notebooks recorded the progress of his spiritual biography and the mystical serendipity that spurred it on, not the teaching program of his pir. Rustam merely copied poems down in the order he found them. More significant, like the storytellers' notebooks, Rustam documented the complex interrelationships between streams of orality and textuality present within Tajik Sufi groups. Both Rustam's and storytellers' notebooks were written collections of oral performance material, mediated by earlier oral performances and written textual artifacts and then subsequently used as technologies of performance. Just as late-nineteenth and early-twentieth-century Iranian storytellers used newly accessible technologies of writing to aid in the transmission of the Persian oral tradition, so, too, Rustam's notebooks reinscribed previous oral performances and enabled written tradition to enter the oral sphere again. Indeed, as Kumiko Yamamoto argues with respect to storytellers' notebooks, "Contrary to the common assumption that writing was the major factor destroying oral culture, in Persia at least, writing served to spread oral culture across a wider audience" (2003, 22). Rustam's notebooks did the same; they facilitated oral performance.

"I was sitting in meditation one day," Rustam said. He spoke about his meditations the way non-Sufis might talk about a curious dream or the plot of a movie they had watched on television the night before. "This ghazal, *'From the benefit of suffering, I . . .,'*" he stopped after singing the first few bars. "It was like I was in the halqa. I saw this ghazal sitting right there in front of me," he said, pointing at the pillow beside him. "I opened my eyes and realized that it wasn't there. There wasn't a book. It was my meditations. I didn't know the ghazal, but I could still sing it."

He paused and then added, "You know that it exists, but you can't figure it out. They'd say it's just a lie." Rustam liked to talk about the inexplicable. For him it provided evidence for the superiority of the path, an observation to me, perhaps, that the miraculous draws people in, echoing the sentiment of the pir in the preceding chapter. Rustam always couched the miraculous as a skeptic might, qualifying it, arguing the other side. The skeptic, he said, would just call it all a lie.

He continued, "If you could see zikr, you'd see clearly that zikr is carrying them, taking them, would see the city all alight, you'd be seeing the words." He motioned as though the chants of zikr were suspended in midair swirling into the sky. "They'd go up to the seventh heaven with the angels."

Rustam beautifully illustrated the relationships among his notebooks, the technologies of performance, and the aural and oral components of his speech. Words, even when spoken, have a physical existence. If one had pure spiritual insight, that is, if one had attained gnosis, the goal of all aspiring mystics, one would see that not only do the words on the page exist but there is also physicality in zikr recitations. As Rustam sings zikr, the words he recites physically ascend to the highest heaven and the abode of angelic beings. The textual artifacts of Rustam's performances, the notebooks, chapbooks, and other texts that form the basis of his performance repertoire, always exist as material objects, be they words on the page in front of him as he performs or words suspended in midair during the course of the performance.

As such, Rustam's notebooks were not only textual aide-mémoire; they were also material tokens of authoritative mystical speech, rendering the abstractness of mystical authority a "thinglike physicality" it lacked as verbal art alone (Green 1999, 50). The notebooks visually assured the gathered adepts that Rustam's speech had authoritative antecedents and were not merely his words alone. Instead, they were the words of long-dead, spiritually accomplished Persian masters. Tellingly, Rustam still wanted the words in front of him even when he had memorized a ghazal's lyrics in their entirety, as he often did.[8] The notebooks were just as much "symbols to be witnessed" as they were books to be read (53). In zikr, when Sufis ascribe agency to forces beyond the perception of the uninitiated, symbols have all the more resonance because of the way they materialize zikr's extrasensory dimensions. In a context in which oral speech physically ascends to heaven, symbol realizes the causative realm, and Sufis accordingly imbue the symbol itself, Rustam's notebooks, with almost magical properties.[9]

This is material communication for sure, but of a different variety than the texts discussed in the preceding chapter. Here Rustam's notebooks' agentive capacities as mediators derived not only from their materiality and the social contexts in which Sufis used them. Rustam's notebooks recorded the speech of revered individuals who had already traversed the mystical path. The textual artifacts of Rustam's zikrs authorized mystical performance, not exclusively through their materiality but also through the saintly wisdom they graphically recorded, even while Rustam improvised, interpolated, and adapted the words he sang during the course of zikr.

Singing Memories

"*Oh, king of the messengers,*" the men sang. It was one of their favorite refrains. Rustam most often saved it for last. His earlier "*There's no God but God*" had already given way to other chants, each seemingly more impassioned than the one preceding it. The increasing intensity was not a feature of Rustam's volume or pacing, but it was almost as if the atmosphere of the room grew denser with each chant, as if anticipation for the next refrain hung heavily in the air. Chants like "*We don't have any friends in the two worlds except for God,*" "*The light of Muhammad is the virtue of God,*" and "*If you're alive or dead, it's by the grace of God. If you're here or gone, it's the glory of God*" provided a template for the men's ecstatic outbursts. If volume was any indication, the room's energy had already peaked. Rustam must have been tired too. Forty minutes or so had passed since he started singing. He still sat in the back of the room, his notebooks, booklets, and other loose papers scattered in front of him.

The pir nodded. Rustam sang out a new ghazal, "*On Muhammad's musky and jasmine scented locks. Oh, king of the messengers.*" He sang, "*It is endeavor and it is effort to gain vision of Muhammad. Oh, king of the messengers."* Rustam didn't just recite the poem as the words were printed on the page in front of him. He only sang nineteen of the twenty-two lines in the original. Of those nineteen, he sang thirteen in their entirety, elided two others, and completely modified the last six, eliminating allusions to the Prophet's night journey, a reference to *Surai Muzammil* from the Qur'an, and an even more esoteric reference to the circumstances in which the Qur'an was revealed to Muhammad.[10] Even more, he added an end rhyme and refrain: *"Oh, king of the messengers."* The end rhyme (*radif*), a standard feature of ghazal poetry, provides coherence to the often kaleidoscopic imagery found in the poems (Bruijn 1997, 54).[11] That is precisely what it did here. Rustam's end rhyme and refrain focused the men back on the primary goal of their cycle of remembrance, the Prophet and the divine, even as the imagery Rustam included in the rest of the poem varied widely.

"Why did you change the ghazal you sang in zikr last night?" I asked Rustam the next day.

"Now, listen," he told me wanting to make sure I was paying attention. "Here," he said, pointing at his notebooks, chapbooks, and poetry books. "In here I only understand part of it myself. I teach the part that I understand. The pir's disciple (*khalifacha*) only teaches what he knows.[12] There are ghazals in here that no one in zikr understands," Rustam said. It was a sentiment he expressed often and one that I included in the preceding chapter as well.

"No one knows?" I interjected. Rustam was prone to hyperbole.

"Absolutely," he said. "No one buys Bedil's works. Read him. You would sit and say, 'What did it say?'"

"Yes, you're right."

"You can't grasp Bedil. You wouldn't understand, wouldn't understand what it is he's saying. You understand?" Rustam said, looking into my eyes. "Because of this, you accordingly separate out simple ghazals, so they'll be understood."

That is exactly what Rustam did in the previous night's zikr. Rustam's intercalations, redactions, and interpolations in performance all worked to simplify the ghazal, especially its theological concepts and mystical vocabulary (Feldman 1993, 263). Rustam chose lines that the men in attendance could easily understand. He did not read the entire poem or even recite lines in their original order. If a line, half line, or single word presented interpretative challenges for its audience, Rustam cut it out (cf. Davis 2001, 28). It was not important that all the disciples should understand the esoteric meanings the poems communicate, but it was essential that the referential content of individual half lines be plain enough for the gathered adepts to follow their meanings. The men had to echo Rustam's end rhyme. Rustam chose lines appropriate for creating the ritual mood (*hol*) and ones that would elicit the most emotive potential. The goal of zikr is precisely that: to facilitate the imprinting (*dogh*) of the pir's ritual grace onto the hearts of those in attendance. The exuberance and ecstatic outcries (*jazb*) of the adepts were evidence to Rustam that he had achieved his goal.

It is not just individual phrases that get in the way of ritual understanding. The entire performance register can also lend potential difficulties to the transmission of ritual grace. Colloquial Tajik, interspersed as it is with Turkisms and Russian vocabulary and syntax, is distinct from literary Persian. That is why Rustam brought up Bedil, because Bedil's poetic dialect, the richness of his Persian literary vocabulary, and the presence of multiform Arabisms hold the potential to limit a ghazal's effectiveness as a ritual vehicle.

"*When the dervishes drink the wine of desire,*" Rustam had sung earlier that night, not long after the zikr began. "*When the dervishes drink the wine of desire, God will be present there and be their guest. God will be present there and be their guest,*" Rustam sang again. "*Oh, he's the sun of Tabriz, the pourer of honey and sugar. Oh, he's the sun of Tabriz, the pourer of honey and sugar.*"

There is inherent danger in interpolation. If the change is too great, the hofiz risks being accused of simply reciting his own words rather than the authoritative speech of mystical masters. The hofiz is supposed to be the conduit of mystical speech, not its originator. A corrective exists in the poetry itself. A ghazal, the predominant genre of Sufi ritual performance, always includes the author's signature. At some point in the last two half lines of the poem, the poet incorporates his or her pen name (*takhallus*), often phrased in the form of self-praise or even as a simple identifier for the poet. In the ghazal Rustam sang, the signature comes in the line "*Oh, he's the sun of Tabriz (Shamsi Tabrizi), the pourer of honey and sugar.* To honor his spiritual mentor, Shams al-Din Muhammad from Tabriz, Rumi took the pen name Shamsi Tabrizi in his lyric masterpiece whose title includes the same name.

Beyond simplification or ritual pragmatics, Rustam's interpolations also lent special authority to his recitations because of the way he ascribed each ghazal he sang to a Persian literary master. Because ghazals must be signed, even amalgamated texts necessarily have a takhallus. There is also a normative Islamic resonance to the attributive practices of Tajik Sufis. In order for a hadith to be read as authentic and authoritative, it must possess an attested, sound (*sahih*) chain of transmission (*isnod*). Reciting a pen name is akin to an isnod of poetic authority, legitimating the soundness of the poetic product. This is where zikr gets its power, from the discursive support provided by attributing poems to spiritually authoritative voices (Berg 2004, 109). In order for poetry performance within zikr to retain and wield such power, hofizes must necessarily attribute their recitations to an authentic, grand sacred past. If poems were merely the words of poetry singers, they would not be true mystical speech. The takhallus is the metadiscursive cue for Rustam's authoritative speech, coding his recitations as traditional and not the exclusive product of individual expression (Urban 1996, 38). Thus coded, Rustam can replicate them and adapt them as he sees fit.

However, one cannot take poetic signatures at face value. Spurious attribution is common across Persianate poetical traditions. In Tajikistan in particular, many poems in oral circulation include spurious authorial attributions.[13] For Tajikistan's Sufis, it actually seemed to matter very little whether a hofiz accurately attributed a line of verse to a long-dead Sufi poet or if the pen name a hofiz recited was authentic. Instead, the importance of (mis)attribution was in the authority it lent to the speech context in which it was embedded, regardless of authorship. It was purported, not authentic, authorship that granted rhetorical power. In this regard, when a hofiz misattributes or conflates centuries of sacred history and equates poets of classical and recent provenances, it is not the results of carelessness, ignorance, or insufficient command of Persian literary idioms. Instead, a hofiz must traditionalize relatively new poems in order for his audience to interpret them appropriately as mystical speech (Hymes 1975, 353), minimizing the intertextual gaps between the Persian mystical canon and the performance text.[14] Traditionalization infuses poetry with a special authority (Bauman 2004, 157). That is exactly what Rustam did. The poems Rustam recited, especially his new ones, had to look, feel, and sound like zikr in order for them to be efficacious. Rustam engaged in an adaptive process during his performance, morphing poems to meet his ritual ends, and concluded his adaptations with a spurious mystical signature, in effect broadcasting Rumi's authorization for his own poetical license.

In that way, Rustam's recitations and the poems that other hofizes sang were "distressed genres" (Stewart 1991, 66–101), forms intentionally crafted to look like older ones. As such, the ghazals of zikr may carry with them nostalgia just as potent as verbally expressed memories, historical narratives, or books. Within ritual there is a gap between the sacred past, the time in which authoritative masters still lived and Tajik Sufism was still strong, and the paradoxical present in which Sufis now live. By imbuing new poems with the contextual cues of the sacred past, the present, too, becomes recontextualized (74). By recontextualizing a ghazal, that is, traditionalizing it, hofizes render the present legitimate. Because of Sufis' nostalgia for that context, the authenticity of poetic authorship makes little difference because, as Susan Stewart puts it (91), the artifact is counterfeit, but the nostalgia is authentic.

The point, then, of traditionalization is to author a complete temporal context, not just an individual poem. The context Rustam sought to author was one dramatically distinct from the paradoxical present. It was one in which Sufis rightly commanded their due and the true mystical reality was manifest.[15] As such, Rustam's traditionalization predominately offered a critique of the present. When he asserted that his poems were traditional, he simultaneously highlighted the insufficiencies of the present and connected his lodge to the rightful past (Mould 2005). What gave his traditionalization all the more resonance was the way it continually reinforced emic notions of how power and knowledge should rightly function in the context of the master-disciple relationship. Performance creates a direct silsila relationship between the poet and the adepts gathered for halqa. As a hofiz recites a poet's verses or verses attributed to a revered mystical master, the poet in practice becomes the group's teaching pir as if the gathered adepts had traveled back to that exemplary moment when the poem was originally recited. Even though a pir is the only one truly authorized to speak during zikr, including a pen name allows the poet to speak directly in the ritual event just as would a living pir. A pen name transforms a poem into a quotation, even when a hofiz modifies half lines toward his performance ends, blurring divisions between author and performer.

Composing Remembrance

"Why do you want to know all this?" the pir asked me. I had grown accustomed to the question. Many of the Sufis with whom I interacted had trouble understanding why a nonbelieving foreigner would care about their acts of daily piety. Mystical literature or religious history seemed legitimate topics of inquiry, but ritual did not. My questions about their acts of devotion seemed misplaced, and they encouraged me instead to look in other places for answers.

"I'm really interested in the ghazals you read, how they're composed," I said. We had been talking that day about the differences between types of zikr.

"The Lord sewed the poem in the poet's heart," he replied. "Can you write a ghazal?" he asked one of his assistants, who was sitting with us in the room.

"No," he said, shaking his head and chuckling.

"Did you see?" the pir said, looking at me. He gestured at the assistant. "That is to say, God revealed secrets appropriate for him." Turning his head back toward me, he said, "God revealed the secrets of language to his saints. We talk like the nightingale. The Lord says, 'You aren't learned. You talk too much.'" He paused. "It's really imprudent for me to talk like this. Only God reveals secrets. God is the Knower (*Olim*)."[16]

While it is not difficult to read the pir's statement as an indirect indictment of my ethnographic project, with its attendant quest for knowledge and my constant questioning akin to the nightingale's persistent chatter, the pir's comments also highlight how Sufis think about the authorship of ritual texts. The pir argued that ghazals, though written by individual poets, always originate with God; they are secrets only revealed to saints. In the same way, Rustam might adapt, change, interpolate, redact, or intercalate poetry, but he denied ever composing the poems he sang.[17] That is, despite his changes, he always argued that the words he recited were decidedly not his own. Instead, they came from God, derived from the classical Persian poetical tradition, from the pens of spiritually mature poets.

Rustam's denials were not just due to the fact that claiming authorship might call into question the pen names he recited in zikr or compromise the authority that these poets lent to his nostalgia-tinged project. Instead, Rustam argued that performers and producers were distinct offices with separate means toward their qualification. A producer must have recognized mystical credentials authorized most often by lineage, scholarship, and/or charisma; a hofiz is chiefly a willing channel for a pir's ritual grace and a possessor of requisite musical skill. Tellingly, Rustam learned his craft from his father, an accomplished master musician in the Central Asian *shash maqom* musical tradition. The distinction between compositional and performance modes also calls attention to the fact that while Sufis attribute composition to mental processes, oftentimes they do not think of performance as a mental activity. That is, the process of adapting a new text happens outside the performance space while performance is mitigated by the hofiz's channeling of ritual grace within a ritual frame (cf. Titon 1988, 288).

While Rustam denied his active role in the composition of his performance texts, he retained creative license within the performance arena predicated on the particular situated needs of each ritual event. For example, with the poem in praise of Abuhanifa, Rustam kept the general integrity of the original verses. He did not alter the general semantic field of the poem. Indeed, his new end rhyme refrain to some degree even amplified the core meanings communicated by the poem. All he did was substitute "The Great Imom" for "Abuhanifa" and repeat the poet's words, imom, and religion in his new line, "The Great Imom is our imom. It's pure religion, it's our religion." After copying the entire poem and his newly composed end rhyme into his notebook, he did not similarly write down the name of the poem's author, nor did he pause to consider any other contextual issues regarding how or where the poem appears in the text he read. For Rustam it was not relevant who originally composed the poem, for what purpose it was composed, or the original textual contexts of its publication. Its textuality rendered it reiterable and decontextualizable (Bauman and Briggs 1990), ready to be recontextualized into the zikr environment.

Tellingly, Rustam and other singers were not at all preoccupied with individual poetic authorship.[18] Rustam said that what he was actually committing to memory when he read poetry was the light of God, not a poem on the page. Textual critics and paleographers may aim to authenticate extant manuscripts and the autographs of Persian texts to deduce which components of a particular poet's oeuvre emanated from that exemplary artist or secretary's stylus and which were later interpolations, accretions, and the excreta of scribal exuberance over subsequent centuries. But distressed genres, like traditionalized oral poetry, mask their authorship. To borrow Bakhtin's oft-quoted phrase, Rustam lived in a world of others' words (1984, 143), but what distinguished his creations from more explicit modes of Persian poetic imitation was the intentionality of his poetic allusions, the degree to which his utterances were "conscious allusions" to a specific prior work or whether he was merely making use of the Persian poetic dialect (Losensky 1998, 102). Persian poetry includes numerous formalized modes and devices for poetic imitation (Lewisohn 1989, 115; Losensky 1994, 230–32).[19] Rustam's practices did not readily approximate any of them. His works were more than simple allusions to other works or even bald instantiations of Persian poetical dialect. His words were not his alone, but they were not the poets' either.

Rustam's artistry was a kind of hybrid form alternating between a strong appreciation for canonistic fixity and a predilection for formulaic oral repetition, all while expunging and modifying problematic author word choice. The result was a dialogic intercalation of authoritative verse, Rustam's voice mixed among the voices of prior poets (Cashman, Mould, and Shukla 2011, 8–10). Rustam's recitations quoted spiritual masters but only indirectly.[20] The poems were allegedly the speech of mystical masters, but they were mediated through Rustam's adaptations and geared toward ritual pragmatics.

Poetry singers base zikr texts on formulaic units, oftentimes learned orally, performed orally, and transmitted primarily in oral/aural channels, but ghazals are not oral-formulaic constructions (Lord 2000; Foley 1995) composed at the time of their performance. Poetry singers do not create ghazals as they sing them.[21] Additionally, a focus on formula potentially dispenses with Rustam's individual artistry or the unique poetic contribution and authorship of other zikr performers. Rustam was more than the nominal author of the poems (cf. Foley 1991, 8). Although he made use of traditional formulae and Persian classical rhetoric, he was still the active shaper of the discourse and as such deserves more credit for his artistry than nominal authorship implies. As T. S. Eliot (1950, 3–11) put it, the measure of the poet comes in how he or she engages with tradition, shapes it, and responds to it, not in the pure novelty of his or her poetry. Rustam's creativity and the meanings he communicated, then, similarly came in the way he dealt with the rhetoric and formulae of Persian poetical tradition, not in the singularity of his lyrics.

Rustam's ghazals shared a metonymic relationship with Persian clas-sical poetical tradition at large and developed a meaning-making capac-ity from it. They held "traditional referentiality"—the idea that meaning derives not from the individual meanings of words but rather from the ways in which those words reference larger tradition (Foley 1991, 1995). Meaning is transmitted just as conventionally as the phraseology, as tra-ditional phrasing invokes a complete context beyond the frame of the sin-gular performance event. That is, each constituent utterance in Rustam's performance represented not the individual meanings of its morphologi-cal constructions but rather indexed poetical tradition writ large, remem-bering it and bringing it to the fore with each recitation to authorize present ritual. Each phrase, each half line of traditionalized, distressed poetry invites adepts to remember the sacred past, invoking memories of it and authoring that authentic context in the pir's lodge. Thinking of ritual poetry performances as episodes of situated metonymy help-fully reframes the issue away from the semantic fields of individual mor-phemes to a more holistic understanding of the texts' oral reception and how their messages are carried for maximal ritual cognizance.

When Rustam first read the poem in praise of Abuhanifa, he stum-bled over the word "reservoir" (*makhzan*). I did too. Rustam later told me that he did not know what it meant. I had to go and look it up in a Persian dictionary. It is not a word you hear in everyday conversation. But Rus-tam's lack of comprehension did not prevent him from appreciating the poem or continuing his adaptation. Similarly, he later simplified the ghazal he sang in zikr, taking out the detailed Qur'anic references and expung-ing problematic word choices. Altogether, Rustam's cavalier attitude toward the referential particulars of the texts foregrounds how individ-ual words operated metonymically and how the totality of poetical tradi-tion in circulation among Tajikistan's Sufis conferred inherent meaning on individual performance pieces irrespective of a text's constituent parts.

It is not that constituent parts make no difference at all in ritual effi-cacy. Rather, the specific words used in a particular ghazal and the audi-ence's knowledge of their meanings and literary connotations are not the primary determinants of the hofiz's choices. Authorship and the meanings of each line mattered less than the weight of Sufi tradition. Tradition was the enabling referent (Foley 1995, 28), as the sacred past, the inspired speech of mystical masters, proverbially spoke into the present ritual moment.

PROVERBS AND REMEMBRANCE

"Recite zikr," the pir said, punctuating a discussion about the special vitality of zikr, as his adepts listened intently. "The poet has said, '*Oh, friend, recite your zikr ever moment. Each time, it's all because of his generosity*,'" the pir chanted, reading from the book in front of him. The men nodded enthusiastically in agreement. They took in the pir's comments with purposefulness as if each thought offered special insight for their individual efforts in seeking the divine.

The pir frequently quoted poetry when he taught. He often made a statement, such as the one about the importance of zikr, admonishing his murids to recite their personal meditations with due diligence, and then quote a few lines of verse that encapsulated his broader points. In place of attributing the verse to a specific poet, he glossed the author simply as "the poet." For the pir, the specifics of authorship did not seem to matter. "The poet has said" was enough to substantiate any argument.

Poetry has a deep cultural resonance among Tajikistan's Sufis.[22] In fact poetical discourse is perhaps the dominant and highest prestige medium for message production in the wider Persian-speaking world. Setrag Manoukian argues that, in Iran at least, "Poetry is the form in which Iranians experience themselves as subjects endowed with the power to act and live in the world" (2011, 205). Poetry is not an instrumental tool but rather the very ground through which sociality, personhood, and subjectivity are constituted (Olszewska 2015, 9–15). The poet, a figure of special erudition and wisdom, commands respect as an authoritative instantiation of both worldly and mystical knowledge. As a particular way of speaking (Hymes 1989), the Persian poetical dialect's conventions, idioms, contexts of use, and so on make it the normative means for communicating the speech of the authoritative sacred past, the focus of Sufi devotion.

The ritual frame of zikr magnifies the potency of poetical discourse to an even greater degree. Ritual is the language of the normative, the hegemonic even (Keane 1997, 6). Indeed, ritual is one of hegemony's most powerful instruments because of the way it reproduces and echoes authority (Bell 1992, 206). Zikr performance offers a powerful, multifaceted vehicle to lend credence to the Sufi project precisely because it uses culturally resonant poetical ways of speaking within a hegemonic ritual frame. Persian poetry is far removed from the colloquial speech register of Sufis because of its oftentimes archaic vocabulary, formulaic structures, and courtly dialect features. It may be complex, but its semantic structure is simultaneously open-ended (Losensky 1996, 3). Poetry is inherently multivalent and able to traverse various speech contexts. When quoted in zikr, its hegemonic claims to authority are given, even as its interpretation is not. Zikr poetry's simultaneous compact and elliptical quality allows it to claim discursive authority (Mills 2013, 231), which renders new Sufi historical imaginations thinkable and possible, even as its meanings remain open to be construed within each zikr performance.

One key reason why zikr exerts an almost hegemonic pull on its audiences is the way quoted poetry approximates proverbial speech. Like proverbs, zikr poetry is contextually dependent "quoting behavior" (Fabian 1990, 27), which uses talk with a historical antecedent to speak pedagogically into the performance context (Briggs 1988, 104).[23] Zikr poetry shares proverbs' multivalent semantic structure, turns on the similar tacit understanding of their audiences, and functions through indirectness (Kirshenblatt-Gimblett 1994, 112). I am not so concerned with how zikr poetry approximates the formal features of internationally dispersed proverb genres, for example, short length and single theme. Rather, my point is that zikr poetry shares similar reservoirs of discursive authority, compactly marshaling the collective wisdom of mystical ages past to speak in support of the hofiz's performative project.

By definition, proverbs are most often authored collectively, authored anonymously, or attributed to "the talk of the elders of bygone times" (Briggs 1988, 4). In contrast, Persian ghazals purportedly are not, their authors' pen names necessarily included in the last two lines of the poem. At the same time, the ghazals sung in zikr are intercalations with an attendant "traditional referentiality" such that poetry, even when (mis)attributed to a long dead Sufi master, retains at its core a proverb-like means of message transmission. Their authorship is still often attributable to anonymous tradition rather than individual artists. Even more, Persian poets have made great use of proverbs and aphoristic constructions in their poetry (Hadissi 2010; Losensky 1996). For example, in the case of Rumi's *Masnavi*, Margaret A. Mills writes, "The language of the *Masnavi* is so densely aphoristic that in many passages it is hard to decide what should *not* count as a proverb or proverbial usage" (1994, 136). To paremiologists, the difficulty in some ways is determining whether a particular proverb originated in the form of poetry or whether a poet made use of a proverb already in circulation at the time of writing.

By the time Rustam began the last ghazal, the poem with the *"Oh, king of the messengers"* refrain, the night's zikr was almost complete. Forty-five minutes or so had already passed. Rustam had sung a ghazal attributed to Rumi.[24] He had recited another slow, intense poem, an amalgamation of mystical phrases drawn from the poetry of various well-known mystical poets, what Rustam called in Russian his improvisation (*improvisatsia*). And finally he presided over the men's ecstatic zikr chants, punctuating their recitation of God's name with half lines of verse. The last ghazal Rustam sang was not a poem from a long-dead Sufi master, nor was it a unique interpolation of esoteric knowledge. In his last ghazal, Rustam quoted Mavlavi Jununi, the nineteenth-century Tajik pir discussed in chapter 3.

"Tomorrow, on the day of resurrection, we'll rise up," Rustam sang.

The other men sang the refrain, *"Oh, king of the messengers,"* with a special intensity, as if they were affirming that they, too, would "rise up" on that day of resurrection.

"On that day, all will gather at the place of judgment to see Muhammad," Rustam continued.

"Oh, king of the messengers."

"To pray for all the downtrodden," Rustam sang.

"Oh, king of the messengers."

Rustam sang the last line, the one that included the poet's signature, *"He ties Muhammad's belt of nobility and greatness,"* the pronoun a self-reference to the poet, Jununi.

"Oh, king of the messengers," the men sang for the last time. Most looked up, recognizing that this was the end.

Rustam sang the final half line, *"May the dust of Muhammad's feet be a salve for Jununi's eyes."*

Just as with the pir's teaching about zikr, Rustam could just have easily have said, "The poet has said," before he sang the last ghazal. This was his zikr's coda, the final poetical proof, validating and affirming the thrust of his earlier recitations, a final appeal to the collective wisdom of mystical ages past expressed through the words of Jununi's ghazal. Poetry, voiced as proverb, provided that final, authoritative link between the lodge that night and the authenticity of the past. Rustam argued, "Why do we get so intoxicated in zikr? It's because we're conversing with the saints." However, the multivalency of poetic and proverbial speech in general, coupled with the esotericism of mystical verse in particular, complicates any simple discussion of how devotees understood what the saints said and how speech affected what they experienced in zikr.

EXPERIENCING REMEMBRANCE

"How many of the pir's followers understand your recitations?" I asked Rustam one morning after zikr. The question was constantly on the minds of the men who read Sufi books, listened to saintly stories, and participated in zikr ritual. Whether it was talk about the theological intricacies of apparent (zohir) and hidden (botin) or simply anxieties about progress along the mystical path, the competing dialectic between the hidden reality of mystical experience and outward zikr practice was perpetually the stuff of Sufi conversation. Participants could see, understand, and interpret what they saw with their eyes and heard with their ears, but the reality of zikr was not apparent to one's senses. Zikr provided access to a hidden, divine realm, a sphere to which one's intellect has no recourse. The chanting of poetry and the recitation of the names of God facilitated access to the real, the real that the present lacked, but zikr's link to the past was an enigmatic one.

I often was surprised at how the men responded to Rustam's singing. It did not seem to matter how esoteric the verses were or how archaic the Persian vocabulary seemed to be; they still enthusiastically engaged his recitations. I had observed firsthand that many of the men did not necessarily have a strong sense of Persian literary convention. As the last chapter's discussion of the esoteric meanings of texts made clear, it is not surprising that the men could not easily describe what a verse meant or why it was efficacious. The referential content of mystical poetry performance is intentionally inexplicable, elliptical even, and oftentimes adepts lack the requisite literary and mystical vocabularies to parse its particulars. At the same time, it was not that the words did not matter at all. Adepts did not respond to each lyric in the same way. The reason comes from how zikr poetry functions as coded speech (Radner and Lanser 1993).[25] Just like the books discussed in the preceding chapter, some in attendance may only understand a poem's explicit content while others can decode its true mystical import.

Rustam described it this way. "Well, twenty or fifteen of them understand. Twenty don't understand. They're the ones coming along, slowly, slowly, slowly." He paused to gather his thoughts. "The Sufi path goes along like this," he said. He raised his right index finger, and then, as if he were painting on an invisible canvas, he began to trace a spiral shape. "It comes, comes, comes," he said, drawing rings as large as the distance between his shoulders. "Gathers together, gathers together, gathers together." His concentric circles steadily became smaller and smaller. "Then, at its time, it comes slowly. Then, one time at zikr the murid understands what it's like," he said, his circles stopping at a point.

Rustam thought that about half the men who heard his singing understood. In the first chapter, a pir argued that many of the ecstatic outcries in zikr are not real. He said that many attendees are not truly intoxicated. They are not acting from their hearts but from their animal spirit (*ruḥi haivonī*). Rustam's point was that knowledge accrues over time. Learning the parameters of mystical speech, understanding what it means, and being able to function appropriately within the group is a slow, iterative process. Through a redundancy of discursive routine, the result of weekly repeating zikr formulae, steadily accruing the norms of mystical comportment, and repeated exposure to ritual texts, adepts attain true understanding. Zikr repetition itself even indexes the past—past zikrs at the lodge, the repeated words of past masters, and the recitations of disciples in ages past (Connerton 1989, 65–68). As Rustam said, the adept will do it over and over, and one time he will get it. The repetitions of zikr were charted alongside the recursive pasts of other expressive modes.

A few moments after he had drawn spirals in the air, Rustam said, "You have to show the ones that don't understand." He quoted a poem to make his point, as he often did when he was trying to explain the intricacies of the Sufi path to me. "Here it's written more simply," he said. This time, he did not use the pir's earlier phrase "the poet has said," but he still proverbially attributed the poem to tradition writ large. He said, "It says, 'Oh, believer, come and worship if you want paradise.'" Then he asked, "What does this poem mean? Do you understand it?"

"Yes," I said.

"If you want paradise, worship," he said, emphasizing the last word. "That's written simply."

Rustam's solution to understanding was zikr. Meaning and understanding come with the experiences one gets from worshipping, from participating in zikr. It is experience itself that engenders knowledge. The two exist alongside each other in a single referential field from which it is difficult to tease out their distinctions. Experience imparts a special kind of knowing apart from objective verification (Hinson 2000, 9–10).

"I've been telling him all about the secrets and mysteries of zikr," Rustam told his pir one day in my presence. The pir had been hesitant to share any insights about zikr with me during our times together, often insisting that the secrets of zikr are only available to the initiated.

"The heart can hear, see, touch, and feel," the pir said. "In short, the heart has the sensory ability of all the apparent (zohir) sense organs. The eyes can't hear, and the ears can't see. When the secrets of the heart are revealed, then the devotee can understand all mysteries."

It takes true mystical insight to see this reality, the reality of what is going on as Rustam sings. The pir sits and through his mystical gaze (*tavajjūh*, lit. "attention") transmits his ritual grace to those listening to Rustam's singing. I often heard the transmission of ritual grace described as being like electricity. Just as a power plant produces electricity, so, too, ritual grace originates only with the divine. High-voltage transmission lines carry the power to smaller substations; pirs are the substations of grace. Smaller lines carry electricity from substations to individual houses, just as a pir transmits grace to the gathered adepts in zikr. That transmission imparts understanding and ritual exuberance, which is the intoxication the adepts seek during zikr. The pir's work manifests itself physically in the bodies of his murids. A person might shake or sob uncontrollably. Another adept might kneel, eyes closed, and sing along with Rustam.

The zikr ended with a prayer. The pir said, "We ask for the gift of righteous favor, the result of the word of God, according to the will of holy Muhammad Mustafo, peace be upon him."

By now the men's exuberance, tears, and uncontrolled movements had ended. They all kneeled with their palms raised in prayer. The pir said, "From the pure and virtuous ones and the beloved of God, we pray for the good repose of the prophets, of the four ones,[26] the masters (*murshid*), the most perfect of perfect masters, the imom, the Great Imom, the Sufis, may they rest in peace, the witnesses, the sympathetic, the pirs, the pirs of the Naqshbandiya, Qodiriya, Chistiya, Suvardiya . . ."

The pir continued, "The great pirs, especially Hazrati Mir Saiid Alii Hamadoni, Hazrati Sulton Uvaisi Hovaling, their excellences, our past pirs, and those yet not passed and still our masters."

As the pir prayed, the men in the room were silent and still. The contrast from several minutes before was striking. The twirling mass of men, sweat dripping and cries so loud that you could have heard them outside on the street, had turned into rows of quiet meditation. The pir said, "May the Lord at our passing grant us paradise, oh pure God. Especially by the faith of the passed ones of this congregation who have raised their hands in prayer. For the ancestors of this ruler of ours, Emomali Rahmon. Oh, pure God, in our Tajikistan, peace and quiet by means of this individual, grant his ancestors, his father and mother, repose."

The pir ended by praying especially for the adepts. He said, "Oh, God, grant a reward for all of us, the people of the path, tomorrow a day of the flag of resurrection underneath the banner of Ahmad. Oh, God, from the intercession of the Qur'an, from the intercession of the messenger, grant us, the enthusiastic, enamored ones, honor, by your grace, oh, God. Amen."

"Amen. God is great," the men said in reply.

The pir's prayer amplified the themes of Rustam's zikr: the sacred past and the power of departed masters. Both the pir's prayer and Rustam's distressed poetry attempted to remedy what was missing or regrettable for the adepts listening in the room—connections to the past, sacred power, respect, poverty, state repression, and more. Zikr rendered such negativity thinkable, interpretable, and ultimately changeable. As a ritual vehicle, zikr provided that bridge as it drew symbolic, linear connections between the poetry of the classical Persian masters, pre-Soviet Tajik poets, and contemporary hofizes. Tradition, value laden with its traditionalizing impulses, enables change, the reconfiguration of Sufi experiences of the world. Zikr posits stability and correct genealogy irrespective of historical disjuncture. Zikr reflexively performs, enacts continuity. The traditional becomes a vital resource for making sense of the paradoxes of the present, for reinscribing the present, reshaping it, and distressing it to make it look like the past. Traditionalization provides a template for agency, at least for forty-five minutes or an hour within the performance space, enabling Sufis to perform the sort of subjectivities they envision.

In the next chapter, Sufis not only perform the past, but they also embody it through public acts of piety in the midst of a Tajik society that finds their anachronisms—their ritual invocations of the sacred past—out of step with its favored modernizing narrative and a state religious bureaucracy that worries about the so-called radicalism Sufi pasts might produce.

chapter 6

░░░░░░░░░░░░░░░░░░░░░░░░░░░░░░░░

Learning to Be Sufi

"The time for that's all passed," Firuz insisted, uncrossing his legs and reaching to pour another cup of green tea. "Anybody can go to a pir now. It doesn't make any difference. You don't have to wear a robe or do your ablutions or anything like that. All that's passed." I could always count on Firuz to have an opinion. Besides interloping at the pir's house, his contagious confidence allowed him easily to dispense with another's piety.

"Well, you know better than I do about all the things Shaikh Temur's disciples do," I replied, sipping the cup of piping hot tea. "They can't eat what they want or come and go without his permission."

A few days before, I had spent an exhausting day a few hours' drive outside the capital with Temur's disciples, digging out small boulders from a mountainside for the foundation of a new mosque. By the time of afternoon prayers, we had only managed to share a few bites of stale bread and an unexpectedly refreshing cucumber. In the hot June sun, the men tirelessly labored without breaks, wearing woolen robes and skullcaps, always sure never to break ritual purity.

"There are lots of different kinds of shaikhs," Firuz continued. "For instance, God says to one 'Here's some barley bread' and to another 'You're going to be rich.' Remember Khoja Ahrori Vali?" Indeed, I did. How could I forget? Firuz had been incessantly talking about the fifteenth-century Naqshbandi pir since our first conversations together. To wit Ahror (1404–89/90) was an important link in the Naqshbandi silsila. He centralized the tariqa, widened its geographic scope beyond Bahouddin's homeland, and incorporated Naqshbandi spirituality into the social fabric of the political and cultural elite (Gross 2002). For Firuz, Ahror represented unabashed strength, the symbiosis of mystical and earthly ambition. Attuned to the observance of shariat and cognizant of his rightful place in the world, Ahror was a model Firuz aspired to emulate.

"Every day, Khoja Ahrori Vali ate a leg of lamb and practiced zikr until daybreak. He did this every day. He slaughtered a lamb and gave it to the Sufis, and they ate and practiced zikr," Firuz said.

Firuz looked out the window and continued the story with a succession of quick sentences, his preferred storytelling mode. "There was this shaikh in China that had these priceless jewel-encrusted slippers. He eventually became so despondent. 'What kind of life is this?' he said as he cursed his fine clothes, his heart filling with fear. His good deeds eventually reached God.

"Khoja Ahrori Vali came and saw the shaikh, now only eating half of a piece of barely bread since he was planning to go sit in seclusion for forty days (chilla).[1] Khoja Ahrori Vali said, 'Come on, let's go sit in seclusion together.'

"The shaikh said, 'Okay, come whenever you're ready. But I have one question. What do the womanly have to say about this manliness?'

"'What do you mean?' Khoja Ahrori Vali said.

"The shaikh replied. 'You go out in a dainty golden waistcoat every day and slaughter a lamb. You go and buy forty loaves of bread with your silver coins and kill a lamb and cook it.'

"So Khoja Ahrori Vali brought this barley-bread-eating shaikh to the place where he did his forty-day seclusions (chillakhona), and this shaikh ate a leg of lamb and even ate another half a leg of lamb. Khoja Ahrori Vali said, 'The latrine is far away. I'm not going to relieve myself outside. I'm not going to come out for forty days.'

"Everyone saw this situation, all the murids. For God's sake, can you imagine all of the gossip? The murids saw that they didn't come out at all to use the bathroom. The murids brought the lamb for the guests, and the shaikhs took off the meat, cleaned it to the bone. Not one of them went outside. It went on like this. They practiced zikr and didn't come out, all total, for forty days.

"When he came out, Khoja Ahrori Vali said, 'This here is manliness, that's how it happens.'

"Think about how much food they ate that month." Firuz said in conclusion, satisfied that he had made his point.

As Firuz finished his story, I struggled to reconcile the anecdote with what I had observed in Tajikistan. I thought about the pious men working to pull rocks off the mountainside, straining in the hot summer sun with inadequate nourishment. I compared images of the weary murids, eager to please the pir through the rigor of their piety, with Firuz's suggestion that different pirs conform to different rules of comportment. Khoja Ahrori Vali's opulence contrasted sharply with the Chinese shaikh's embrace of poverty, yet both men still experienced the divine.

That afternoon's activities on the mountain might have struck the casual Tajik Muslim as anachronistic—the dress, the manners of comportment, the men's quietist concerns—all so out of step with the majority of contemporary Tajik society. Indeed, some might have even echoed Firuz's comment "The time for that has passed." Of course for many Sufis the time obviously has not. Growing the beard of the outwardly pious, donning dress uncharacteristic of that of one's family and friends, and actively participating in Sufi reading circles all operate as forms of bodily nostalgia just as potent as many of the other discursive memory practices Sufis also engage.[2] In earlier chapters, Sufis expressed visions of the sacred Persian past through narrative, disseminated it through books, or invoked it within the bounds of ritual performance. In this chapter, Sufis embody memory through their efforts to cultivate an ethical life by adhering to intricate rules of pious comportment (*adab*) and participating in group teaching events (*dars*).[3]

BODILY NOSTALGIA

Even though I had been spending time with adepts for almost a year, the look of the sport-utility vehicle (SUV) took me aback. If ever there were a car that the traffic police might suspect of militant activity, this would be it. The men's long black beards, shaved heads topped with prayer caps and turbans, and tunic shirts akin to those standardly worn in Muslim South Asia marked its occupants as exceptional. To someone from central casting, the passengers would have seemed just as at home in a Taliban training camp across the border in Afghanistan as they did in aspirational, urbane Dushanbe. Policemen routinely stopped those with even the slight appearance of cultivating piety, forcibly shaving beards and refusing admittance to official buildings and government offices. I had grown increasingly weary of the extortion and harassment my pious friends and acquaintances routinely faced due to policemen's overzealous enforcement of often arcane traffic rules.

Khurshed got out of the dusty SUV packed with eight bearded men, an enterprising traffic policeman's dream. More than most, Khurshed seemed to take pride in how he stood out from others on the street. His sartorial attention matched the intensity of his convictions. The same passion that motivated him to tell me about his uncle's Soviet era devotion or berate me for my inattention to spiritual things also gave him a haughtiness, which seemed to cushion him from verbal harassment or traffic policemen's hefty fines.

"Ben, you know that the Sufi path has rules," he said, holding a beige robe and white prayer cap in his hands. "You should put these on." He looked at the ground with an uncharacteristic meekness that suggested he was uneasy about asking. "Do you know how to do ablutions? You're going to need to do them when you get there."

"Okay," I said, putting my arms through the sleeves of the robe. I was unsure of how to respond. Khurshed knew full well that I was not a Muslim, a cause of frequent acrimony between us.

Another dusty SUV arrived, and the pir's first assistant (*khalifai avval*)—the second-ranking member of the group—climbed out. The men ran toward him, bowed, kissed his hands, and hurried back to the car, never turning their backs. With his faded and torn quilted robe, the portly, gray-bearded man more closely resembled an impoverished farmer than someone deserving of overt displays of obeisance.

An hour or so later, we reached a small village of about twenty houses surrounded by high mud walls. The pir's L-shaped mud house sat high above the rest adjacent to a construction site, the foundation of a mosque. The men tied their robes together with twine. Grabbing their tools, they dispersed without instruction to begin their work.

"Come on," Khurshed almost whispered as he directed me to the side of the compound. I could still hear the hesitation in his voice. At a metal tank, he filled a small jug with water and handed it to me, gesturing for me to follow him to a line of wooden outhouses, one roped off with a velvet cord. "That one's for the pir," he said, anticipating my question. "Make sure and dry yourself," Khurshed timidly added as I went inside the dark stall, his face still betraying the awkwardness he felt. I came out, and Khurshed pointed to another stall. "Go ahead and do your ablutions," he said, gesturing below his waist. "Clean yourself well," he added.

When I came out after what I thought was an appropriate interval, he said, "Do you want me to refill the pitcher?"

"I still have some," I said, watching as mild frustration filled Khurshed's face. It was only later that I learned the water in the pitcher would not have been even close to enough. I should have washed three times.

Khurshed filled the pitcher again and walked me through each individual step. With more confidence in his voice, he said, "Now, your hands, right, then left . . . now, your teeth . . . your forehead to your neck." When I had finished, I followed Khurshed to where the men were already cleaving rocks off a cliff.

The Sufi way for the men on the mountain existed through the body in the form of group-specific norms of comportment. Dress, ritual purity, deference to mystical superiors, and other "somatic modes of attention" attenuated each adept's place in the group and his individual progress along the mystical path (Csordas 1993). Embodied action was a way for the men to engage directly with the Sufi project. The important thing for Khurshed and the other murids on the mountainside was that I shared a sort of "kinesthetic empathy" with them (Sklar 1994), that I bodily conformed by feebly attempting to replicate their ritual purity. Even the most visceral activity did not escape their notice as both Firuz's story about Khoja Ahror's seclusion and Khurshed's meticulousness in the outhouse attest.

As Firuz suggested, Sufi somatic modes of attention, that is, the kinds of behaviors that occurred on the mountainside, purposively engaged the past (Connerton 1989). The clothes the men wore and the esteem in which they held their pir sharply diverged from the Tajik everyday. For some, their extreme reverence was indicative of how murids acted prior to the advent of state-enforced secularism and their pious garb of typical male dress before Eastern Bukhara's integration into the Russo-Soviet sphere. To Firuz the men's refusals to adhere to Tajik sartorial and behavioral norms appeared as time out of joint (Freeman 2010, 19). Firuz may have accusingly maintained that "the time for that has passed," but many Sufis proudly embraced their asynchrony. Their attention to their bodies performed the past and embodied sacred memory in the present (Stoller 1995, 37–45). Their intentional anachronisms allowed them the possibility of creating alternative worlds (Dinshaw 2012, 5–7), ones that subverted the normative. It is precisely this longing for the past remade in the present that makes Sufi somatic modes of attention nostalgic. They are bodily nostalgias—nostalgic memory carried by and developed onto the body.

In one frame, the men on the mountainside wore a sort of nostalgia-tinged costume, distinct from the vast majority of Tajik Muslims and "extraordinary in semantic elaboration" (Shukla 2015, 14). That seemed to be Firuz's estimation. The men's clothes and pious comportment were self-conscious presentations of self that amplified the various identities they assumed and chose to perform—as Sufi, Muslim, someone who is pious, and so on. In another frame, the men's intentional anachronisms and bodily nostalgias were much more potent than semantic messages and forms of expressive communication, more than simple vehicles that allowed them to return to an idealized past (197). Instead, their embodied memory practices were the means whereby a Sufi self could emerge. The men's prayer caps, turbans, and beards—though still performances of identity—provided a means for cultivating a self not available in everyday life and that transcended it.[4]

Khurshed at one point described it to me like this. "We're like children, and we need a teacher (*tarbiiatgar*). For instance, you could say that we're like soldiers. The pir is the commander. Right now we're just normal soldiers, but the pir will help us become supermen (*universal'nyï askar*)." If the goal is to become "supermen," the task is compounded by the fact that everyday life easily subverts that lofty goal. Khurshed added, "Shaiton is in everyone, he tempts everyone. God gave him permission to take everyone who would follow him to hell, but everyone who follows God would go to paradise. This is free will (*ikhtiër*). For example, if you eat a lot you won't be able to pray evening or morning prayers. You'll miss two of the five daily prayers because your *nafs* will make you sleep."[5] Later he clarified what this means in practice, demonstrating with an erect posture, "In the tariqat, in one day you can eat three times, using three fingers and with seven mouthfuls." At another point, Khurshed said, "The tariqat isn't about reason. It isn't only talking. It's in action. God said, 'Put on the turban, grow a beard, prepare for me a robe, comport yourself (*adabī kun*)!'"

Khurshed's comments encapsulated the relationship between embodied practices and ethical cultivation. He suggested that even the most mundane of daily behaviors, such as how one eats, directly implicate one's progress along the mystical path. In the same way, the adepts' hard labor in the hot sun was not just a reflection of their membership in the group or an exterior performance of devotion to their pir. Instead, their embodied anachronisms were what enabled them to foster a correct Sufi way of being in the world. By working in the hot sun while maintaining ritual purity and fasting from substantive nourishment, they quite literally worked to create the Sufi disposition they so craved. For Khurshed and the other men, all their activities became "the potentialities—the ground if you will—through which the self is realized" (Mahmood 2005, 31). As Khurshed often phrased it, it was his conduct (*suluk*) that supported his morality (*akhloq*).

Khurshed's embodied ethics were just as nostalgic as sharing memories, telling historical narratives, reading and publishing Sufi texts, or singing mystical poetry. He conflated ideas about the Persian sacred past with the performance of daily behaviors. Khurshed and the other men's actions hearkened back to an imagined past in which mystical knowledge flowed freely between knowledgeable pirs and their intimate associates and norms of piety were respected even by those uninitiated into the Sufi path. When disciples recited ritual formulae previously uttered by earlier generations of Central Asian Sufis and read from worn books held by their mystical forebears, they became intimately connected to this not so distant Central Asian Muslim past. Embodied memories cultivated ethical personas in much the same way that oral and written hagiography substantiate an ideal self in the hearer or reader (Ruffle 2011, 5). At the same time, a Sufi way of being in the world is predicated on more than simple bodily action. It also comes via the concurrent transmission and reception of ritualized knowledge.

RITUALIZED KNOWLEDGE

"I'm not sure why you want to come to dars. This is all high knowledge, specialized. It isn't just Muslim knowledge. So for someone who's not a Muslim to try to understand, it's like the one at the bottom trying to understand what's at the top," Abdullo said as he maneuvered the Uzbekistan-made Daewoo hatchback over ruts and mud-filled puddles one early winter Saturday morning not long after the conclusion of morning prayers.

I would have liked to know Abdullo better. He spoke directly with conviction and carried himself with an uncommon warmth that fostered easy camaraderie. He was the kind of person who could give you bad news and you would thank him for it. After hearing about my interest in Sufism, an acquaintance at the Islamic University had introduced me to Abdullo, his former classmate. Like many Tajik men, Abdullo had spent time working as a laborer in Russia. In Tajikistan, he tended his family's small plots west of the city and offered prayers at village functions. As he pulled the car to a stop outside a half-built cinderblock wall, I wondered what I was supposed to make of his statement. Earlier in the week, he had been much more receptive to my visit, going as far as offering to make a special trip into the city to pick me up.

We got out of the car and walked through a gap into a sparse yard—a fuel tank, a well, and construction debris. "Stay here while I tell Hazrati Pir you're here," Abdullo said over his shoulder, opening a bare wooden door and going into the house. Until another murid arrived a few minutes later, I was alone in the quiet yard.

"Aren't you coming in?" the man said, mouth agape, obviously curious at the unfamiliar foreigner standing notebook in hand alone in the pir's yard.

Abdullo eventually swung the door open and gestured for me to come inside, trying not to draw attention to what he was doing. Inside the pir, with a long flowing beard and tightly wrapped turban, sat on cushions behind a low wooden dais. Twenty or thirty men sat, heads bowed, on dark cushions hugging the bare walls. Two of them knelt in front of the pir, engaged in conversation. "Amen," the pir said, finishing the conference with whispered prayers.

The men in turn knelt before the pir and kissed his hand. Each time a murid came up to the dais, the pir asked about the disciple's daily diligence in practicing his assigned recitations and meditations. The pir rebuked failure or assigned new formulae to recite. It was impossible to overhear more than a snippet of each conversation. "Did you do it?" the pir said to one man. He nodded. The pir's blessing followed. Some interactions were tinged with emotion as tears welled up in the men's eyes. Smiling, they whispered things like "Thank you, Hazrati Pir!" or "Yes, yes, a thousand times over!" Shame filled, other murids did not dare meet the pir's gaze.

A cell phone ring punctured the hushed tones of the pir's next prayer. A man, not dressed like the others, pulled the phone out of his pocket and answered it. "Hello?" he said, almost shouting. He walked out of the room, slamming the wooden door behind him.

The pir stopped a blessing in midsentence. "Who brought him?" the pir said with seeming anger.

No one dared answer.

At one point, the pir wrote something on a scrap of paper and handed it to a younger man, hunched over facing the dais. The man got up and walked back to his seat, shuffling backward so as not to turn his face

from the pir. Persian-script jottings served as personal ritual instructions for the coming weeks, what murids called their vazifa. A murid had
to master them in order to receive new ones. The man sat, inspected the
words on the paper, and excitedly showed it to the men seated next to
him along the back wall, beaming with pride. They nodded, mumbling
words of affirmation softly so as not to disturb another conference,
which had already begun.

Abdullo allowed me to copy down all the vazifa he had ever received.
After each conference, he had recorded the pir's instructions on his
mobile phone. In total he shared vazifa that he had received every three
or four weeks over the course of the past two years, including ones from
two different pirs. One of the first ones was "29.05.09 Naqshbandiya.
The subtle center of the heart. Its light is yellow. It is the seat of the
arrival of Hazrati Odam. (Its zikr is 'Olloh.')"[6]

The pir's instructions were for Abdullo to recite daily the zikr formula
"Olloh" while keeping his attention on the subtle center (*latif*) of his
heart (*qalb*). Activation of one's six subtle centers (*lato"if*) is one of
the key methods whereby a murid progresses along the mystical path
(Buehler 1998, 103). Each of the subtle centers has a physical location
within the body, a uniquely colored radiance, and a spiritual exemplar to
whom an adept directs specific ritual formulae.[7] Accordingly, the heart
exudes a yellow-colored radiance during zikr and is under the guidance
of the prophet Odam.

One time, I asked Abdullo how many vazifa there were. "Altogether,
about four hundred," he said.

Another murid, listening intently to our discussion, interjected, "The
pir knows sixteen hundred."

"Getting one once a month, it would take more than a lifetime for you
to learn them all," I suggested.

"Some people can learn one every three or four days," Abdullo said.

Abdullo's comments amplify how greater ritual diligence leads to
greater knowledge. If working to build the mosque's foundation was primarily about cultivating a Sufi way of being in the world, so, too, the
recitation of zikr formulae enabled the men to develop the spiritual disposition that they so earnestly sought. Another Sufi described the purpose of vazifa like this. "God only wants our mental faculties (*hushu ëd*).
He doesn't want anything else. He wants our focus to be on him. You can

be praying in the mosque, you can wear a prayer cap, have a beard. But inside you can be squirming, not experiencing God's grace." The man suggested that it was not enough that adepts wear the correct clothes or trim their beards to appropriate lengths. They also had to develop their mind. Following rules of comportment and diligently reciting ritual formulae went together as means for learning how to be a Sufi. Ritual instructions existed alongside the nostalgias of the mountainside as within dars adepts treated pious comportment, bodily nostalgias, and ritualized knowledge as different means to the same end.

Dars, a highly articulated event, inextricably linked behavior and knowledge. Each of the adepts' actions, from their posture while waiting for lessons to begin to their individual conferences with the pir, were choreographed precisely, and any deviance, such as the cellphone interruption, risked provoking the pir's anger. When describing dars, adepts often stressed the rules governing who sits where, when it was appropriate to approach the pir, and the specifics of the formulae enjoined on them during their personal conferences with the pir. The knowledge they emphasized referred not to the passive reception of religious precepts but rather to a knowledge that was enacted in ritual. Vazifa, literally a "task," meant ritualized knowledge, a knowledge encapsulated by repeated symbolic behavior (Chamberlain 1994, 125–30; Buehler 1998, 26–28). Their knowledge was formalized action.

I asked one man how his actions allowed him to progress along the mystical path. He replied:

> It's the pir who brings you to the next step. If you engage in acts of worship (*ibodat*) and do your vazifa from one Ramazon to the next, then, God willing, you may move to the next step. You have to really memorize the formula. Say the president of Tajikistan comes and gives you a task and leaves to go to America for twenty days. You might rest for fifteen days and then during the last five actually work on it. People do that with God too. They wait. God is different. You can't escape from God. You feel it.

What the man described was a sort of corporeal knowing (Stoller 1997, 66), the idea that understanding comes in copying the world through the body. Ritual diligence led to God; knowledge came from the body. The man's ritualized knowledge was not primarily an objectified knowledge that circulated in texts or the inscribed loci often invoked in discussions of Muslim pedagogy. It was not the simple memorization of vazifa, something theoretically within the grasp of any individual with access to the formulae. Instead, the man's knowledge encompassed both textual components and an "embodied knowledge" that "cannot be put into words, it can only be experienced in practice" (Lambek 1997, 136). It was a knowledge bodily performed and lived (Lambek 1993). In addition to vazifa, dars also included instruction on mystical texts such as *The Letters of Imom Rabboni*, Rumi's *Masnavi*, or portions of Bedil's *Devon*.

LEARNING A MYSTICAL DISPOSITION

After the last man had shuffled back to his cushion, the pir opened a large, worn lithographed tome that had been resting on the dais and began to read: "Statements were issued to Muhammad Mumin, the son of Khoja Ali Khon, to explain the changing of mystical states and the elimination of earthly desires."

For several years, the pir had regularly read from *The Letters*.[8] By the time I attended dars, he had reached letter 64 in volume 2 of the compiled letters. Some men read along in their tattered copies of the work. One white-bearded man held a weathered, hand-copied manuscript filled with ornate penmanship and framed in flowery red borders. Others carried small paperback books, which included short summaries. "If there's not time to read the entire letter," Abdullo told me.

"The world is the believer's prison," the pir continued.[9] He looked up and explained Sirhindi's statement: "This is the man set free from his nafs (*odami itloq*). It means the annihilation of the self (*fanoi odam*), not annihilation into the divine."

The pir read the letter in its entirety, stopping only to define unfamiliar terminology and quote poetry related somehow to the themes the letter engaged. He shifted easily between reading and explaining Sirhindi's complex philosophy.

"Be attentive to this important conversation," the pir read, finishing the letter. "May you understand it in the coming week," he added in benediction, closing the book. He scanned the men's faces and said, "Do you have questions?"

"What's the meaning of *alhamdulillo*?" one younger man said, notebook in hand. The man had taken notes throughout the entirety of the pir's lesson.

"Essentially, you have to understand the Arabic meaning of *shukr*. Shukr are words given in thanks, words. *Alhamdulillo*, a feeling of thanks, a feeling."

"What zikr do the Qodiriya recite?" another man said, not waiting for the pir to invite additional questions.

"There are many different zikr: the zikr of human nature (*zikri nasuti*), loud zikr (*zikri jahri*)," the pir answered. "*Olloh, hu, lo iloho*, and others. We know that the Naqshbandiya only use *Olloh*. But they're all equivalent, all are God's speech and have merit."

The man with the notebook asked another question: "Have all of the saints attained the annihilation of the self?"

"Yes, of course," the pir said, lingering on *of course*. The hint of frustration in his voice matched his tone during the conferences that came before. It seemed like both a well-deserved reproach to an overeager teacher's pet and bridled frustration at the man's seeming forgetfulness. "Remember Ibn Arabi.[10] When he was just nineteen years old, he could tell about all of the saints that were to come," the pir said.

The pir ended dars without an announcement, apparently satisfied that there were no additional questions. He closed his book and began whispering to the man seated next to him. Most adepts grabbed their books, slowly got up from their cushions, and silently filed out the door, walking backward.

Abdullo took me back to the car. "You know that in order to learn anything, you have to become a Muslim," he said, returning to what he had said before dars.

No doubt Abdullo intended his comments as a not so subtle rebuke of my perceived lack of faith. At the same time, they also highlighted the incongruence between the knowledge of dars and the sort of knowledge Abdullo assumed I was seeking. Abdullo emphasized their contrasting pragmatics, in which what becomes primary is "what is *accomplished* in the act of utterance, in contrast to what information is being conveyed" (Silverstein 2008, 131). That is, dars teaches adepts more than the particulars of Sirhindi's mystical theosophy in a straightforward, linear accounting of reality in the form of a contemporary nonfiction text. Instead, those in attendance gain mastery over a mystical vocabulary and a Sufi interpretive frame, knowledge only available to the initiated. Dars engenders this total mystical disposition, not unlike hard labor on the mountainside or the memorization of ritual formulae.

Teaching within dars had the same ritualized quality as the transmission of vazifa with its attendant formulism. Tellingly, in my conversations with adepts after dars, they often stressed the terms they learned during their time with the pir, in contrast to themes or larger points of spiritual or profane application. They quoted the pir's short Tajik-colloquial explications of Sirhindi's terminology in the letters and more often than not ignored their topical foci. Their questions focused on the meanings of *alhamdulillo* (praise/thanks to God) or the distinctions between different Qodiri and Naqshbandi zikr formulae. More important, the men wanted to ensure that I understood and followed the rules of pious comportment that dars inculcated.

The significance of ritualized knowledge, with respect to both learning vazifa and the pir's lessons about Sirhindi's letters, is not unique to the present moment. Historically, the experience of reading Sirhindi's letters operated less as an investigation into puzzling out Sirhindi's ideas than as an exercise in fostering a mystical way of being in the world. Naqshbandi pirs in South Asia most often read the letters aloud to their disciples, commenting and expanding on their lexical meanings where appropriate and building on their content in relation to the life of the group and the pir's personal experiences of the mystical enterprise (Buehler 2011).[11] Accordingly, it is not nearly as simple as saying that if one knows the lexical meanings of the letters one can understand Sirhindi's purpose in a given letter and by extension the knowledge dars communicates.

Beyond being another critique of the ethnographic enterprise, Abdullo's incredulity at my naïveté in thinking I could attend dars similarly encapsulates this idea. Of course, I might be able to stumble through a letter's more straightforward meanings using dictionaries and other lexical aids, but the idea that I would understand the letters' allusions, the representations of mystical reality they describe, and their references to the wider world of Naqshbandi spirituality was ludicrous. Indeed, it is precisely this wider constellation of Central Asian religious history that dars indexes. The rules of comportment, ritual formulae, and the transmission of Sirhindi's mystical precepts all hold echoes of the sacred Persian past. Within dars, adepts bodily performed that past as they sought to cultivate an ethical life according to precepts no longer, or perhaps never, valued in wider Tajik society.

Dars, then, is just as anachronistic, nostalgia-filled even, as was the men's work on the mountainside. Its anachronisms came into even sharper focus for me when three teenagers uninitiated in the specifics of ritual comportment attended dars for the first time. That morning a man wept loudly at a high pitch for several long, awkward minutes. Many in the room seemed uncomfortable at the extended display of emotion; most men turned their gaze toward the floor or closed their eyes in meditation. The teenagers looked at each other incredulously as they attempted to hold back their laughter. None of the boys went forward to visit with the pir while I was there, and they left before dars had ended. They seemed to find the pir's instruction of embodied, ritualized knowledge jarring. Perhaps their unease was generational; as teenagers their temporal maps were different than the older men, who sought out the anachronism. With more historical consciousness, the teenagers might have echoed Firuz's comment that the "time for that has passed." Even so, in addition to their unfamiliarity with the embodied norms of the group, their discomfort was especially acute because they lacked individual relationships with the pir. Embodied nostalgias and ritualized knowledge always exist in concert with an ongoing, intimate relationship with an accomplished mystical guide.

SOCIALITY AND THE TRANSMISSION OF KNOWLEDGE

"Children ought to respect their fathers and mothers. Else, they'll face disownment," the pir intoned gravely. It was the same register one might hear during a Friday sermon or university lecture. Ibrohim and I had come at the invitation of the pir's brother. Though a proud skeptic when in his office at the institute, Ibrohim relished his role in introducing me to pirs and accompanying me to social functions when he could. He maintained relationships with wide networks of religious personnel across central Tajikistan and cultivated an easy rapport with them. In their presence, Ibrohim transformed open defiance into deference, while pirs greeted him as they might a long-lost friend.

When we arrived in the village that evening not long before the final call to prayer, the meal had ended and the pir had already begun his talk. A hundred or so mostly white-bearded men relaxed in the warm evening air and ate from plates of rice and bowls of sliced watermelon, resting on colorful cushions in the compound's courtyard. The wizened pir held court at the far end of the courtyard, only the oldest men sitting near him.

"Brother, what were you saying?" the pir said to a man seated beside him, the pir's earlier didactic tone now more conversational.

"My eldest son came back," the man began in a hoarse voice. "He's in Russia and doesn't take care of me," he continued.

"Does he recite his daily prayers?" the pir said with seeming concern in his eyes. The man slightly lowered his gaze and replied inaudibly.

"You shouldn't blame your son but yourself," the pir told him. "It's because you didn't train him that he doesn't recite his daily prayers." The pir's accusation surprised me. It came gently, the pir's voice tempering the apparent harshness of his words. "I'll admonish him in the village in front of folks," he added to murmurs of approval from some of the men sitting nearby. The pir then offered a one-word explanation for the son's wayward behavior: disrespect, his keyword for the evening.

Ibrohim whispered to me, "Hazrati Pir often helps the older men in his villages." Despite what Ibrohim thought about the intellectual basis of the pir's prescriptions, he valued the stabilizing influence men like the pir played amid the volatility and social disruption of post-Soviet economic change. Men like the pir may have been distinct from the "real" pirs of Ibrohim's history books, but Ibrohim believed they still played a vital role in village life.

"Abu Huraira converted to Islam, but his mother didn't," the pir continued.[12] "His mother cursed the Prophet, peace be upon him, and Abu Huraira wept. He went to the Prophet, peace be upon him, and asked him to pray that his mother would become a Muslim. When he arrived home, she was saying the declaration of faith so loudly that he could hear it from outside his house."

Many of the men replied, "*Moshollo* (wonder, praise)." Others simply smiled or chuckled softly to themselves.

The pir finished by reminding the men of a larger point: "This is an example of children respecting their parents."

The call to prayer rang out a few moments later from a loudspeaker at the not so distant village mosque.[13] I never found out whether the apparently tight choreography was planned or pure serendipity. Nonetheless, the muazzin's invocation served as a poetic coda to the talk, validating the pir's pronouncements and broadcasting his wisdom into space, almost as if by divine proclamation. Most of the men slowly got up, warmly greeted their fellow attendees, and walked toward the mosque for prayers.

"My son is leaving tomorrow to go to Russia," I overheard one man say to the pir as he was leaving. The pir raised his hands and prayed for physical and spiritual protection.

Teaching and pious comportment are always enmeshed in wider contexts of sociality. It is only through intimate companionship that a pir can transact embodied knowledge and impress upon his disciples the spiritual dispositions he holds. That late summer evening, relaxing over plates of cold rice and lukewarm tea, the village men enacted just that intersection of teaching and relationship. The men sat on the veranda and enjoyed the pir's hospitality while he instructed them on the virtues of living a respect-filled life, a life that the man's example suggested was tragically atypical of many of the labor migrants traveling to Russia. The son's lack of respect necessitated the pir's intervention. The pir also interceded on another disciple's behalf, praying for his son's protection and financial benefit as he traveled to Russia for work.

This is the mutual intimacy of companionship (*sūhbat*, lit. "conversation"), both what the men on the veranda called their regular evening discussions with the pir and a term denoting a highly articulated Naqshbandi notion of spiritual companionship (Schimmel 1975, 366; Weismann 2007, 29), which plays out across a wide spectrum of Sufi teaching contexts.[14] For instance, Khurshed commented in chapter 4 that he could only learn what his pir taught him. Similarly, Abdullo's pir did not allow anyone to come to dars with whom he could not interact directly. At the end of the lessons that I attended, the pir asked anyone with whom he not talked to come to the dais, the precise activity the skeptical teenagers seemed purposely to avoid. Dars, like companionship, only occurred through intimate relationships.

Many critics of Sufi intimacy accuse pirs of merely manipulating gullible men for financial gain, not unlike earlier Soviet era polemics that accused pirs of being a drain on the economic resources of peasants (Ro'i 2000, 393–405). I frequently encountered individuals who, on hearing about the nature of my research, immediately said things like "Pirs just take money," "Mullahs are only about money," "Prayers are free, so why do you have to pay for a prayer?" or "Religion (*din*) is about God, not nation or money." In a private moment, Ibrohim put it even more bluntly, "All the shaikhs in Tajikistan are new. They are all after money or power."

Such accusations parody pir-murid sociality and the transmission of mystical knowledge as merely transactional—intangible spiritual benefits in exchange for a pir's real financial gain. Reductionist claims ignore the way companionship mutually benefits both pirs and their disciples. The transmission of embodied knowledge may only occur because a murid has financially supported his pir, but benefits do not accrue to the pir alone. Abdullo's pir moved from his home in a distant village to a humble house in the Dushanbe suburbs because of his disciples' generosity, but in return they expected him to interact with them regularly, teach them the litanies of the path, and offer prayers on their behalf when they had some important concern. Beyond the hospitality the pir provided on the veranda, the two men sought a direct financial benefit from their relationship with the pir. Children are supposed to care for their aging parents. The pir's efforts were to ensure that one son would fulfill his financial duties at home and another would send home the fruit of his labor as a migrant in Russia.

Even so, it is impossible to reduce pir-murid interactions to the simple financial gain that comes from amassing a group of loyal cadres or the immediate (in)tangible benefits gained from having an influential patron. Indeed, most of the pirs with whom I interacted lived humbly, gave any excess offerings beyond their immediate living expenses to the village poor, and willingly shared the hospitality of their table with those that arrived on their doorsteps. Most murids I encountered emphasized the spiritual benefits of devotion and were quick to stave off potential criticism by suggesting that their pirs rightly distributed charity to those in need. They interpreted pirs' spiritual and monetary largesse as the result of their disciples' generosity.

Rustam once told me about a time when his pir was sharing a meal with some of his followers who lived in a distant village. Rustam liked to stress the ways in which his pir's power manifested itself beyond the forum of poetry singing. That day the men saw that the pir had three thousand euros, two thousand dollars, and a few Tajik somoni in his front shirt pocket. One of the men approached the pir, saying he needed some money for his son's wedding. To his great chagrin, the pir refused. Later that day a beggar woman asked the pir for some money so she could feed her children. Surprising everyone, the pir immediately took out all his money and gave it to the woman. Later the men were worried that when it became time to find a car to take them back to the city they wouldn't have enough money to pay the fare. The men found one anyway and haggled over the price, despite the fact that they didn't have any money with which to pay the driver. Just as they were setting off, a man flagged down the car and got in, recognizing the pir. The man had been on his way to the city so he could give his offerings to the pir. He handed the pir two thousand dollars, and the pir gave it straightaway to the murid who had asked for money for his son's wedding.

Rustam's story neatly highlighted the give-and-take inherent in the pir-murid relationship. Bodily nostalgias and lessons in mystical cultivation only become operational in contexts of intimate, mutual reciprocity. Yet still, as with any form of public religiosity in contemporary Tajikistan, personal piety easily runs afoul of the shifting moods of the state religious bureaucracy; even quietism and fixations on a long-distant sacred past can be potentially threatening to security forces charged with controlling civil society. It is the anachronisms of the pir-murid relationship with the attendant loyalty the relationship inspires that members of the religious bureaucracy fear the most.

BODILY NOSTALGIAS, EMBODIED KNOWLEDGE, AND THE STATE

"I used to give lessons on the *Masnavi.*" He paused. "But not anymore. It's illegal to have gatherings (mahfil)." The pir was someone deeply respected by both pious Tajiks and members of the religious bureaucracy, in my experience a rare combination. Whenever I asked Sufis about prominent teachers whom I should meet, the pir's name invariably came up.

Knowing that the pir regularly taught his disciples, I shifted the subject slightly. "When *do* your disciples (murids) come?" I said, hoping he would tell me about the lessons he gave.

"I don't have any disciples. I just have a few students (*shogirds*)," he replied. "I don't have anyone give me their oath (baiat) or even take their hand."[15] He clarified, "I only take their hand if they are truly seeking vazifa, if they come in a posture of forgiveness. If they're seeking, then I give them vazifa." Then, presumably directed to me, he added, "If they pray their daily prayers."

Reframing my previous question, I said, "How often do your students come?"

"Whenever they want," he said. "A group of older men gather to read together. We read and discuss jurisprudence."

The white-bearded pir, with friends across the political spectrum, could afford to be more candid with me than most about state-sponsored repression of Muslim teaching circles. Still, he demurred. He denied that he and his students engaged in any of the intricate norms of comportment standard to Central Asian Naqshbandi spirituality. He did not have disciples, he claimed, instead only a few students. He used to teach the *Masnavi* but no longer. Hence there was no transmission of mystical knowledge. He did not accept anyone's oath of allegiance. Instead, he merely shook hands with his students, informally agreeing to teach them. There was no regular instruction, no ongoing relationship. Students simply came whenever they wanted, not at the behest of the pir, nor to complete ongoing teaching rubrics.

On the one hand, the pir's answers to my questions were unsurprising. Regardless of what actually occurred during the times he met with village men, he did not know me well, nor could he intuit the aims or potential audiences of my ongoing research. At the same time, the pir's statements directly gestured at the wider climate of religious repression at the time of my interview. His comments illustrated some of the well-founded fears of the pious. The whims of the state security services and resulting waves of persecution directly threatened Sufi embodied comportment, the transmission of mystical knowledge, and a murid's intimate relationship with his pir. The pir, no doubt, feared how local security services might respond to what went on at his home.

Pirs are especially easy targets for the religious bureaucracy because they work within informal teaching networks, a specific focus of Tajikistan's repressive religious politics. When I met with the pir, the law on parental responsibility, discussed in chapter 1, had recently been introduced. In anticipation of its passage, security officials had already begun enforcing some of its mandates. In Tajikistan, with its rubber-stamp parliament, introduced legislation was as good as settled law. While the state religious bureaucracy tightly controlled formal Islamic education, legions of informal madrasas operated around the country in which boys, and sometime girls, studied Arabic, the Qur'an, and more. Dars was both a euphemism for informal madrasa studies and the lessons pirs gave. Though addressed to separate audiences and with distinct topical foci, the dars of pirs shared the same informal networks as the dars targeted by the legislation.

The religious bureaucracy's efforts against dars may simply reflect a Soviet-inflected fear about the alleged political potency of the pir-murid relationship. Echoes of the legendary Naqshbandi leader Shamil's (1797–1871) decades-long fight against encroachments by the Russian Empire in the nineteenth-century Caucasus still reverberate in contemporary Central Asia (Knysh 2002). Alternatively, fears may stem from anxiety about the supposed threat the Soviet Union faced from "muridism" during the last decades of the Soviet project (Bennigsen and Wimbush 1985). Still more, it may be the result of a fear of client-patron relationships that in many ways mirror the client-patron relationships supported by the nepotistic parochialisms of the Tajik elite (Hammoudi 1997). Both cannot exist while mimicking each other and operating with the same potential bases of social support.

Perhaps even more poignantly, pirs and teaching networks have become targets because of their seeming peculiarity, their anachronisms. Though most members of the state's security services likely don't have the ability to parse the particulars of Sufi bodily nostalgia, they nonetheless recognize that the quiet, inward projects of Tajikistan's Sufis stand in stark contrast to ideas about Islam put forward by the state's religious bureaucracy. The dress, manners, and ritual concerns of dars are all components of an intentional anachronism that butts against official state conceptions of Tajik modernity and the Central Asian religious present.[16] Bodily nostalgias remain threatening, as they publicly mark ideologies, broadcasting them into public space and directly encroaching on the hegemonic secularism perpetuated in the Tajik public sphere.

This is not to say that pirs' lessons or their followers' comportment are openly or intentionally antagonistic. Rather, Sufis in Tajikistan, like other members of the religious classes, merely adapt to the political circumstances of the present moment. State security forces do not target them because of their advocacy for specific policy prescriptions or even something as extreme as overt regime change, but rather because they fear the results of the unregulated transmission of religious knowledge. They imagine the coalescence of social networks outside state control as potentially destabilizing to Tajik domestic politics.

As such the present political environment inextricably shapes Sufi comportment and dars (Roche 2013), not as antagonistic responses to episodes of harsh repression but rather as bodily nostalgias, purposeful anachronisms, and forms of expressive culture that cultivate a Sufi self outside the boundaries of state-sanctioned religiosity. Comportment and dars, like other Tajik Sufi memory practices—telling historical narratives, publishing religious literature, and performing rituals—facilitate complex negotiations in which Sufis work to conceptualize what a life in twenty-first-century Central Asia rightly entails after the traumatic disjuncture of the Soviet era and the political and social uncertainties of the last few tumultuous decades.

Epilogue

During the spring of 2014, I had hoped to chat with several bookseller acquaintances at Dushanbe's central Hoji Yaqub mosque. I wanted to get a sense of how things had changed for them since my last visit several years before. There were many new books I had not seen previously, and I couldn't find many of the most popular texts from earlier years. I had been chatting amicably with one bookseller when I asked him about these changes. Quite surprisingly to me, he ended our discussion.

"Would it be okay if I came back and talked to you about some of these things again sometime?" I said, thinking maybe he would be more forthcoming in private.

"We shouldn't talk anymore. It's all political," he replied offhandedly in a manner uncharacteristic of our earlier chats.

"I'm not asking about politics. I just want to hear about what's changed in the past three years."

As if answering some of my potential questions, he told me, "There used to be lessons and freedom. Now there are neither lessons nor freedom. See, our conversation has come back to politics."

The bookseller's comments succinctly captured the politics of talking about the past and, by extension, of the Sufi expressive memories I have documented. It was obvious to the bookseller that his talk about the past made a pragmatic claim on the present. By just talking about what was, he implicitly offered an evaluation of what is. Pious Tajiks used to meet in teaching circles freely, unofficial madrasas operated without the interference of the state religious bureaucracy, and those that wanted to could easily purchase texts for teaching and personal study. By the time of my conversation with the bookseller in 2014, most unofficial madrasas had been shuttered, and pirs no longer met as easily with their disciples. The bookseller was not alone in his pessimism.

In 2010 I had been surprised to learn that Rustam and his friends had started preparing a DVD to send to President Rahmon. They were encouraged by what they had heard in some of Rahmon's speeches; he occasionally gestured toward mystical themes. The government had even sponsored the restoration of a few shrines. I heard several of the men in Rustam's group confidently say that Rahmon knew about Sufism. It almost seemed as if the president was somehow already familiar with what they were doing. They intended their DVD to include recordings of some rituals along with supporting verses from the Qur'an and other stories. They felt that if the president could only learn about what they truly did, they wouldn't have any more problems.

During my last visit, I asked Rustam if they had ever sent the DVD.

"No," he chuckled. "That wouldn't have been a good idea."

Rustam and his friends have since tried even harder to deflect unsolicited attention, Rahmon's included. Rustam went to Russia for a time, but he moved back home. Ibrohim no longer works at the institute. He took a higher-paying job outside academia. He said it didn't have anything to do with the politics of it all. It was just about making more money. But it definitely didn't hurt that he no longer had to worry so much about what he said and wrote. I still occasionally talk to Firuz. He plays music whenever he can get a gig and continues to tell stories. I'm not sure what happened to Khurshed. I worry about him, not least because several of his friends were arrested along with Eshoni Temur in 2015. Khurshed's limited social media presence is gone. The last time I was in Dushanbe, he wasn't staying in the same house as before, and both his cell phone numbers had been disconnected. It is possible he is just working in Russia. Or maybe he was arrested along with the others. I don't know.

Since the time of my last fieldwork, I have heard about a number of village pirs who have been fined or harassed for giving informal lessons in their homes. As the case of Eshoni Temur demonstrates, the story is perhaps even bleaker for more prominent pirs. Even Shaikh Bahodir was killed in Kabul, a victim of entirely different political circumstances. Bahodir's death reverberated among his Tajik followers. The idea that Afghanistan, a place of seeming hope to some Tajik Sufis, where Sufism could flourish in the midst of extreme insecurity and unhindered by state interference, was not immune to anti-Sufi violence struck a nerve and led some to question the way they imagined their futures in Tajikistan.

That is the rub in Sufi tradition. Tradition, in the sense of making the future out of the past, carries with it a hopeful strain. As tradition mines the past, it also points toward a future trajectory. It is precisely this future that remains more oblique for Tajikistan's Sufis and holds even less promise than it has in recent memory. Instead, it is the past that holds real possibility and lends the opportunity for taking action and reconfiguring Sufi experiences of the present. That is why Sufis need recourse to recursive histories. Purposeful anachronisms, inhabiting multiple times, and nostalgia remedy the paradoxes that Sufis live. Sufis continue to look to the past as their cultural reservoir, not to the future (cf. Piot 2010; Shaw 2013), because the hopefulness required to envision a future remains foreclosed and only the province of the governing elite.

Tajik Terms and Phrases

All terms and phrases reflect local usage among Sufis.

Adab: pious comportment, ethical behavior

Aḣli baĭt: the members of the Prophet Muhammad's household

Aḣli tariqat (also *aḣli tasavvuf*): literally, "the people of the path"; that is, Sufis

Aḣli zoḣir: literally, "the people of the apparent"; that is, non-Sufis

Avlië: saint

Avliëgī: sainthood

Baĭat: a formal pledge of allegiance by a prospective *murid* to a *pir*, signifying the beginning of a *pir-murid* relationship

Botin: hidden, esoteric knowledge, the opposite of *zoḣir*

Dars: lesson, Sufi teaching

Ėshon: an honorific given to religious figures in Central Asia, often used as a synonym for *saĭid*

Faĭz: God's grace, particularly the grace emanating from the *pir* during *zikr*

Fiqeḣ (or *fiqh*): Islamic jurisprudence

Ghazal: a lyric poem

Ghazalkhonī: poetry singing

Ḣajj: pilgrimage to Mecca

Ḣalqa: a group of Sufis or a Sufi gathering

Ḣalqai zikr: a gathering to recite *zikr*

Ḣanafī: a follower of the Ḣanafī school of Islamic jurisprudence

Ḣazrat: an honorific for religious figures

Ḣazrati Pir (also *Ḣazrati Buzurgvor*): respectful term of address for a *pir*

173

Ḣofīz: a poetry singer

Ḣojī: someone who has completed the *hajj*

Ḣu: one of the names of God recited in *zikr*

Ḣujra: a teaching circle, a group of Sufis

Ilm: mystical knowledge

Imom: a prayer leader in a mosque

Imomi khatib: the leader of a congregational mosque

Ishq: love, especially divine love or love for one's *pir*

Karomot: miracle

Khalifa: successor, the assistant/deputy of a Sufi *pir*

Khati irshod: a letter from a *pir* authorizing one to teach

Khonaqoḣ: a Sufi lodge

Kolkhoz: a collective farm

Kumitai Din: the State Committee for Religious Affairs (Komitai Oid
   ba Korḣoi Din)

Lato"if: the subtle centers of the body activated through *zikr*

Lavḣal maḣfuz: the book of fate

Maḣfil: meeting, a Sufi gathering

Makhdum: an honorific for a learned religious figure

Maqom (also *zina*): a stage in the Sufi path

Masjidi jomeḣ: a congregational mosque where Friday sermons are
   delivered

Masjidi panj vaqta: a small mosque for daily prayers

Muftī: a senior religious official authorized to issue legal opinions

Murid: a disciple, an initiate

Muroqiba: contemplation, meditation, a vision

Nafs: the soul, one's base instincts, the place of carnal desire

Namoz: the five daily prayers

Pir: a Sufi master

Rūza: fasting during the month of Ramazon

Saïid: a descendent of the Prophet Muhammad

Shaïkh: a Sufi *pir*

Shajara (also *Shajaranoma*): genealogy, a genealogical tree

Shariat: the law, Sufi gloss for the five pillars of Islam (saying the
   statement of faith, reciting *namoz*, fasting during the month of
   Ramazon, giving alms, and going on *hajj*)

Shirk: polytheism, attribution, the sin of attributing undue powers or
   qualities reserved for God alone to another figure

Shogird: a student of a *pir*
Silsila: the chain of mystical transmission between master and disciple
Somonī: the currency of Tajikistan
Sūhbat: conversation, spiritual companionship
Suluk: conduct, ethics, the Sufi path
Takhallus: a pen name
Tariqat (sing. *tariqa*): the Sufi path, transnational Sufi teaching
    hierarchies, groups of Sufis
Tariqatī: a Sufi
Tasavvuf: mysticism, Sufism
Tasavvufī: a Sufi
Tavajjūh: attention, mystical gaze
Tavakkal (also *tavakkul*): total trust in God
Tazkira: literary compendium, biographical dictionary of Sufi saints
Ṭūmār: storyteller's notebook
Tūra: an honorific given to religious figures in Central Asia, often used
    as a synonym for *saïid*
Ulamo: Muslim scholars
Uvaïsī: a Sufi who has achieved initiation into a *tariqa* without the
    guidance of a living *pir*
Vazifa: duty, a mystical task given by a *pir* to a disciple, Sufi recitations
Viloīat: saintly power
Zakot: alms-giving
Ziërat: pilgrimage
Zikr: recollection of the name of God
Zikri jahrī: voiced recollection of the name of God
Zikri khufī (also *zikri qalbī*): silent recollection of the name of God
Zohir: apparent, outsider knowledge, the opposite of *botin*

Notes

INTRODUCTION

1. "Tojikiston piri tariqat dorad?," Saïidqosimi Qiëmpur, Radioi Ozodī, February 8, 2013, http://www.ozodi.org/a/24896207.html; "Javob ba maqolai 'Tojikiston piri tariqat dorad?,'" Radioi Ozodī, April 8, 2013, http://www.ozodi.org/a/24950926.html.

2. In 2010 civil servants and university students, among others, were compelled to purchase shares to finance the Rogun Dam's eventual construction, projected to cost as much as $2 billion (Menga 2015).

3. There is a certain banality to emphasizing the challenges one faces when translating terms for Sufi practice into English, yet it still bears repeating. Two competing forces are at work. One is the seeming chasm between Sufi experiences of mystical reality and mere metaphor. The second is the Orientalist legacy of transposing concepts from Christianity to the study of Islam. *Tariqat* (sing. *tariqa*) most often appears in English as "orders" or "brotherhoods," analogues to Christian monastic orders, yet tariqat more closely approximates "paths" in English. Similar precise alternatives do not always exist. For example, I retain the use of "saint" for the Tajik word *avlië*, despite the differences between Sufi and Christian concepts of sainthood, because no other English terms as readily capture its range of meanings (Kugle 2006, 31–32).

4. For more on female Sufi groups in Central Asia (but not in Tajikistan), see Louw (2007); Peshkova (2014); Sultanova (2011).

5. Ironically, the inverse was true during the last decades of the Soviet Union's existence. Sovietologists frequently argued that Sufis represented an existential threat to the stability of the Soviet regime (e.g., Bennigsen and Wimbush 1985).

6. "Statement at the Official Meeting on the Occasion of the 25th Anniversary of State Independence of the Republic of Tajikistan," Press Service of the President of the Republic of Tajikistan, September 8, 2016, http://www.prezident.tj/en/node/12953.

7. There has been a sustained call to rethink post-Soviet (Chari and Verdery 2009; Boyer and Yurchak 2010; Gilbert et al. 2008). Diana Ibañez-Tirado (2015) has usefully brought that discussion to Tajikistan, highlighting the mismatch between Soviet and post-Soviet as mutually exclusive frames in charting Kulob residents' experiences of time. I, too, share Ibañez-Tirado's concern with Tajiks' alternative temporalities, though I see Sufis as living a pastness, which Ibañez-Tirado's collaborators may not. On experiences of time in Tajikistan, see also Remtilla (2012); Mostowlansky (2017). One corrective has been to dispense with chronology and resituate our emphasis on epistemology (Stenning and Hörschelmann 2008, 317). Post-Soviet, then, as "thickly," not "thinly" applied (Stoler 2016, 344), becomes a kind of metadiscursive frame, as an analogue to other posts, including post-colonialism.

8. I am grateful to Paolo Sartori for this point.

9. I have found Ann Laura Stoler's (2016) work on postcolonial recursive histories helpful in thinking through the way pasts linger on in the present, yet my argument does not depend on Central Asia being "postcolonial." See Verdery (2002); Kandiyoti (2002).

10. Tradition, too, has been a primary heuristic for the study of Islam after the Soviet experience, both for understanding the rhetoric put forward by Central Asian elites and for understanding the experiences of individual Muslims (Khalid 2007; Hilgers 2009, 67–94; Stephan 2010).

11. Some political science literature has grasped the process of tradition but curiously not its critique of the immutable heritage of the past. In this frame, some scholars have termed the introduction of practices with analogues that existed prior to the Soviet experience as "retraditionalization" (Gal and Kligman 2000; Commercio 2015).

12. Tellingly, Deema Kaneff (2004, 151) notes that "folklorization," mediated displays of culture, renders temporal regimes linear.

13. Recent work has complicated folklorists' justifiable urge to celebrate the folk's refusal to be dominated. See, for example, Gilman (2009, 168–77); McDonald (2013, 25–28).

14. This is not to suggest that Muslims in Tajikistan never resist state power. See Lemon (2016, 98–106).

Chapter 1. Sufis in Tajikistan

1. Sufis make a sharp distinction between Sufism (*tasavvuf*) and the law (*shariat*). For many the shariat refers to those practices that all Muslims standardly perform; for example, reciting the five daily prayers (*namoz*), fasting during the month of Ramazon (*rūza*), giving alms (*zakot*), and going on pilgrimage to Mecca (*hajj*).

2. Luqman is a composite legendary figure found across Arabic, Persian, and Turkish folklore; he figures in pre-Islamic Arabian legends, a Qur'anic sura

that bears his name, and Persian and Turkish literature, including the wider medieval Alexander romance traditions.

A similar, well-known story about Luqman and Iskandar (Alexander the Great) can be found in a printed Tajik collection of stories about Luqman compiled in the early Soviet era (Nuraliev 1991, 73–82). In the tale, Iskandar conquers the distant land of darkness. In tribute, the king gives Iskandar some magical flour and instructs the world conqueror to take it home and bake bread from it himself. Iskandar instead asks his princess to bake the bread, but she does not follow his instructions. Every time she puts the bread in the hearth it falls into the ashes. She eventually gives up and bakes Iskandar another loaf of bread from regular flour. That day Aflatun (Plato) and Luqman were in the king's kitchens. They divided the half-baked, ash-covered bread and ate it themselves. Both immediately possessed immense wisdom.

Another, similar story about Luqman's wisdom is found in Rumi's *Masnavi* (2007, 89–91). In Rumi's tale, Luqman's master always sought to eat the food that Luqman left so that the master would become "enraptured." One time the master gave Luqman slices of melon. As Luqman ate the melon, his rapture became evident. The master saved the last slice for himself. Yet when he ate it, it was sour, like fire in his throat.

3. Others have similarly attested to the proliferation of teaching circles in this era. See Dudoignon and Qalandar (2014, 86–95); Roche (2013); Tasar (2012, 171–72).

4. Some sources include the spelling Abdurrahmonjon.

5. A belabored debate that still animates many scholarly discussions about the nature of Muslim life in Soviet Central Asia has been the division between state-recognized, official currents of Muslim religiosity and the unofficial, often underground, "parallel" practices that operated without the approval of state religious bureaucrats. In 1943 the Muslim Spiritual Directorate for Central Asia and Kazakhstan (SADUM), along with similar directorates for other regions of the Soviet Union, was set up to administer mosques, train imoms (prayer leaders), and adjudicate all religious matters in the Soviet Central Asian republics. Significantly, Sufi practices—pilgrimages to shrines, devotion to pirs, and so on—fell outside SADUM's purview and were relegated to the so-called unofficial or parallel spheres of religious practice. The directorate often issued polemics, vilifying Sufi practices as "ishanism," evidence for heterodoxy among "backward" Central Asians (Ro'i 2000, 393–405). For many Soviet era commentators, Sufism became a chief metric for the "unofficial" (Gross 1999).

Will Myer (2002) has dutifully outlined that the genealogy of dichotomies goes back at least to the era of late colonialism, convincingly arguing that this conception of Islam is based on the colonial experience of Cold War Europe. When European, and later American, theorists looked toward the "colonies" of the Soviet underbelly, they drew on analogous examples from their own colonial experiences, namely, nationalist discontent on the Indian subcontinent and resistance in French Africa. Thus, the experience of colonial administrators with a Muslim native population in French Algiers became the frame with which to view potential cleavages in a Soviet administrative and society-transforming capacity in Central Asia.

Although the bifurcation of Soviet era Islam continues to exist in scholarly studies of Soviet era Islam (e.g., Ro'i 2000), official versus unofficial Islam was a colonial administrative construct and the product of Soviet ideology rather than a reflection of lived Muslim reality in Central Asia (Gross 1999; DeWeese 2002). It is even problematic to speak of official Islam as a unitary entity, or even state-controlled, due to the fact that state functionaries perpetuated diverse agendas and interpretations of Islam, sometimes at odds with official ideology (Saroyan 1997). Additionally, the lived experiences of many Soviet-era Central Asian Muslims operated somewhere in between the two currents, in what Eren Tasar (2017) has usefully termed the "gray spaces" of Soviet-era Islam.

Despite the division's problematic construction, the tensions embodied in bifurcated Islam have carried over into state rhetoric about the boundaries of correct and incorrect Islam today (Rasanayagam 2006). Echoes of the official and unofficial reverberate in the way governing elites in Tajikistan construct the distinctions between acceptable Islam, the "good" Muslims, and troublesome piety, so-called bad Islams (cf. Peshkova 2014, 152).

6. Salmoni Forsi was a companion of the Prophet Muhammad and the first Persian convert to Islam.

7. See chapter 5 for the distinctions between different types of zikrs.

8. The diagram portrayed the subtle bodily centers (*lato"if*). See chapter 6 for a more detailed discussion of the centers.

9. Varieties of ritual practice, adherence to unique forms of proper behavior and comportment (*adab*), relationships with the ulamo, exposure to distinct bodies of mystical literature, and inclusion in discrete circles of knowledge transmission may help to better characterize different streams of Sufi practice in Central Asia irrespective of practitioners' self-identification into larger, transnational teaching hierarchies. Dual and concurrent initiations may historically have been more characteristic of Sufi practice in Central Asia rather than singular adherence to one specific teaching path. This is not the well-documented historical practice of an adept seeking out initiations from pirs who represent distinct paths (cf. Ernst and Lawrence 2002, 28). At least since the eighteenth century, the phenomenon of "bundled" lineages has likely characterized much Central Asian Sufi practice (DeWeese 2012), in which a pir simultaneously transmits streams of practice with historical origins from discrete lineages to the extent that group self-identification no longer corresponded with the labels of their practices.

10. The *ahli baït*, literally "the people of the house," are members of the Prophet Muhammad's household.

11. Literally, Ibrohim said, "They've completed the spiritual centers, *ma'rifat* [knowledge, a step on the Sufi path], and moved up the ladder through the stages of the Sufi path."

12. See also Epkenhans (2017, 177–82).

13. Another striking aspect of tariqat taxonomic flexibility is that some important Sufi families, like the Turajonzodas, are listed as either Naqshbandi or Qodiri depending on the source. For example, Svatopluk Soucek (2000, 307) calls them Naqshbandi in his epic history of the region. Even Hoji Akbar's adviser and confidant at the peace talks mediated by the United Nations (UN) at the conclusion of the civil war, Sergei Gretsky (1994, 16), refers to them as successors of a Naqshbandi pir. In a much more recent article, Stéphane Dudoignon (2011, 75) lists Hoji Akbar as a son of a Naqshbandi eshon. Vitaly Naumkin (2005, 232) calls attention to the Turajonzodas' affiliation in the Qodiriya yet spuriously refers to their pir as "Khaliljon, a famous pir from Kurghanteppa," details that Olivier Roy (2000, 149) also includes in his book on Central Asia after the Soviet experience.

I would suggest that the discrepancies in tariqat identification are not a result of academic or editorial carelessness but rather that the Turajonzodas likely did/ do emphasize particular aspects of their biographies to different audiences depending on the circumstance. These shifting emphases are more than political marriages of convenience, as they further suggest the "bundling" of mystical lineages (DeWeese 2012).

14. *Hazrat* is an honorific for religious figures. Adepts frequently refer to their pir as "Hazrati Pir."

15. That is, they need to travel to Afghanistan and serve in Bahodir's household for three months before they can receive authorization to teach.

16. An alternate Persian spelling is *tavakkul*. While both spellings/ pronunciations are accepted in standard Tajik Persian, *tavakkal* was more commonly used among the Sufi groups in which I participated.

17. See chapter 2 for more about Temur's arrest.

18. The sentiment is broadly attested in classical Persian poetry. For example, an almost identical verse is often attributed to the poet Hofiz: "Don't go into the tavern without a pir, because each of them is the Alexander of the age."

19. Sufis use multiple terms to refer to sacred sites. The most common are *mazor* (shrine), *ziëratgoh* (lit. place of pilgrimage), *maqbara* (mausoleum), and *qadamjoi* (lit. stepping place, a site where a holy person has stepped).

20. For comparative examples of state appropriation of shrine space in Central Asia, see Privratsky (2001); Louw (2007); Thum (2014); O'Dell (2017).

21. Recent ethnographic scholarship on politics in Central Asia has emphasized the ways in which the state is "performed" (Rasanayagam, Beyer, and Reeves 2014; Heathershaw 2014; Fjæstad and Kjærnet 2014). Building on the work of Judith Butler (1990), scholars have argued that the state is not a preexisting

entity but rather is performed into being through repeated acts of signification. I find this conception particularly helpful in thinking through the discursive effects of the symbolic politics enacted by Rahmon's regime and established dialogically with Sufi groups (Tedlock and Mannheim 1995).

22. Most Tajiks still refer to the state's security services by the Soviet-era acronym, "KGB." Hizb ut-Tahrir is an Islamist political movement with roots in the Middle East and aspirations to establish the historical Caliphate. Officially nonviolent, it is nonetheless illegal across Central Asia and a frequent bogeyman of the region's repressive regimes.

CHAPTER 2. NOSTALGIA AND MUSLIMNESS

1. The story does not seem to be attested in literary Persian, though, of course, Mahmud and his slave Ayoz are important figures in mystical Persian poetry. Also interestingly intertextually is Mahmud's largesse and patronage of Sufi pirs. Tradition relates that Mahmud quite stingily neglected to pay the poet Firdavsi what he had been promised to author the Persian epic the *Shahnameh*. In place of each promised gold coin, Firdavsi received a silver one.

2. Rey Chow refracts entanglements through a slightly different lens. She calls them a "condition of overlapping recurrences" (2012, 2) and the "linkages and enmeshments that keep things apart, the voidings and uncoverings that hold things together" (12). Chow's *entanglement* is also an especially apt term for nostalgic talk in that it also has the connotation of an attachment from which one cannot easily be extricated. That is precisely the case with Sufi nostalgic memories about the past. Additionally, Jason Whitesel and Amy Shuman's refinement and application of Barad's notion of entanglements fruitfully emphasizes how discourses can "intersect, overlap, and complicate each other" (2016, 40). Rather than thinking of these as contradictions, or in the case of Sufi talk as temporal constructions or mere episodes of historical imagination, *entanglements* better accounts for the complexities of nostalgic memory (52). Drawing on a different scholarly genealogy, yet oriented toward the Tajik experience, Till Mostowlansky productively utilizes the concept of entanglement to interrogate modernity in the high mountain plateau of eastern Tajikistan. Mostowlansky (2017, 13) still sets up entanglements as nonlinear but contra and distinct from the multiple temporalities and overarching pastness I discuss among Sufi groups.

3. In that Sufi poetics draws upon resources from Muslim tradition, I should also emphasize the fact that religion as a category is inherently nostalgic in that religious discourse fundamentally involves acts of mythopoesis. Practitioners invest particular events in sacred history with some special significance, and these events then become "the norm against which other social arrangements and forms of behavior are judged and found wanting" (McCutcheon 1997, 22).

4. Alexei Yurchak (2006, 4) emphasizes that at the center of the late socialist world there existed a seeming contradiction. The Soviet system was "both

stagnating and immutable, fragile and vigorous, bleak and full of promise." The Soviet Union was seen as an "eternal state" with the permanence and immutability that the concept implies, yet at the same time its fall seemed unsurprising to many Soviet citizens. Yurchak theorizes that nostalgia emerged at the center of this paradox by enabling assertions of longing for "the very real humane values, ethics, friendships, and creative possibilities that the reality of socialism afforded" (8). Even more, religious nostalgia has been a particularly robust category of nostalgic longing common across the individual countries of the former communist bloc (see Balzer 2006, 78; Pedersen 2011, 7).

5. The predominant thrust of Sufi devolutionary discourse centers on an apocalyptic idea, a sort of "restoration myth" in which the present order is seen as degraded and in need of restoration (Cook 1997, 42). Such discourses of decline are also modeled in Persian Sufi literature widely available in Tajikistan. For example, in the Tajiki Persian edition of the sixteenth-century Naqshbandi text the *Rashahot* the editors lament the lack of spiritual exemplars and the difficulties in finding a perfect pir (*piri komil*) in contemporary Tajikistan (Safī 2009, 12). The editors implore their countrymen to seek out such a figure but then regretfully admit that they too have been unable to find such a man and thus remain without the guidance of a living pir. Strikingly, they write that Mavlono Alii Safi (d. 1532–33), the author of the five-hundred-year-old text, also compiled his work as an example to his contemporaries of the spiritual devotion of ages past he argued now was absent from his present age. Another interesting parallel to this concept can be found in the Persian poet Attor's (1145/46–1221) *Conference of the Birds*. Thirty birds set out in search of the *simurgh*, the phoenix, the allegorical representation of the perfect pir. In the end, the birds find that there is no simurgh (lit. "thirty birds" in Persian), but only thirty birds, just themselves. The perfect pir, then, is not to be found in a distant figure but rather in the collective as a whole.

6. Kathryn Babayan (2002), Shahzad Bashir (2003), and A. Azfar Moin (2012) all offer compelling portraits indicating that cyclical and millenarian conceptions of time existed among Sufi circles in early modern Iran, Central Asia, and Persianate South Asia. Despite the temporal and cultural distance between the early modern periods and contemporary Sufi life in the greater Persianate sphere, these accounts all demonstrate that logics of time, predicated on millenarian impulses, were embedded in the regional Sufi milieu and continued to influence various movements across the wider region from the late medieval period until the modern era.

7. The "*hus*" are the loud zikr of "*hu*," one of the names for God, literally in Arabic "he." A *sovkhoz* is a Soviet state farm.

8. I suspect my disgust at the Tajik state's religious policies implicates some broader longing I might have for an authentic pre-Soviet Sufism devoid of hostile government interference. It is especially important to pay attention to issues

of ethnographic reflexivity in the study of nostalgia (Gille 2010, 287), as nostalgia is intrinsic to the ethnographic enterprise (Behar 2003; Cashman 2006; Berliner 2015). More broadly, scholarly discussions and interpretations of tradition might in some ways always be evidence of our "anxiety about the vanishing past" (Boym 2001, 19).

For many, even the study of "folklore" itself evokes nostalgic sentiment in perpetuating what many see as varieties of highly unreflective populisms (Kirshenblatt-Gimblett 1998, 298). Nostalgic discourses have been implicated in the formation of folkloristics in complex ways. Indeed, many of American folklore studies' early antiquarian cohorts were searching and longing for what they perceived as authentic pasts (Bendix 1997; Bauman and Briggs 2006). Even so, critical discussions of nostalgia are for the most part remarkably absent from disciplinary discussions given its centrality to its history and the critiques leveled against the academic study of expressive culture from other scholars in the academy. Furthermore, it is important to engage nostalgic expressive forms critically due to the fact that nostalgia often is coterminous with the folks' treatments of tradition, history, memory, and narrative.

9. The most common disjuncture scholars working in post-Socialist studies have explored is an economic one. The failures of post-Socialist neoliberal economic reforms have been accompanied by unfulfilled economic desires, lingering from fantastical visions of what the consumerist paradise of the West might have entailed (Todorova 2010a, 11). Nostalgia operates here as a signifying practice that foregrounds economic fantasies of the Soviet era past or alternatively as kitsch or a camp-filled response to the newly commodified reality of the capitalist present (Berdahl 1999; Bach 2002). Tajikistan's Sufis do not primarily express an economic nostalgia but rather a nostalgic longing for features of the past social order.

10. A turban (*salla*) and robe (*ïaktak*) are part of the traditional garb of pious Tajik Muslim men.

11. The Great Master (H̱azrati Buzurgvor, lit. "His Greatness") is another honorific for a Sufi pir. In this case, Khurshed is referring to his pir.

12. H̱anifī is the school of Islamic jurisprudence most common in Central Asia.

13. Regretfully, this may no longer be the case. As described in the last chapter, since 2010–11, when I conducted interviews with them, Tajikistan's religious bureaucracy has moved against the Turajonzodas' influence. The Turajonzodas are now perhaps as marginalized as others. Thus, nostalgia may now be their mode of operation too.

14. Balogardon is an honorific, meaning "protective" or "warding off misfortune."

15. An Uvaïsī is a Sufi who has achieved initiation into a tariqa without the guidance of a living pir. Instead, he traces his silsila via the Prophet Muhammad or a vision from an exemplary dead master. See Baldick (1992).

16. *Maqom* are the stages or stations a disciple advances through while progressing along the Sufi path (Schimmel 1975, 98–186).

17. The word the pir uses here is *talqin*, lit. explanation or interpretation. In Sufi terminology, talqin refers to instruction a murid receives from his pir (Schimmel 1975, 169). Here, the pir is describing how Uvaïsï need not receive instruction from a living pir.

18. *Tavajjūh* (lit. "prayer or pleading") is the term Sufis use for a pir's mystical gaze. Through his gaze, a pir can affect mystical change in a disciple's heart. *Vazifa* are the duties and mystical obligations a pir gives his disciples. These include specific zikr formulae, prayers, reading tasks, and so on. "The level of Imomi Siddiq" is a maqom of high mystical accomplishment. Imomi Siddiq refers to Abu Bakr (d. 669), the first caliph and after the Prophet Muhammad the next rung in the Naqshbandi silsila.

19. Traditionally before eating, a child or some other junior member of the host's household pours water over guests' hands to wash them using a pitcher. The dirty water collects in a basin placed below the guests' hands. Here, later in the story as the water pours over Hofiz's hands, the water in the pitcher never runs out and the basin never fills with dirty water.

20. The *ahli zohir* (lit. "the people of the apparent") are non-Sufis, that is, those not *ahli tariqat* (the people of the tariqat).

21. The *imomi khatib* is the official who leads prayers and administers the local mosque. The *muftī* is a senior religious official authorized to issue legal opinions.

22. Traditionally, the place of least honor is the place closest to the door or farthest away from the guest of honor. In this case, Hofiz is seated in the place of least honor, that is, "at the foot of the imom."

23. The book of fate (*lavhal mahfuz*) is a book preserved in heaven containing the fates of all of the people in the world.

24. Carl Ernst (1997, 62) notes that one common trope of sainthood is self-effacement. If the mystical quest is primarily about the annihilation of one's ego, then one necessarily cannot assert one's relative authority over another. Thus, true saints, those who have completely annihilated their egos, may not even recognize the extent of their own sainthood.

25. As Daphne Berdahl argues, "Nostalgia is about the production of the present rather than the reproduction of a past" (1999, 202).

26. Svetlana Boym (2001), perhaps the best-known theorist of post-Socialist nostalgia, outlines distinctions between what she terms reflective and restorative forms of nostalgia. Her reflective nostalgia operates at the level of individual memory, memory lingering on in wistful or ironic reflection on the past. She sees reflective nostalgia in a positive light and as often culturally productive and for the most part politically innocuous. In contrast, her restorative nostalgia is ideologically suspect in the way it supports efforts to reconstruct the symbols,

rituals, and mythologies of the past. Restorative nostalgia moves outside the realm of ideas and actively supports the politically troublesome and sometimes violent mythmaking projects of many new post-Socialist nationalist histories.

27. Susan Stewart likewise writes that nostalgia is always ideological because "the past it seeks has never existed except as narrative, and hence, always absent, that past continually threatens to reproduce itself as a felt lack" (1993, 23). The past has no reality beyond a mere ideological one. The "threat" for Stewart is that nostalgia will "erupt" in spaces of temporal disjuncture, continuously reproducing itself without closure, a desire for the past continuously reproducing itself as more desire for the past. Stewart is right to emphasize that nostalgic talk is ideological in the ways it makes pragmatic claims on the present, yet nostalgia is not socially debilitating for Tajikistan's Muslims, threatening to reproduce nostalgic desire with no end in sight. Instead, nostalgia operates as a strategic political weapon, offering Tajikistan's Sufis the possibility of reconceptualizing contemporary history via their nostalgic talk (Berdahl 1999).

Chapter 3. Narrating the Past

1. An early version of part of this chapter appeared in 2016 as "Historical Narrative, Intertextuality, and Cultural Continuity in Post-Soviet Tajikistan," *Journal of Folklore Research* 53 (1): 41–65.

2. Akhi Faraji Zanjoni (d. 1065) was a contemporary of Al-Hujwiri, who lists him among the prominent mystics of Quhistan, Azerbaijan, Tabaristan, and Kumish. See Ohlander (2008, 279–80).

3. The story originally appeared in Abdurrahmoni Jomi's (1414–92) *Nafaho-tuluns* (1990, 17).

4. Cats figure prominently in Muslim narrative traditions. Interestingly, Annemarie Schimmel (1983) does not include this story in her collection of cat narratives from various Muslim traditions, even though she includes numerous Sufi tales in her chapter "Der Derwisch und die Katze."

5. The term I use for theses stories deserves some explanation in that "historical narrative" is neither an emic distinction Sufis make nor a canonistic genre of international folkloristics. In etic terms, the stories approximate something like historical or local legends (Dégh 2001, 51–52). Even terms like *family saga* (De Caro 2013) or (vernacular) *historical discourse* (Briggs 1988, 59–99; Beiner 2007) resemble the features of some of the narratives.

The narrators of these tales would most likely classify their narrations simply as *qissa*, undifferentiated stories. That is not to suggest that Tajik folklorists would not differentiate between the story texts. For Tajik scholars, the texts would likely approximate *rivoīat* or *naql*. Rivoīat carries the weight of "legend" yet is devoid of all fantastical elements, and rivoīat are always understood by their narrators to be unequivocally true (Rahmonī 2008, 86–87; Rahimov 2009, 132–36). Naql are in many ways analogous to memorates or personal experience narratives (Rahmonī 2008, 87–88; Raḣimov 2009, 136–38). Naql are topically consistent with the tales under discussion in this chapter, yet not all of the texts here are told in the first person.

I recognize the ethnocentrism inherent in etic genre identification (Ben-Amos 1976), yet at the same time genre identification is by nature an analytical activity (Stahl 1989, 13–14) and as such requires analytical descriptors not always necessary for members of the speech community that tell the stories. The terms *historical narrative* and *oral hagiography* capture the storytellers' orientations to the substance of their tales and the social work accomplished with each narrative's telling better than the term *story*.

6. Emir Muzaffar Khan was the ruler of the Bukharan emirate from 1860 until his death in 1885. The emirate spanned the territory between the Syr Darya and Amu Darya rivers, territory mostly within the boundaries of contemporary Uzbekistan and Tajikistan.

7. Rohati is Jununi's village, the same village in which the storyteller lives.

8. These four half lines of verse are ostensibly quoted as Jununi's poetry. However, I was unable to locate them within any of Jununi's published works.

9. The dates of his birth and death differ depending on the source. The only internal evidence from any of his extant works comes in the epilogue to one of his poetry collections, yet even the internal evidence is suspect in that the epilogue is likely a later addition to the text. The epilogue relates the information that the text was completed during the reign of Emir Muzaffar and that the poet was fifty-two years old upon the work's completion (Junūnī 1376, 701). Emir Muzaffar's reign lasted from 1860 to 1885. Thus, Jununi could not have been born prior to 1808 or later than 1832. Sufi Mirzo, the son of Boboi Abdusalom, who was one of Jununi's closest disciples, told a researcher about attending Jununi's funeral when he was twelve years old and related that Jununi had died at the age of seventy-seven. Mirzo died in 1973, when he was ninety-eight. This would mean that Jununi passed away in the year 1887 with a birth date of around 1810 (Nodiri 2004, 39–40). However, many of Jununi's contemporary devotees maintain that he was born in the year 1216 of the Islamic calendar, approximately 1800 CE. It is this earlier date that the editors of Jununi's works prefer. Yet the testimony of Sufi Mirzo and internal evidence from his texts would suggest that he was born closer to 1810.

10. Mavlavi is an honorific for an Islamic scholar. Jununi (The Mad) is the pen name he used in his poetry.

11. Stéphane Dudoignon (2011, 70) reports, "Jununi is today listed among the authors who were the most widely read and commented on in the Sufis' gatherings of the Soviet period." My interviews suggest otherwise. Outside of the saint's direct descendants and successors in his silsila, I couldn't find anyone who admitted to knowing of him until after 1997, when his poetry was first published.

12. The first of Jununi's works to be published, the *Mine of (Mystical) States* (*Kulliëti ma'dan-ul hol*), appeared in Tehran during 1997 with the financial support of the Turajonzoda family. A complete collection of his mystical poetry, the *Devoni Jununi*, also in its original Persian script, was published in Dushanbe in 2002. Two years later, the third installment of his mystical oeuvre was released, the *Lovers' Treasury* (*Ganjul oshiqin*). Finally, a Tajiki Cyrillic version of the *Mine of (Mystical) States* was issued in 2009. Since their original Persian script printings, various Tajik state publishing houses have also released Tajiki Cyrillic chapbook editions of Jununi's poetry.

13. An interesting analogue of Sufi stories about Jununi and Tursunzoda is Carole McGranahan's discussion of stories about Mao in Tibet. As she notes, such stories are not evidence of Tibetans "coming to terms with Mao in the context of the People's Republic of China or communism but instead in the context of a fractured Tibet and a revitalized Tibetan Buddhism" (2012, 238). That's similarly the case with stories about Jununi and Tursunzoda. They also suggest a "cultural and historical reckoning" with Tursunzoda in the context of contemporary Muslim life and the new reputation of someone like Jununi.

14. For example, see Briggs (1988, 17–18); Goffman (1974, 496–559).

15. Charles L. Briggs (1988, 71–72) similarly observes how the past can work as a framing device to mark a performed text as distinct from its wider speech context. Erving Goffman (1974, 506) writes that these replayings are often short and embedded within other talk, and for that reason their frame is often overlooked.

16. The narrator's story also shares some rhetorical similarities with personal experience narratives related to the exploits of Jununi's literary contemporaries. The well-known father of Tajik literature, Sadriddin Aini, was similarly summoned to the emir's court, this time Emir Muzaffar's successor, Abdulahad, not long after gaining some recognition as a poet (Perry and Lehr 1998, 10–11). Aini initially refused the emir's patronage, but he eventually relented after the emir threatened legal action. The parallels between Aini's and Jununi's experiences at court speak to the motif's rhetorical force and historical resonance, as a well-regarded poet was expected to serve in the emir's court. However, the parallels between the schoolteacher's story and the circumstances of Aini's life may run even deeper. The narrator is well versed in Tajik literature, and as such he knows Aini's biography and works, a key component of Soviet era and post-Soviet school curricula. Because the narrator is intimately familiar with the model of patronage the emir standardly proffered to important poets, his legend's similarity to common folk motifs suggests the active construction of Jununi's legacy.

In addition to the emirs of Bukhara and their ulamo, contemporary devotees of the saint extend such historical positioning to other persons of authority recognizable to Tajiks at large. For example, I also heard stories linking Jununi to Abdulhasani Panjakenti (Jununī 2004, 38). Panjakenti is a well-known figure of historical Central Asian Islam and particularly popular in the Tajik border regions around the Uzbek city of Samarkand, the same area from which he hailed. One of the administration subdivisions (*jamoat*) of the Panjakent region is even named for him. The legitimation provided by connecting Jununi to an eponym of a state administrative division further puts Jununi into a coherent historical frame to which authority has already been naturalized.

17. The motif is similar to J.1169.8, "The prophet's first disciple" (Thompson 1955, 4:82). Interestingly, Thompson's source was Albert Wesselski's 1911 text *Hodscha Nasreddin*, a compilation of oral narratives, which circulated in Persianate Central Asia. Nasreddin (in Tajikistan also called Moshfeqi) is the witty protagonist of a humorous body of stories told across greater Central Asia and the Middle East.

18. Henry Glassie (1982, 652) has similarly observed that narrators continually "rehearse" history in repeated performances.

19. What is significant here is not the common fact that the past legitimates the present but rather the way in which the past is connected to it. Here the past does not share, what Valerio Valeri (1990) calls a "paradigmatic" relationship with the present as a representation or typification of the past. Rather, its connection is "syntagmatic," as connected in a direct temporal chain.

20. Drawing on the work of William McNeill, Guy Beiner usefully resituates the relationship between oral tradition and folk histories, calling it a "synthesis of memory and history that constitutes a *mythistory*" (2007, 33, emphasis in original).

21. Michael Jackson takes it a step further. He argues, "All stories are, in a sense, untrue. They rearrange and transform our experiences. . . . When one tells stories, therefore, one is never simply giving voice to what is on one's own mind or in one's own interests; one is realizing, or objectifying, one's own experience in ways that others can relate to through experiences of their own" (2013, 14–15).

22. Liliya Karimova similarly observes that pious Tatar women tell personal narratives that "[enable] the women to create a continuously moral character that was not at odds with their present-day Muslim piety" (2016, 125). For newly pious Tatar women, narrative provides a way to create continuity between their Soviet and post-Soviet selves.

23. See Epkenhans (2011) for more about Turajonzoda's remarks.

24. An alternate explanation may be that during the intervening years Tajiks' orientation toward Soviet history changed. That is, the years not long after the dissolution of the Soviet Union were characterized by marked anti-Soviet attitudes. However, in subsequent years, as economies faltered and the stability of the Soviet period was systematically dismantled, many former Soviet citizens replaced their earlier anti-Soviet attitudes with more nostalgic attitudes toward the stability and economic certainty of the Soviet period, the kinds of memories

discussed in the last chapter. So, too, the editors' attitudes may have similarly tracked these more general changes.

25. The editors neglect to provide a reference to these two half lines of poetry from Jununi's work. I was also unable to locate them in the text.

26. To this point, I have favored terms such as *self-understanding, identification*, and *groupness* to specify particular varieties of social practice devoid of the reifying features of the term *identity* (Brubaker and Cooper 2000). However, Mol's notion of "sacralized identity" (2007) still holds some explanatory value because of the way it captures how a community's self-understanding of its groupness operates within a religious framework. It is that aspect of Mol's theory that I draw on here and not Mol's wider functionalist explanations of religion and attempts to advance a broader sociological theory of religious meaning.

27. Rahmon is a prolific author, like his fellow heads of state in Central Asia, allegedly authoring numerous books. See http://president.tj/taxonomy/term/5/141.

28. While I make use of the Foucauldian terminology of *counterdiscourse*, I do not deploy it toward his same ends. I conceive of counterdiscourse, in a much broader sense, as simply an emic discursive stance in opposition to another (or other). As such, my use of the term should not imply an explicit examination of the relations of power in which such claims are embedded or a specific Foucauldian conception of agency (or the lack thereof).

Chapter 4. Material Sainthood

1. Jununi was a common pen name (*takhallus*) for Persian-language poets in Central Asia during the nineteenth and early twentieth centuries. Even the most famous Soviet era Tajik poet, Sadriddini Aini, used the takhallus for a time during his youth (Bečka 1980, 66). As such, some *tazkira* and Soviet era anthologies reference poets with the pen name Jununi. However, the author of the booklets is not among them.

2. In the decades prior to Central Asia's absorption into the Soviet Union, Bukhara was relatively awash in literati anthologizing their regions' poets (Hodizoda 1968). Similarly, scholars working during the Soviet period meticulously cataloged poetry specimens they had collected during ethnographic expeditions into the mountains of the republic and from manuscripts they had forcibly taken from villagers' homes. Jununi is absent from them all.

3. Copies of Jununi's manuscripts are not in any of the manuscript collections now controlled by the Tajik government in Dushanbe, housed in either the National Library of Tajikistan or the Oriental Studies Institute of the Tajik Academy of Sciences. Two extant manuscripts are held in the library of the Oriental Studies Institute of the Uzbek Academy of Sciences. Those two manuscripts are cataloged as numbers 1563 and 2913 (Semenova 1954, 2:356). The first manuscript is dated 1907, and the second is assumed to be in the author's own hand.

No other information is given. Tellingly, Jürgen Paul and Baxtiyar Babadjanov (2002) do not list either manuscript in their catalog of Sufi manuscripts housed in the Library of the Oriental Studies Institute of the Uzbek Academy of Sciences. All the other known surviving copies, and perhaps the only manuscripts ever created of all of Jununi's writings, are held by the Turajonzodas.

4. See Schwab (2011) for an accounting of similar publication efforts in Kazakhstan.

5. In other chapters, I use *text* more clearly in the Bakhtinian sense "as any coherent complex of signs" (Bakhtin 1986, 103; Hanks 1989). Here I am concerned specifically with material objects—books, booklets, notebooks, parchments, and so on—what Michael Silverstein and Greg Urban (1996, 2) have termed "textual artifacts."

6. Folklorists' focus has often been on what Michael Owen Jones aptly terms material behavior. He argues, "Material behavior—short for 'material aspects and manifestations of human behavior'—refers to activity involved in producing or responding to the physical dimension of our world" (1997, 202). Folklorists have treated material behavior as an analogue to language practices and as such have investigated it as a communicative event (Glassie 1997) to be analyzed in performative terms (Kapchan 2003). Where folklorists have also ventured to explore the relationship of books to material behavior, they have considered topics such as scrapbooking as performance (Christensen 2011), books as icons of personal narrative (Byrd 2008), and folklore as augmented by book culture (Hayes 1997). My focus here is more akin to Cynthia Byrd's (2008) notion of "booklore," folklore performed through the book itself.

7. Drinking wine is a common trope of Persian mystical poetry. Drawing on the legacy of court poets, for whom wine was a regular though morally suspect aspect of courtly life, mystical poets transformed wine drinking into a metaphor for the search for transcendence, drunkenness became spiritual intoxication, and the tavern became the Sufi lodge. Umar Khaiyam's (1048–1131) poetry was widely read during the Soviet period. Though written within a medieval Islamic milieu, its idioms, including wine, conflicted less with Soviet ideology than those of more explicitly Muslim poets such as Fariduddin Attor (1145/46–1221) and Shamsiddin Shohin (1865/66–1895/96), who did not figure prominently in school curricula until the end of the Soviet period.

8. Vernon Schubel (1999, 76–77) goes so far to classify this larger constellation of religious material as a genre unto itself, calling it "post-Soviet hagiography."

9. Jürgen Paul (2002) argues that in Uzbekistan various distinct hagiographical traditions have likewise been marshaled to support a singular project. In the case of Uzbekistan, Sufi texts became about instilling national, not necessarily Muslim values.

10. Maria Louw takes it a step farther, arguing that in Uzbekistan saints (*avliё*) embodied special agency, "everything perceived to be missing in intersubjective encounters" (2007, 98).

11. Idi Qurbon, the feast of sacrifice, sometimes also referred to as Idal Akha, is one of the two most important Muslim holidays.

12. In Jacques Derrida's (1976) terms, the pir's preference for the original utterance, that is, his "phonocentrism," vis-à-vis what is captured within the newly published text suggests his fear of the potential "open interpretability" of written texts (Messick 1993, 205). Devoid of the direct testimony of their producers, written texts potentially exist separate from human interactions, and as such their meanings remain potentially open to misinterpretation.

13. The *Letters of Imom Rabboni* (Maktuboti Imom Rabboni) is comprised of the collected letters of Shaikh Ahmad Sirhindi (1564–1624), an important Naqshbandi pir and the founder of the Mujaddidi line of the Naqshbandi lineage. Sirhindi has been a lynchpin figure in the history of Sufism in Central Asia, and his writings concerning the "renewal" of Naqshbandi thought in the Indian subcontinent have been among the most widely circulated and studied within Sufi groups (Friedmann 2000).

14. Mikhail Bakhtin's characterization of voicing is somewhat distinct from my argument here. He argued that poetical discourse can never be "double-voiced" in the way that discourse in the novel can (1981, 324–30). However, with respect to poetical discourse, Bakhtin was specifically referring to metaphorical speech. The Sufi distinction between apparent and hidden discourse is more than the difference between a literal and metaphorical interpretation of a given text. Botin meanings may sometimes be communicated metaphorically, but oftentimes botin exists independent of metaphor.

15. The title plays on the duel meanings of the word *shajarāt*. Literally meaning "trees," here it refers specifically to genealogical trees, and their "fruits" are the progeny of those intimate with God, that is, saints. The book is a biographical dictionary of Sufi figures compiled in South Asia during the late sixteenth and early seventeenth centuries.

16. Khizr is an important figure in Sufi tradition. Qur'anic commentators equated him with an anonymous helper to the prophet Musa included in the Qur'an. In Sufi literature, Khizr is often invoked as the prototypical mystical guide (Krasnowolska 2009). In the story the pir's business associate read, "'Imād al-dīn Jūnpūrī, known as a companion and friend of Khizr, left at his pir's instruction to wash the pir's clothes in the river. While there, he missed a set appointment with Khizr. When Khizr arrived, Junpuri apologized but continued washing, telling Khizr it was more important to serve his pir."

17. This idea builds on other folkloristic arguments related to the "iconicity" of narrative (e.g., McDowell 1982), yet I do so by drawing on another of Peirce's terms. *Icon* specifically refers to the "likeness" of a sign (Sebeok 1994, 28–30). Narratives, even more specifically personal narratives, are representations of the events they are alleged to recount (Labov 1997). In that frame, since narratives mirror the events they describe, they become icons of those events. My

argument here is similar but distinct. Sufi stories very well may represent the events they recount and, thus, be icons of them. But, Sufi stories are also indices, in Peirce's formulation, of their saintly objects. Indices point to their sign, just as the stories point to the power of their protagonists. In addition to recapitulating events, Sufi stories index saintly power.

18. Interestingly, Webb Keane (1997, 79) has even argued that indexical signs might more readily instantiate authority than other types of signs do because of the way they embody causal effects and thus lend their meanings more plausibility.

19. The bookseller was referring to a law passed in 2010 that limited mosque attendance to males over the age of eighteen.

20. Vernon James Schubel has noted that in Uzbekistan not long after the dissolution of the Soviet Union Sufism was divorced from the pir-murid relationship and had become in many ways a "literary, intellectual tradition" (1999, 85). While the situation in Tajikistan is somewhat distinct (and almost twenty years have passed since Schubel's writing), nonetheless there also remain severe restrictions on public Muslim religiosity, though perhaps not to the same degree as in Uzbekistan. Many Soviet era pirs have passed away without their assistants taking their places, and at the same time literature on historical Sufism is abundantly available to the Tajik reading public.

Chapter 5. Remembering God

1. Portions of this chapter appeared in 2013 in "The Guide after Rumi: Tradition and Its Foil in Tajik Sufism," *Nova Religio* 17 (1): 1–23.

2. "Saying blessings" is distinct from the formalized poetical genre of *na'ati sharif*, praise poetry to the Prophet Muhammad. At the shrine, pilgrims are enjoined to recite the names of God using prayer beads (*tasbeh*) or specific suras from the Qur'an rather than more overt displays of devotion to the Prophet and the people of his house (*ahli bait*).

3. Historically, loud zikr emerged across the majority of Sufi paths (Algar 1976), including forms with dancing, music, and ecstatic vocal formulae, all of which induced states beyond the corporeal. In contrast, strains of the Naqshbandiya proscribed loud, favoring silent recitation alone (Togan 1999). A standard explanation claims that the Naqshbandis' preference for silent zikr was due to their general sobriety, restraint, and attentive observance of shariat (e.g., Algar 1976, 43). However, in Central Asia in particular, and likely elsewhere too, the picture is more complex. As early as the eighteenth century, discrete silsila identifiers lost their descriptive utility and ritual practice became a more potent mark of Sufi identity (DeWeese 2012). Additionally, pirs "bundled" initiations from multiple paths, and some lineages were subsumed under a common Naqshbandi idiom. The result was that, in Central Asia at least, there were some Naqshbandis who practiced loud zikr, while others did not. See also Algar (1971).

In the modern period, there are groups who self-identify with various Sufi lineages, Qodiriya, Naqshbandiya, and Yasaviya, that practice forms of loud zikr
(Louw 2007, 110; Pasilov and Ashirov 2007; Privratsky 2001, 104; Sultanova
2000; Sultanova 2011, 41).

4. Manja Stephan (2017, 263) analogously documents how many Tajiks who
have opted to study Islam outside of the country see their time abroad as an
"antidote to their experiences of everyday life at home" in Tajikistan. That is,
pious education creates transcendence—a geographic one, not dissimilar from
the temporal one I have documented.

5. Here "religion" (*mazhab*), alternatively "doctrine," "teaching," or "sect,"
refers to Abuhanifa's specific school of jurisprudence.

6. The poem was authored by a regional poet, Ihromiddin Abdulhaizoda,
as part of the "Year of the Great Imom" celebrations in Rasht, Tajikistan—the
government-sponsored commemorations discussed in chapter 3. In addition to
the ways in which Rustam adapted the poem for zikr, his uncritical adoption of
state frames of reference for the celebration of Abuhanifa's life is also suggestive
of Sufi orientations toward the political. Rather than dismissing such celebrations as mere state propaganda, Rustam integrated them into the Sufi ritual
environment (Epkenhans 2011, 93). As before, Sufi expressive culture is predicated on the very order it seeks to disrupt (Heathershaw 2014, 42).

7. I never heard Rustam or any other hofiz use either term. Rustam preferred to call them *tetrad'*, Russian for notebook. Benjamin Koen (2009, 139)
says that among Pamiri Ismailis in Tajikistan *ţūmār* refers to a prayer amulet. In
contrast, in Tajik Badakhshan poetry singers, or *maddohkhon*, use the term *baëz*
for objects similar to the *ţūmār* of the Iranian storytelling tradition (van den
Berg 2003, 6).

8. Stuart H. Blackburn (1988, 31–47) observes a similar phenomenon at
work in Tamil ritual. The story text as inscribed onto palm leaves has to be present at the time of a ritual performance in order for it to be efficacious, even to
the point that lithographed copies of the same text are insufficient.

9. There is an important distinction between the "magical" and "religious."
Richard Firth Green's (1999) focus on the "magical" particularly resonates with
ideas about how symbols operate within Sufi groups because of the way they are
invested with extrasensory agency. However, in Tajik usage *jodu*, or "magic,"
implies a dark force. Here I do not conceive of the extrasensory dimensions of
Sufi practice in that frame, although Tajik critics of the path might.

10. The Qur'anic reference comes from surai Najm, verse 9. In A. J. Arberry's
(1955, 244) interpretation it reads, "Two bows' length away, or nearer." The "two
bows" are the distance the angel Gabriel was from the Prophet Muhammad as
the Qur'an was revealed. The poem Rustam recited directly quotes the Arabic,
"The two bow lengths of Muhammad." But Rustam combined the first half line
of one verse with the second half line of another. The result was a layering of

metaphor that is difficult to render into colloquial English. His combination changes "the bow" in the Qur'anic reference (*qavs*) to its more colloquial Tajik meaning of "arch" in combination with the word "abode" (*obod*). In another case, Rustam eliminated the common Persian mystical trope of "heaven" (*arsh*) and the "throne" (*kursī*). He substituted "every night" for "heaven," so in the second half line "throne" becomes less the "throne of heaven" than simply a chair to be ornamented with Muhammad as its pillow.

11. Rustam's ghazal included both an end rhyme (*radif*) and a refrain (*naqarot*). Per standard Persian literary convention, the second line of each ghazal couplet ends with the same words, an end rhyme, whereas refrains are a feature exclusive to ghazal singing (*ghazalkhonī*). I never heard Rustam or any other hofiz separate out the difference between the two or use the term *refrain*. Rustam simply called his refrains end rhymes. See Berg (2001, 69–71) for a parallel example of end rhyme and refrain in Tajik Badakhshan.

12. *Khalifacha* literally means a "representative" or "successor." Within Sufi groups, khalifacha are attendants to the pir, his inner circle of disciples. The diminutive -*cha* suffix distinguishes them from the pir's primary assistant, his *khalifa*.

13. Gabrielle van den Berg (2004, 112) found that a full 71 percent of the poems she collected in Tajik Badakhshan were spurious in their attributions. Similarly, Benjamin D. Koen (2003, 197) found that verses orally recited for devotional healing purposes and attributed to the masters of classical Persian poetry had a much more tenuous relationship with their literary progenitors than was perhaps explicit to the performers themselves. Additionally, Jean During (1990, 183) observed that Chisti Sufis in Pakistan similarly altered canonized Persian mystical verse to uniquely suit their own musical and ritual ends by adding spurious attributions to newly improvised poetical creations.

14. Rhetorics of tradition, not limited to ritual, are vital components of contemporary Islam in Tajikistan. For example, Manja Stephan (2010, 55–80) has observed traditionalizing processes in relation to conceptions of Muslim space in Dushanbe, and Colette Harris's (2006, 37–62) work on youth culture in Tajikistan has considered the ways in which Muslims conceptualize and actively create Tajik tradition.

15. As Earl Waugh puts it, the goal of Moroccan Sufi ritual "is to make present the realities of the mythic domain in an expressive, existential manner" (2005, 15).

16. The Knower is one of God's names.

17. Joel C. Kuipers argues that "textual performances deny their situated character" (1990, 4). Rustam's comments are similar to the sentiments of performers and authors in many traditions, for example, Sufi poetry singers in Egypt and Morocco (Frishkopf 2003; Waugh 1989, 186; Waugh 2005, 34) and Uyghur hagiographers (Thum 2014, 65–69). The Serbo-Croatian bards Albert

Bates Lord (2000) studied also maintained that their texts were fixed, that they did not change the texts in the course of a performance.

18. Compare this to Waugh's statement about Egyptian Sufi singers: "[The singer] introduces material on the basis of theme; source is secondary to the message he wishes to deliver" (1989, 126).

19. Intercalation is also a common poetic mode among non-Persian-speaking Sufi groups (Frishkopf 2003, 5).

20. This is a quality that Voloshinov (1986, 122) sees as especially characteristic of verbal art. It is in reported speech, framed via indirect quotations, that a performer maximally orients past speech toward the needs of the present speech context.

21. This is in stark contrast to Lord's (2000) foundational study on Yugoslav epic traditions and the oral origins of Homeric epic. Sufi practices are distinct from Lord's principle of the simultaneity of composition and performance in his definition of what oral poetry entailed. For Lord, oral poetry was always composed orally. Ruth Finnegan's (1992, 73–86) complementary emphasis on the role of prior memorization of oral poetry helpfully resituates Lord's theories in relation to the oral-written dynamics of Sufi performance, as does John Miles Foley's (2002, 43–45) description of "voiced texts," texts performed orally, received aurally, but whose features are relatively stable and often have a prior existence in print.

22. Muslim religious poetry performance has offered a robust site for ethnographic investigation. Some important studies have considered tribal poetry in Egypt (Abu-Lughod 1986), poetry performance on the Arabian Peninsula (Caton 1990), cassette poetry circulation in Yemen (Miller 2007), the interconnections of history and poetry in contemporary Iran (Manoukian 2011), and poetry among Afghan intellectuals living in Iran (Olszewska 2015).

23. Proverbs need not always be quotations. Instead, proverb situations are occasions for what Erik Aasland (2014) calls "deictic projection." One of many possible projections is a temporal one, one like zikr poetry performance, during which the past speaks as a quote into the present.

24. The ghazal includes Rumi's takhallus. However, it does not seem to be attested in Furuzanfar's (Rūmī 1383) critical edition of Rumi's poetry. Most likely the poem is not a genuine work of the poet (Berg 2003).

25. Radner and Lanser's (1993) work specifically deals with coding strategies that enable women to communicate with other women in ways undetectable to male power holders. Although Radner and Lanser's conception of coding is limited to the way subordinate actors approach centers of power, their conception applies just as well to the speech of those in power as it does to the subaltern. Although the benefits of enigmatic language during the Soviet period are readily apparent, ritual language is still (at the least) biform and its audience composition complex. Some members of the audience are competent to decode

the inherent esotericism of the poetical texts, and others have yet to be initiated into that knowledge and thus are still liminal in their relation to group power centers.

26. The "four ones" are the successors of the Prophet Muhammad: Abu Bakr, Umar, Usmon, and Ali ibn Tolib.

CHAPTER 6. LEARNING TO BE SUFI

1. *Chilla* literally means "forty." For Sufis it refers to a forty-day period of meditation completed in seclusion from others. Some Sufi lodges have a dedicated place for forty-day periods of seclusion and prayer, a *chillakhona*.

2. Embodied actions can be discursive (Young 1993, 1994), but Sufi bodily nostalgias should not be reduced to narrative descriptions or texts. I do not exclusively think of Sufi embodiment, as Foucault might, as signs or enouncements (*énoncés*). Instead, I see them as, in Diana Taylor's words, "embodied praxis and episteme" (2003, 17). They are knowledges performed and perpetuated through the body, what Taylor has called the performatic, the "nondiscursive realm of performance" (6).

Taylor's performatic also offers an important contrast to ideas of an overarching Islamic discursive tradition like Talal Asad's (1986), particularly as Asad's ideas hold less utility outside the Arab heartland (Silverstein 2011, 14). The performatic, along with the nondiscursive knowledges that bring it into sharper relief, potentially provides a means of thinking about various articulations of Muslim religiosity more tenuously connected to the textual traditions of classical Islam.

3. A number of scholars have discussed Muslim pedagogy in contemporary Tajikistan (Abramson 2010; Epkenhans 2010; Stephan 2010, 211–46; Roche 2013). What I describe in this chapter shares many of the same elements as the informal teaching networks considered in this literature, but there are significant differences. Sufi teaching networks are small informal circles of students. Many pirs have no formal training. The genealogy of the teacher is often more important than any credential. And group meetings frequently begin or end at the insistence of the authorities. The disciples, who are not primarily children but mostly middle-aged and older men, often move between teachers.

4. Recent anthropological scholarship concerning Muslim life has usefully resituated attention to modes of ethical subject cultivation (Mahmood 2005; Hirschkind 2006; Silverstein 2011; Schwab 2012). These studies, among others, have shifted the frame of scholarly reference to think through the ways Muslims actively fashion new moral selves and ethical subject positions. Saba Mahmood's notion of "embodied ethics" is particularly apt for thinking through the social work of Sufi efforts at pious cultivation. This conception of ethics "refers to those practices, techniques, and discourses through which a subject transforms herself in order to achieve a particular state of being, happiness, or truth" (Mahmood 2005, 28). See also Silverstein (2011, 14).

5. *Nafs* is the soul, one's base instincts, and the place of carnal desire.

6. "*29.05.09 Naqshbandīia. Latoifi kalb. Nurash zard. Takhti kudumi khaz-rati odam. (zikrash ollokh).*" The typographical inconsistencies in the transcription were copied directly from the Abdullo's cell phone. By necessity, most Tajik speakers use a Russian-language typeface on their cell phones and simply adapt the Russian script to Tajik. As such, *qalb*" becomes *kalb* and *hazrat* becomes *khazrat.*

7. The six centers and their corresponding bodily locations are *khufī* (the secret place), the right upper part of the chest; *sir* (secret, mystery), the upper left part of the chest; *ikhfo* (hiding), the middle of the chest; *rūh* (spirit), the lower right quadrant of the chest; *qalb* (heart), two finger lengths below the left part of the chest; and *nafs* (the soul), the forehead. Among Tajik Sufis, the preferred term is *khufī* (Atozoda 2000, 26). However, the normative Naqshbandi term is *khāfī*, "the secret place," or what Buehler (1998, 105) terms the arcanum. The colored radiance and prophetic exemplar for *khufī* is black and the prophet Iso, white and Musa for *sir*, green and the Prophet Muhammad for *ikhfo*, red and both Ibrohim and Nuh for *rūh*, yellow and Odam for *qalb*, and finally brown but no corresponding prophet for nafs.

8. These are the collected letters of Shaikh Ahmad Sirhindi (1564–1624), the founder of the Mujaddidi line of the Naqshbandi lineage. See chapter 4, note 13.

9. To say the least, it is a challenge to translate portions of Sirhindi's letters into idiomatic English. Beyond the fact that Sirhindi wrote in medieval Indo-Persian, an amalgam of Persian distinct from classical or modern Persian literature, Sirhindi used specialized mystical terminology, borrowing concepts from the everyday universe of sixteenth-century South Asia to describe the mystical enterprise. I have done my best to approximate the experience of hearing lines of Sirhindi's letters read, even as I have, no doubt, made unavoidable translation mistakes.

10. Ibn Arabi (1165–1240) was a prolific Sufi scholar and philosopher understood by many Tajik Sufis to be the epitome of earthly wisdom and scholarly erudition.

11. It is worth noting that the broad contours of Naqshbandi South Asian pedagogy, one of the chief influences on Sufi pedagogical routines in Central Asia, are fundamentally distinct from historical pedagogical traditions in other parts of the Muslim world surveyed by anthropologists. For example, in Morocco students were not permitted to ask questions of their teachers (Eickelman 1992), whereas in Iran there existed a complex tradition of disputation between teachers and students (Mottahedeh 2009). In Yemen questions were more muted, and teachers answered by reciting again the portions of the texts the students had not understood (Messick 1993, 84–92). Among Bektashi Sufis in Albania, interaction between teacher and student was of paramount importance (Trix 1993).

12. Abu Huraira (d. 678, 679, or 680) was a companion of the Prophet Muhammad famous for relaying more deeds and sayings of the Prophet, later recorded in Hadith, than any other of the Prophet's companions.

13. This was the only time I ever heard the call to prayer electronically amplified in Tajikistan. It is illegal for mosques to amplify the call to prayer in any way.

14. A parallel concept of *robita*, or "binding," also exists, in which a disciple keeps the attention (tavajjūh) of his heart directly on his pir and the pir reciprocates by focusing his heart on the murid (Meier 1995). I never heard Tajik murids discuss robita beyond its more colloquial meanings of connection or relationship. However, the mutual reciprocity inherent in the spiritual concept of robita closely approximates the kinds of profane reciprocal intimacies operational within Sufi groups.

15. The pir contrasted two distinct ways of expressing one's loyalty and allegiance to a pir. Baīat is a formal pledge of allegiance by a prospective murid to a pir, signifying the beginning of a pir-murid relationship. It is the murid's outward commitment of submission to a pir's guidance and the disciple's diligence in performing assigned vazifa. In contrast, *dast giriftan* is merely a simple handshake, a more informal arrangement, which potentially abrogates the hierarchical nature of teaching within a Sufi lodge.

16. Maria Louw (2007, 2) writes about the way official discourses in Uzbekistan similarly marked "extremists" and "Wahhabis" as anachronistic, arguing that such groups were trying to turn the societal clock back several hundred years.

References

Aasland, Erik. 2014. "Now You See Me Now You Don't: Deictic Projection and the Dynamics of Proverb Performance." *Western Folklore* 73 (1): 38–68.

Abashin, Sergei. 2014. "A Prayer for Rain: Practising Being Soviet and Muslim." *Journal of Islamic Studies* 25 (2): 178–200.

Abdujalilkhoja, Hoji Saïid. 2009. *Az nasabnomai Saïidzodagoni Movarounnahr (Bahr-ul-ansob) Qismi 4–5*. Dushanbe: Sharqi ozod.

Abdulhaev, Raqib. 2009. *Ta"rikhi Muhojirat Dar Tojikiston (Solhoi 1924–2000)*. Dushanbe: Donish.

Abrahams, Roger D. 2003. "Identity." In *Eight Words for the Study of Expressive Culture*, edited by Burt Feintuch, 198–222. Urbana: University of Illinois Press.

Abramson, David M. 2000. "Socialism's Bastard Children." *Political and Legal Anthropology Review* 23 (1): 49–64.

———. 2010. "Foreign Religious Education and the Central Asian Islamic Revival: Impact and Prospects for Stability." Washington, DC: Central Asia-Caucasus Institute and Silk Road Studies Program.

Abu-Lughod, Lila. 1986. *Veiled Sentiments: Honor and Poetry in a Bedouin Society*. Berkeley: University of California Press.

———. 1990. "The Romance of Resistance: Tracing Transformations of Power through Bedouin Women." *American Ethnologist* 17:41–55.

Adams, Laura L. 2010. *The Spectacular State: Culture and National Identity in Uzbekistan*. Durham, NC: Duke University Press.

Algar, Hamid. 1971. "Some Notes on the Naqshbandī Tarīqat in Bosnia." *Die Welt Des Islams* 13 (3–4): 168–203.

———. 1976. "Silent and Vocal Dhikr in the Naqshbandī Order." In *Akten des VII: Kongresses für Arabistik und Islamvissenschaft*, 44–45. Göttingen: Vandenhoeck and Ruprecht.

———. 1990. "A Brief History of the Naqshbandi Order." In *Naqshbandis: Cheminements et situation actuelle d'un ordre mystique Musulman*, edited by

Marc Gaborieau, Alexandre Popovic, and Thierry Zarcone, 3–44. Istanbul: Editions Isis.

Alimardonov, Amriyazdon. 2009. "The Written Heritage of Badakhshan." In *Écrit et culture en Asie Centrale et dans le monde Turco-Iranien, Xe–XIXe siècles*, edited by Francis Richard and Maria Szuppe, 127–43. Paris: Association pour l'avancement des études Iraniennes.

Alver, Brynjulf. 1989. "Historical Legends and Historical Truth." In *Nordic Folklore: Recent Studies*, edited by Reimund Kvideland and Henning K. Sehmsdorf, 137–49. Bloomington: Indiana University Press.

Anderson, Benedict R. 1991. *Imagined Communities: Reflections on the Origin and Spread of Nationalism*. New York: Verso.

Arberry, A. J. 1955. *The Koran Interpreted*. New York: Touchstone.

Arendt, Hannah. 1958. *The Human Condition*. Chicago: University of Chicago Press.

Asad, Talal. 1986. *The Idea of an Anthropology of Islam*. Washington, DC: Center for Contemporary Arab Studies, Georgetown University.

Assmann, Jan. 2006. *Religion and Cultural Memory: Ten Studies*. Stanford, CA: Stanford University Press.

Atozoda, Ismoil, ed. 2000. *Kashf-ul-Asror: Gulchini ghazaliët az devoni Shaïkh Abdurrahimi Davlat*. Dushanbe: Humo.

Babadjanov, Bakhtiyar. 2004. "Debates over Islam in Contemporary Uzbekistan: A View from Within." In *Devout Societies vs. Impious States? Transmitting Islamic Learning in Russia, Central Asia, and China through the Twentieth Century*, edited by Stéphane A. Dudoignon, 39–60. Berlin: Klaus Schwarz Verlag.

Babadjanov, Bakhtiyar, and M. Kamilov. 2001. "Muhammadjan Hindustani (1892–1989) and the Beginning of the 'Great Schism' among the Muslims of Uzbekistan." In *Islam in Politics in Russia and Central Asia (Early Eighteenth to Late Twentieth Centuries)*, edited by Stéphane A. Dudoignon and Hisao Komatsu, 195–219. New York: Kegan Paul.

Babayan, Kathryn. 2002. *Mystics, Monarchs, and Messiahs: Cultural Landscapes of Early Modern Iran*. Cambridge, MA: Harvard University Press.

Bach, Jonathan P. G. 2002. "'The Taste Remains': Consumption, (N)ostalgia, and the Production of East Germany." *Public Culture* 14 (3): 545–56.

Bakhtin, M. M. 1981. *The Dialogic Imagination: Four Essays*. Edited by Michael Holquist. Translated by Caryl Emerson and Michael Holquist. Austin: University of Texas Press.

———. 1984. *Problems of Dostoevsky's Poetics*. Translated by Caryl Emerson. Minneapolis: University of Minnesota Press.

———. 1986. *Speech Genres and Other Late Essays*. Translated by Vernon McGee. Austin: University of Texas Press.

Baldick, Julian. 1992. *Imaginary Muslims: The Uwaysi Sufis of Central Asia*. London: I. B. Tauris.

Balzer, Marjorie Mandelstam. 2006. "Sustainable Faith? Reconfiguring Shamanic Healing in Siberia." In *Spiritual Transformation and Healing: Anthropological, Theological, Neuroscientific, and Clinical Perspectives*, edited by J. D. Koss-Chiono and Philip Hefner, 78–100. Lanham, MD: AltaMira.

Barad, Karen Michelle. 2007. *Meeting the Universe Halfway: Quantum Physics and the Entanglement of Matter and Meaning*. Durham, NC: Duke University Press.

Bashir, Shahzad. 2003. *Messianic Hopes and Mystical Visions: The Nurbakhshiya between Medieval and Modern Islam*. Columbia: University of South Carolina Press.

Battaglia, Debbora. 1995. "On Practical Nostalgia: Self-Prospecting among Urban Trobrianders." In *Rhetorics of Self-Making*, edited by Debbora Battaglia, 77–96. Berkeley: University of California Press.

Bauman, Richard. 1972. "Differential Identity and the Social Base of Folklore." In *Toward New Perspectives in Folklore*, edited by Américo Paredes and Richard Bauman, 31–41. Austin: University of Texas Press.

———. 1984. *Verbal Art as Performance*. Prospect Heights, IL: Waveland.

———. 1986. *Story, Performance, and Event: Contextual Studies of Oral Narrative*. New York: Cambridge University Press.

———. 2004. *A World of Others' Words: Cross-Cultural Perspectives on Intertextuality*. Malden, MA: Blackwell.

Bauman, Richard, and Charles L. Briggs. 1990. "Poetics and Performance as Critical Perspectives on Language and Social Life." *Annual Review of Anthropology* 19:59–88.

———. 2006. *Voices of Modernity: Language Ideologies and the Politics of Inequality*. New York: Cambridge University Press.

Bayart, Jean-François. 2005. *The Illusion of Cultural Identity*. Chicago: University of Chicago Press.

Bečka, Jiří. 1968. "Tajik Literature from the 16th Century to the Present." In *History of Iranian Literature*, edited by Jan Rypka, 483–605. Dordrecht: D. Reidel.

———. 1980. *Sadriddin Ayni: Father of Modern Tajik Culture*. Naples: Istituto Universitario Orientale, Seminario di Studi Asiatici.

Behar, Ruth. 2003. "Ethnography and the Book That Was Lost." *Ethnography* 4 (1): 15–39.

Beiner, Guy. 2007. *Remembering the Year of the French: Irish Folk History and Social Memory*. Madison: University of Wisconsin Press.

Bell, Catherine M. 1992. *Ritual Theory, Ritual Practice*. New York: Oxford University Press.

Ben-Amos, Dan. 1976. "Analytical Categories and Ethnic Genres." In *Folklore Genres*, edited by Dan Ben-Amos, 215–42. Austin: University of Texas Press.

———. 1984. "The Seven Strands of Tradition: Varieties in Its Meaning in American Folklore Studies." *Journal of Folklore Research* 21 (3): 97–131.

Bendix, Regina. 1997. *In Search of Authenticity: The Formation of Folklore Studies*. Madison: University of Wisconsin Press.

Bennigsen, Alexandre, and S. Enders Wimbush. 1985. *Mystics and Commissars: Sufism in the Soviet Union*. Berkeley: University of California Press.

Berdahl, Daphne. 1999. "'(N)Ostalgie' for the Present: Memory, Longing, and East German Things." *Ethnos: Journal of Anthropology* 64 (2): 192–211.

Berg, Gabrielle van den. 2001. "Poetry from Tajik Badakhshan: Form and Performance." *Edebiyât* 12:59–72.

———. 2003. "The Classical Persian Ghazal and Rumi in the Oral Poetry of the Ismailis of Tajik Badakhshan." In *Mais comment peut-on être Persan?*, edited by C. van Ruymbeke, 3–13. Leiden: Peeters.

———. 2004. *Minstrel Poetry from the Pamir Mountains: A Study on the Songs and Poems of the Ismailis of Tajik Badakhshan*. Wiesbaden: Reichert.

Bergne, Paul. 2007. *The Birth of Tajikistan: National Identity and the Origins of the Republic*. New York: I. B. Tauris.

Berliner, David. 2015. "Are Anthropologists Nostalgist?" In *Anthropology and Nostalgia*, edited by Olivia Angé and David Berliner, 17–34. New York: Berghahn Books.

Bhabha, Homi K. 1994. *The Location of Culture*. New York: Routledge.

Blackburn, Stuart H. 1988. *Singing of Birth and Death: Texts in Performance*. Philadelphia: University of Pennsylvania Press.

Bleuer, Christian. 2012. "State-Building, Migration, and Economic Development on the Frontiers of Northern Afghanistan and Southern Tajikistan." *Journal of Eurasian Studies* 3 (1): 69–79.

Borbieva, Noor O'Neill. 2017. "The Ascendance of Orthodoxy: Nation Building and Religious Pluralism in Central Asia." In *Islam, Society, and Politics in Central Asia*, edited by Pauline Jones, 151–72. Pittsburgh, PA: University of Pittsburgh Press.

Boyer, Dominic. 2012. "From Algos to Autonomous: Nostalgic Eastern Europe as Postimperial Mania." In *Post-Communist Nostalgia*, edited by Maria Todorova and Zsuzsa Gille, 17–28. New York: Berghahn Books.

Boyer, Dominic, and Alexei Yurchak. 2010. "American Stiob, or What Late-Socialist Aesthetics of Parody Reveal about Contemporary Political Culture in the West." *Cultural Anthropology* 25 (2): 179–221.

Boym, Svetlana. 2001. *The Future of Nostalgia*. New York: Basic Books.

Briggs, Charles L. 1988. *Competence in Performance: The Creativity of Tradition in Mexicano Verbal Art*. Philadelphia: University of Pennsylvania Press.

Briggs, Charles L., and Richard Bauman. 1992. "Genre, Intertextuality, and Social Power." *Journal of Linguistic Anthropology* 2 (2): 131–72.

Bronner, Simon J. 2000. "The Meaning of Tradition: An Introduction." *Western Folklore* 59 (2): 87–104.

Brubaker, Rogers, and Frederick Cooper. 2000. "Beyond 'Identity.'" *Theory and Society* 29 (1): 1–47.

Bruijn, J. T. P. de. 1997. *Persian Sufi Poetry: An Introduction to the Mystical Use of Classical Persian Poems.* Richmond, Surrey: Curzon.

Buehler, Arthur. 1998. *Sufi Heirs of the Prophet: The Indian Naqshbandiyya and the Rise of the Mediating Sufi Shaykh.* Columbia: University of South Carolina Press.

———. 2011. "Translators Preface: Disclaimers and Confessions." In *Revealed Grace: The Juristic Sufism of Ahmad Sirhindi (1564–1624)*, translated by Arthur F. Buehler, ix–xxii. Louisville, KY: Fons Vitae.

Bunzl, Matti. 1998. "Counter-Memory and Modes of Resistance: The Uses of Fin-de-Siècle Vienna for Present-Day Austrian Jews." In *Transforming the Center, Eroding the Margins: Essays on Ethnic and Cultural Boundaries in German-Speaking Countries*, edited by Dagmar C. G. Lorenz and Renate S. Posthofen, 169–84. Columbia, SC: Camden House.

Burawoy, Michael, and Katherine Verdery, eds. 1999. *Uncertain Transition: Ethnographies of Change in the Postsocialist World.* Lanham, MD: Rowman & Littlefield.

Butler, Judith. 1990. *Gender Trouble: Feminism and the Subversion of Identity.* New York: Routledge.

Byrd, Cynthia. 2008. "Booklore: The Folklore Surrounding the Diaries and the Ephemera of Edith Workman Minnix." PhD diss., University of Pennsylvania.

Cashman, Ray. 2006. "Critical Nostalgia and Material Culture in Northern Ireland." *Journal of American Folklore* 119 (472): 137–60.

———. 2008. *Storytelling on the Northern Irish Border: Characters and Community.* Bloomington: Indiana University Press.

Cashman, Ray, Tom Mould, and Pravina Shukla. 2011. "Introduction." In *The Individual and Tradition: Folkloristics Perspectives*, edited by Ray Cashman, Tom Mould, and Pravina Shukla, 1–26. Bloomington: Indiana University Press.

Caton, Steven C. 1990. *"Peaks of Yemen I Summon": Poetry as Cultural Practice in a North Yemeni Tribe.* Berkeley: University of California Press.

Chakrabarty, Dipesh. 2008. *Provincializing Europe: Postcolonial Thought and Historical Difference.* Princeton, NJ: Princeton University Press.

Chamberlain, Michael. 1994. *Knowledge and Social Practice in Medieval Damascus, 1190–1350.* New York: Cambridge University Press.

Chari, Sharad, and Katherine Verdery. 2009. "Thinking between the Posts: Postcolonialism, Postsocialism, and Ethnography after the Cold War." *Comparative Studies in Society and History* 51 (1): 6–34.

Chow, Rey. 2012. *Entanglements, or Transmedial Thinking about Capture.* Durham, NC: Duke University Press.

Christensen, Danille Elise. 2011. "'Look at Us Now!' Scrapbooking, Regimes of Value, and the Risks of (Auto)Ethnography." *Journal of American Folklore* 124 (493): 175–210.

Commercio, Michele E. 2015. "The Politics and Economics of 'Retraditionalization' in Kyrgyzstan and Tajikistan." *Post-Soviet Affairs* 31 (6): 529–56.

Connerton, Paul. 1989. *How Societies Remember*. New York: Cambridge University Press.

Cook, David. 1997. "Moral Apocalyptic in Islam." *Studia Islamica* 86:37–69.

Csordas, Thomas J. 1993. "Somatic Modes of Attention." *Cultural Anthropology* 8 (2): 135–56.

Danzer, Alexander M., and Oleksiy Ivaschenko. 2010. "Migration Patterns in a Remittances Dependent Economy: Evidence from Tajikistan during the Global Financial Crisis." *Migration Letters* 7 (2): 190–202.

Darvozī, Shaīkh Qamariddini, and Mirzohusaīni Badalipur. 2003. *Zindaginomai Hazrati Eshoni Abdurahmonjon ibni Eshoni Porsokhoja*. Dushanbe.

Davis, Dick. 2001. "Interpolations to the Text of Šāhnāmeh." *Persica* 17:35–49.

De Caro, Frank. 2013. *Stories of Our Lives: Memory, History, Narrative*. Logan: Utah State University Press.

Dégh, Linda. 2001. *Legend and Belief: Dialectics of a Folklore Genre*. Bloomington: Indiana University Press.

Derrida, Jacques. 1976. *Of Grammatology*. Baltimore, MD: Johns Hopkins University Press.

DeWeese, Devin. 2002. "Islam and the Legacy of Sovietology: A Review Essay on Yaacov Ro'i's *Islam in the Soviet Union*." *Journal of Islamic Studies* 13 (3): 298–330.

———. 2011. "Survival Strategies: Reflections on the Notion of Religious 'Survival' in Soviet Ethnographic Studies of Muslim Religious Life in Central Asia." In *Exploring the Edge of Empire: Soviet Era Anthropology in the Caucasus and Central Asia*, edited by F. Mühlfried and S. Sokolovskiy, 35–58. Berlin: Lit Verlag.

———. 2012. "'Dis-ordering' Sufism in Early Modern Central Asia: Suggestions for Rethinking the Sources and Social Structures of Sufi History in the 18th and 19th Centuries." In *History and Culture of Central Asia/Istoriia i Kul'tura Tsentral'noi Azii*, edited by Bakhtiyar Babadjanov and Kawahara Yayoi, 259–79. Tokyo: University of Tokyo.

Dinshaw, Carolyn. 2012. *How Soon Is Now? Medieval Texts, Amateur Readers, and the Queerness of Time*. Durham, NC: Duke University Press.

Dudoignon, Stéphane. 2004. "Faction Struggles among the Bukharan Ulama during the Colonial, the Revolutionary, and the Early Soviet Periods (1868–1929): A Paradigm for History Writing?" In *Muslim Societies: Historical and Comparative Aspects*, edited by Sato Tsugitaka, 62–96. New York: Routledge-Curzon.

———. 2011. "From Revival to Mutation: The Religious Personnel of Islam in Tajikistan, from De-Stalinization to Independence (1955–91)." *Central Asian Survey* 30 (1): 53–80.

Dudoignon, Stéphane A., and Sayyid Ahmad Qalandar. 2014. "'They Were All from the Country': The Revival and Politicisation of Islam in the Lower Wakhsh River Valley of the Tajik SSR (1947–1997)." In *Allah's Kolkhozes: Migration, De-Stalinisation, Privatisation, and the New Muslim Congregations in the Soviet Realm (1950s–2000s)*, edited by Stéphane A. Dudoignon and Christian Noack, 47–122. Berlin: Klaus Schwarz Verlag.

Dundes, Alan. 1989. *Folklore Matters*. Knoxville: University of Tennessee Press.

During, Jean. 1990. *Musique et mystique dans les traditions de l'Iran*. Paris: Institut français de recherche en Iran.

Eickelman, Dale F. 1992. *Knowledge and Power in Morocco: The Education of a Twentieth-Century Notable*. Princeton, NJ: Princeton University Press.

Eliot, T. S. 1950. *Selected Essays*. New York: Harcourt, Brace.

Epkenhans, Tim. 2010. "Muslims without Learning, Clergy without Faith: Institutions of Islamic Learning in Tajikistan." In *Islamic Education in the Soviet Union and Its Successor States*, edited by Michael Kemper, Raoul Motika, and Stefan Reichmuth, 313–48. New York: Routledge.

———. 2011. "Defining Normative Islam: Some Remarks on Contemporary Islamic Thought in Tajikistan—Hoji Akbar Turajonzoda's *Sharia and Society*." *Central Asian Survey* 30 (1): 81–96.

———. 2017. "Islam, Religious Elites, and the State in Tajikistan." In *Islam, Society, and Politics in Central Asia*, edited by Pauline Jones, 173–98. Pittsburgh, PA: University of Pittsburgh Press.

Ernst, Carl W. 1992. *Eternal Garden: Mysticism, History, and Politics at a South Asian Sufi Center*. Albany: State University of New York Press.

———. 1997. *The Shambhala Guide to Sufism*. Boston: Shambhala.

Ernst, Carl W., and Bruce B. Lawrence. 2002. *Sufi Martyrs of Love: Chishti Sufism in South Asia and Beyond*. New York: Palgrave Macmillan.

Fabian, J. 1990. *Power and Performance: Ethnographic Explorations through Proverbial Wisdom and Theater in Shaba, Zaire*. Madison: University of Wisconsin Press.

Feldman, Walter. 1993. "Mysticism, Didacticism, and Authority in the Liturgical Poetry of the Halvetî Dervishes of Istanbul." *Edebiyât* 4 (2): 243–65.

Finnegan, Ruth. 1992. *Oral Poetry: Its Nature, Significance, and Social Context*. Bloomington: Indiana University Press.

Fjæstad, Kristin, and Heidi Kjærnet. 2014. "Performing Statehood: Afghanistan as an Arena for Central Asian States." *Central Asian Survey* 33 (3): 312–28.

Flueckiger, Joyce Burkhalter. 2005. "The 'Deep Secret' and Dangers of Karamat: Miraculous Acts, Revelation, and Secrecy in a South Indian Sufi Tradition." *Comparative Islamic Studies* 1 (2): 159–76.

Foley, John Miles. 1991. *Immanent Art: From Structure to Meaning in Traditional Oral Epic*. Bloomington: Indiana University Press.

———. 1995. *The Singer of Tales in Performance*. Bloomington: Indiana University Press.

———. 2002. *How to Read an Oral Poem*. Urbana: University of Illinois Press.

Freeman, Elizabeth. 2010. *Time Binds: Queer Temporalities, Queer Histories*. Durham, NC: Duke University Press.

Friedmann, Yohanan. 2000. *Shaykh Ahmad Sirhindi: An Outline of His Thought and a Study of His Image in the Eyes of Posterity*. New Delhi: Oxford University Press.

Frishkopf, Michael. 2003. "Authorship in Sufi Poetry." *Alif: Journal of Comparative Poetics* 23:78–108.

Gal, Susan, and Gail Kligman. 2000. *Reproducing Gender Politics, Publics, and Everyday Life after Socialism*. Princeton, NJ: Princeton University Press.

Gatling, Benjamin. 2013. "The Guide after Rumi: Tradition and Its Foil in Tajik Sufism." *Nova Religio* 17 (1): 1–23.

———. 2015. "Abdulhaï Mujaxarfī and the Contemporary Reception of Pre-Soviet Tajik Poetry." In *Iranian Languages and Literatures of Central Asia: From the Eighteenth Century to the Present*, edited by Matteo De Chiara and Evelin Grassi, 207–31. Studia Iranica 57. Paris: Association pour l'avancement des études Iraniennes.

———. 2016. "Historical Narrative, Intertextuality, and Cultural Continuity in Post-Soviet Tajikistan." *Journal of Folklore Research* 53 (1): 41–65.

Giehler, Beate. 2014. "Maxim Gorki and Islamic Revolution in a Southern Tajik Cotton Plain: The Failure of Soviet Integration in the Countryside." In *Allah's Kolkhozes: Migration, De-Stalinisation, Privatisation, and the New Muslim Congregations in the Soviet Realm (1950s–2000s)*, edited by Stéphane A. Dudoignon and Christian Noack, 123–47. Berlin: Klaus Schwarz Verlag.

Gilbert, Andrew, Jessica Greenberg, Elissa Helms, and Stef Jansen. 2008. "Reconsidering Postsocialism from the Margins of Europe: Hope, Time and Normalcy in Post-Yugoslav Societies." *Anthropology News* 49 (8): 10–11.

Gille, Zsuzsa. 2010. "Postscript." In *Post-Communist Nostalgia*, edited by Maria Todorova and Zsuzsa Gille, 278–89. New York: Berghahn Books.

Gilman, Lisa. 2009. *The Dance of Politics: Gender, Performance, and Democratization in Malawi*. Philadelphia, PA: Temple University Press.

Glassie, Henry. 1982. *Passing the Time in Ballymenone: Culture and History of an Ulster Community*. Philadelphia: University of Pennsylvania Press.

———. 1997. *Art and Life in Bangladesh*. Bloomington: Indiana University Press.

———. 2003. "Tradition." In *Eight Words for the Study of Expressive Culture*, edited by Burt Feintuch, 176–97. Urbana: University of Illinois Press.

Goffman, Erving. 1974. *Frame Analysis: An Essay on the Organization of Experience*. New York: Harper & Row.

Green, Garth L. 2007. "Authenticity, Commerce, and Nostalgia in the Trinidad Carnival." In *Trinidad Carnival*, edited by Garth L. Green and Philip W. Scher, 62–83. Bloomington: Indiana University Press.

Green, Nile. 2004a. "Emerging Approaches to the Sufi Traditions of South Asia: Between Texts, Territories, and the Transcendent." *South Asia Research* 24 (2): 123–48.

———. 2004b. "Stories of Saints and Sultans: Re-membering History at the Sufi Shrines of Aurangabad." *Modern Asian Studies* 38 (2): 419–46.

———. 2006. *Indian Sufism since the Seventeenth Century: Saints, Books, and Empires in the Muslim Deccan.* New York: Routledge.

Green, Richard Firth. 1999. *A Crisis of Truth: Literature and Law in Ricardian England.* Philadelphia: University of Pennsylvania Press.

Gretsky, Sergei. 1994. "Qadi Akbar Turajonzoda." *Central Asian Monitor* 1:16–24.

Gross, Jo-Ann. 1999. "The Polemic of 'Official' and 'Unofficial' Islam: Sufism in Soviet Central Asia." In *Islamic Mysticism Contested: Thirteen Centuries of Controversies and Polemics*, edited by Frederick de Jong and Bernd Radtke, 520–40. Leiden: Brill.

———. 2002. "The Naqshbandīya and Khwāja ʿUbayd Allāh Aḥrār." In *The Letters of Khwāja ʿUbayd Allāh Aḥrār and His Associates*, edited by Ason Urunbaev, translated by Jo-Ann Gross, 1–22. Leiden: Brill.

———. 2013. "Foundational Legends, Shrines, and Ismaʿili Identity in Tajik Badakhshan." In *Muslims and Others in Sacred Space*, edited by Margaret Jean Cormack, 164–92. New York: Oxford University Press.

Hadissi, Korosh. 2010. "A Socio-Historical Approach to Poetic Origins of Persian Proverbs." *Iranian Studies* 43 (5): 599–605.

Hafstein, Valdimar T. 2012. "Cultural Heritage." In *A Companion to Folklore*, edited by Regina F. Bendix and Galit Hasan-Rokem, 500–519. Malden, MA: Wiley Blackwell.

Hammoudi, Abdellah. 1997. *Master and Disciple: The Cultural Foundations of Moroccan Authoritarianism.* Chicago: University of Chicago Press.

Handler, Richard. 1988. *Nationalism and the Politics of Culture in Quebec.* Madison: University of Wisconsin Press.

Handler, Richard, and Jocelyn Linnekin. 1984. "Tradition, Genuine or Spurious." *Journal of American Folklore* 97 (385): 273–90.

Hanks, W. F. 1989. "Text and Textuality." *Annual Review of Anthropology* 18:95–127.

Hann, Christopher M., ed. 2002. *Postsocialism: Ideals, Ideologies, and Practices in Eurasia.* New York: Routledge.

Haring, Lee. 1988. "Interperformance." *Fabula* 29:365–72.

Harris, Colette. 2006. *Muslim Youth: Tensions and Transitions in Tajikistan.* Boulder, CO: Westview.

Hayes, Kevin J. 1997. *Folklore and Book Culture.* Knoxville: University of Tennessee Press.

Heathershaw, John. 2009. *Post-conflict Tajikistan: The Politics of Peacebuilding and the Emergence of Legitimate Order.* New York: Routledge.

————. 2014. "The Global Performance State: A Reconsideration of the Central
    Asian 'Weak State.'" In *Ethnographies of the State in Central Asia*, edited by
    Madeleine Reeves, Johan Rasanayagam, and Judith Beyer, 29–54. Blooming-
    ton: Indiana University Press.
Heathershaw, John, and Sophie Roche. 2011. "Islam and Political Violence in
    Tajikistan: An Ethnographic Perspective on the Causes and Consequences of
    the 2010 Armed Conflict in the Kamarob Gorge." *Ethnopolitics Papers* 8:1–21.
Herzfeld, Michael. 1982. *Ours Once More: Folklore, Ideology, and the Making of
    Modern Greece*. Austin: University of Texas Press.
————. 2005. *Cultural Intimacy*. New York: Routledge.
Hierman, Brent. 2010. "What Use Was the Election to Us? Clientelism and Polit-
    ical Trust amongst Ethnic Uzbeks in Kyrgyzstan and Tajikistan." *Nationalities
    Papers* 38 (2): 245–63.
Hilgers, Irene. 2009. *Why Do Uzbeks Have to Be Muslim? Exploring Religiosity
    in the Ferghana Valley*. Berlin: Lit Verlag.
Hill, Jane H. 1998. "'Today There Is No Respect': Nostalgia, 'Respect,' and Oppo-
    sitional Discourse in Mexicano (Nahuatl) Language Ideology." In *Language
    Ideologies: Practice and Theory*, edited by Bambi B. Schieffelin, 68–86. New
    York: Oxford University Press.
Hinson, Glenn. 2000. *Fire in My Bones: Transcendence and the Holy Spirit in
    African American Gospel*. Philadelphia: University of Pennsylvania Press.
Hirsch, Francine. 2005. *Empire of Nations: Ethnographic Knowledge and the
    Making of the Soviet Union*. Ithaca, NY: Cornell University Press.
Hirschkind, Charles. 2006. *The Ethical Soundscape: Cassette Sermons and
    Islamic Counterpublics*. New York: Columbia University Press.
Hobsbawm, Eric. 1983. "Introduction: Inventing Traditions." In *The Invention of
    Tradition*, edited by Eric Hobsbawm and Terrence Ranger, 1–14. New York:
    Cambridge University Press.
Hodizoda, Rasul. 1968. *Adabiëti Tojik dar nimai duvvŭmi asri XIX: Qismi avval*.
    Dushanbe: Donish.
Hokiroh, Muhammad. 2010. *Hazrati Pir "Dil ba ëru dast ba kor."* Dushanbe:
    Moturidiyon.
Howard, Robert Glenn. 2013. "Vernacular Authority: Critically Engaging 'Tradi-
    tion.'" In *Tradition in the 21st Century: Locating the Role of the Past in the
    Present*, edited by Robert Glenn Howard and Trevor Blank, 72–99. Logan:
    Utah State University Press.
Hull, Matthew S. 2012. *Government of Paper: The Materiality of Bureaucracy in
    Urban Pakistan*. Berkeley: University of California Press.
Hymes, Dell. 1975. "Folklore's Nature and the Sun's Myth." *Journal of American
    Folklore* 88 (350): 345–69.
————. 1981. *"In Vain I Tried to Tell You": Essays in Native American Poetics*.
    Philadelphia: University of Pennsylvania Press.

————.1989. "Ways of Speaking." In *Explorations in the Ethnography of Speaking*, edited by Richard Bauman and Joel Sherzer, 2nd ed., 433–51. New York: Cambridge University Press.

Ibañez-Tirado, Diana. 2015. "'How Can I Be Post-Soviet If I Was Never Soviet?' Rethinking Categories of Time and Social Change, a Perspective from Kulob, Southern Tajikistan." *Central Asian Survey* 34 (2): 190–203.

Jackson, Jason Baird, ed. 2016. *Material Vernaculars: Objects, Images, and Their Social Worlds*. Bloomington: Indiana University Press.

Jackson, Michael. 2013. *The Politics of Storytelling: Variations on a Theme by Hannah Arendt*. Copenhagen: Museum Musculanum Press.

Jomī, Abdurrahmoni. 1990. *Nafahotuluns*. Dushanbe: Adib.

Jones, Andrew M., and Nicole Boivin. 2010. "The Malice of Inanimate Objects: Material Agency." In *The Oxford Handbook of Material Culture Studies*, edited by Dan Hicks and Mary C. Beaudry, 333–51. New York: Oxford University Press.

Jones, Michael Owen. 1997. "How Can We Apply Event Analysis to 'Material Behavior,' and Why Should We?" *Western Folklore* 56 (3–4): 199–214.

Junūnī, Mavlavī. 1997 [1376]. *Ma'dan al-Hāl*. Edited by 'Abdālnabī Sitārzādih and Mahmūdjān Tūrahjānzadih. Tehran.

————. 2004. *Ganj al'āshiqīn*. Edited by Ismā'īl 'Abdulūhāb zādeh Qahārī. Dushanbe.

Jununī. 2009. *Kulliëti Ma"dan-ul Hol*. Edited by Asadulloi Abdukhon and Tolibi Didor. Dushanbe: Safat.

Kandiyoti, Deniz. 2002. "How Far Do Analyses of Postsocialism Travel? The Case of Central Asia." In *Postsocialism: Ideals, Ideologies, and Practices*, edited by Christopher M. Hann, 238–57. New York: Routledge.

Kaneff, Deema. 2004. *A Model Village: The Politics of Time in a "Model" Bulgarian Village*. Oxford: Berghahn Books.

Kapchan, Deborah A. 2003. "Performance." In *Eight Words for the Study of Expressive Culture*, edited by Burt Feintuch, 121–45. Urbana: University of Illinois Press.

Karimova, Liliya. 2016. "(Re)constructing Muslim Identities from the Soviet Past: Muslim Tatar Women's Stories of Soviet Moral Selves." *Central Asian Affairs* 3 (2): 117–41.

Kassymbekova, Botakoz. 2016. *Despite Cultures: Early Soviet Rule in Tajikistan*. Pittsburgh, PA: University of Pittsburgh Press.

Keane, Webb. 1997. *Signs of Recognition: Powers and Hazards of Representation in an Indonesian Society*. Berkeley: University of California Press.

Keller, Shoshana. 2001. *To Moscow, Not Mecca: The Soviet Campaign against Islam in Central Asia, 1917–1941*. Westport, CT: Praeger.

Kemper, Michael, and Stephan Conermann, eds. 2011. *The Heritage of Soviet Oriental Studies*. New York: Routledge.

Khalid, Adeeb. 2000. "Society and Politics in Bukhara, 1868–1920." *Central Asian Survey* 19 (3–4): 364–93.

———. 2007. *Islam after Communism: Religion and Politics in Central Asia.* Berkeley: University of California Press.

Kirshenblatt-Gimblett, Barbara. 1994. "Toward a Theory of Proverb Meaning." In *The Wisdom of Many: Essays on the Proverb,* edited by Wolfgang Mieder and Alan Dundes, 111–39. Madison: University of Wisconsin Press.

———.1998. "Folklore's Crisis." *Journal of American Folklore* 111 (441): 281–327.

Knysh, Alexander. 2002. "Sufism as an Explanatory Paradigm: The Issue of the Motivations of Sufi Resistance Movements in Western and Russian Scholarship." *Die Welt Des Islams* 42 (2): 139–73.

Koen, Benjamin D. 2003. "Devotional Music and Healing in Badakhshan, Tajikistan: Preventive and Curative Practices." PhD diss., Ohio State University.

———. 2009. *Beyond the Roof of the World: Music, Prayer, and Healing in the Pamir Mountains.* New York: Oxford University Press.

Krasnowolska, Anna. 2009. "ḴEŻR." *Encyclopædia Iranica.* http://www.iranica online.org/articles/kezr-prophet.

Kugle, Scott Alan. 2006. *Rebel between Spirit and Law: Ahmad Zarruq, Sainthood, and Authority in Islam.* Bloomington: Indiana University Press.

Kuipers, Joel C. 1990. *Power in Performance: The Creation of Textual Authority in Weyewa Ritual Speech.* Philadelphia: University of Pennsylvania Press.

———. 2013. "Evidence and Authority in Ethnographic and Linguistic Perspective." *Annual Review of Anthropology* 42:399–413.

Kumo, Kazuhiro. 2012. "Tajik Labour Migrants and Their Remittances: Is Tajik Migration Pro-Poor?" *Post-Communist Economies* 24 (1): 87–109.

Labov, William. 1997. "Some Further Steps in Narrative Analysis." *Journal of Narrative and Life History* 7:395–415.

Lagerkvist, Amanda. 2013. *Media and Memory in New Shanghai: Western Performances of Futures Past.* New York: Palgrave Macmillan.

Lambek, Michael. 1993. *Knowledge and Practice in Mayotte: Local Discourses of Islam, Sorcery, and Spirit Possession.* Toronto: University of Toronto Press.

———. 1997. "Knowledge and Practice in Mayotte: An Overview." *Cultural Dynamics* 9 (2): 131–48.

Latour, Bruno. 1999. *Pandora's Hope: Essays on the Reality of Science Studies.* Cambridge, MA: Harvard University Press.

———.2005. *Reassembling the Social.* New York: Oxford University Press.

Lawrence, Bruce. 1982. "The Chishtiya of Sultanate India: A Case Study of Biographical Complexities in South Asian Islam." In *Charisma and Sacred Biography,* edited by Michael A. Williams, 47–67. Chico, CA: Scholars.

———.1993. "Biography and the 17th Century Qādiriya of North India." In *Islam and Indian Regions,* edited by Anna Libera Dallapiccola and Stephanie Zingel-Ave Lallemant, 1:399–415. Stuttgart: Steiner.

Lemon, Edward. 2014. "Mediating the Conflict in the Rasht Valley, Tajikistan." *Central Asian Affairs* 1 (2): 247–72.

———. 2016. "Governing Islam and Security in Tajikistan and Beyond: The Emergence of Transnational Authoritarian Security Governance." PhD diss., University of Exeter.

Lemonnier, Pierre. 2012. *Mundane Objects: Materiality and Non-Verbal Communication*. Walnut Creek, CA: Left Coast Press.

Lévi-Strauss, Claude. 1966. *The Savage Mind*. Chicago: University of Chicago Press.

Lewisohn, Leonard. 1989. "The Life and Poetry of Mashreqi Tabrizi." *Iranian Studies* 22 (2–3): 99–127.

Liu, Morgan Y. 2011. "Central Asia in the Post–Cold War World." *Annual Review of Anthropology* 40:115–31.

Lord, Albert Bates. 2000. *The Singer of Tales*. 2nd ed. Cambridge, MA: Harvard University Press.

Losensky, Paul E. 1994. "'The Allusive Field of Drunkenness': Three Safavid-Moghul Responses to a Lyric by Bābā Fighānī." In *Reorientations/Arabic and Persian Poetry*, edited by Suzanne Pinckney Stetkevych, 227–62. Bloomington: Indiana University Press.

———. 1996. "Fanā and Taxes: A Brief Literary History of a Persian Proverb." *Edebiyât* 7:1–20.

———. 1998. *Welcoming Fighani: Imitation and Poetic Individuality in the Safavid-Mughal Ghazal*. Costa Mesa, CA: Mazda.

Louw, Maria Elisabeth. 2007. *Everyday Islam in Post-Soviet Central Asia*. New York: Routledge.

Magliocco, Sabina. 2004. *Witching Culture: Folklore and Neo-Paganism in America*. Philadelphia: University of Pennsylvania Press.

Mahmood, Saba. 2005. *Politics of Piety: The Islamic Revival and the Feminist Subject*. Princeton, NJ: Princeton University Press.

Manoukian, Setrag. 2011. *City of Knowledge in Twentieth Century Iran: Shiraz, History, and Poetry*. New York: Routledge.

Marat, Erica. 2009. "Labor Migration in Central Asia: Implications of the Global Economic Crisis." Silk Road Paper. Johns Hopkins University—SAIS: Central Asia—Caucasus Institute Silk Road Studies Program.

McCutcheon, Russell T. 1997. *Manufacturing Religion: The Discourse on Sui Generis Religion and the Politics of Nostalgia*. New York: Oxford University Press.

McDonald, David A. 2013. *My Voice Is My Weapon: Music, Nationalism, and the Poetics of Palestinian Resistance*. Durham, NC: Duke University Press.

McDowell, John H. 1982. "Beyond Iconicity: Ostension in Kamsá Mythic Narrative." *Journal of the Folklore Institute* 19 (2–3): 119–39.

———. 2000. *Poetry and Violence: The Ballad Tradition of Mexico's Costa Chica*. Urbana: University of Illinois Press.

McGranahan, Carole. 2012. "Mao in Tibetan Disguise: History, Ethnography, and Excess." *HAU: Journal of Ethnographic Theory* 2 (1): 213–45.

Meier, Fritz. 1995. *Meister und Schüler im Orden der Naqšbandiyya*. Heidelberg: C. Winter.

Mendoza-Denton, Norma. 2008. *Homegirls: Language and Cultural Practice among Latina Youth Gangs*. Malden, MA: Blackwell.

Menga, Filippo. 2015. "Building a Nation through a Dam: The Case of Rogun in Tajikistan." *Nationalities Papers* 43 (3): 479–94.

Messick, Brinkley. 1993. *The Calligraphic State: Textual Domination and History in a Muslim Society*. Berkeley: University of California Press.

Miller, Flagg. 2007. *The Moral Resonance of Arab Media: Audiocassette Poetry and Culture in Yemen*. Cambridge, MA: Center for Middle Eastern Studies, Harvard University.

Mills, Margaret A. 1994. "Folk Tradition in the Masnavī and the Masnavī in Folk Tradition." In *Poetry and Mysticism in Islam: The Heritage of Rumi*, edited by Amin Banani, Richard Hovannisian, and Georges Sabagh, 136–77. London: Cambridge University Press.

———. 2008. "What('s) Theory?" *Journal of Folklore Research* 45 (1): 19–28.

———. 2013. "Gnomics: Proverbs, Aphorisms, Metaphors, Key Words, and Epithets in Afghan Discourses of War and Instability." In *Afghanistan in Ink*, edited by Nile Green and Nushin Arbabzadah, 229–51. London: Hurst.

Mills, Margaret A., and Ravshan Rahmoni. 2015. "Gashtak: Oral/Literary Intertextuality, Performance, and Identity in Contemporary Tajikistan." In *Orality and Textuality in the Iranian World*, edited by Julia Rubinovich, 316–41. Leiden: Brill.

Moin, A. Azfar. 2012. *The Millennial Sovereign: Sacred Kingship and Sainthood in Islam*. New York: Columbia University Press.

Mol, Hans. 1977. *Identity and the Sacred: A Sketch for a New Social-Scientific Theory of Religion*. New York: Free Press.

Montgomery, David W. 2016. *Practicing Islam: Knowledge, Experience, and Social Navigation in Kyrgystan*. Pittsburgh, PA: University of Pittsburgh Press.

Montgomery, David W., and John Heathershaw. 2016. "Islam, Secularism, and Danger: A Reconsideration of the Link between Religiosity, Radicalism, and Rebellion in Central Asia." *Religion, State, and Society* 44 (3): 192–218.

Mostowlansky, Till. 2017. *Azan on the Moon: Entangling Modernities along Tajikistan's Pamir Highway*. Pittsburgh, PA: University of Pittsburgh Press.

Mottahedeh, Roy P. 2009. *The Mantle of the Prophet: Religion and Politics in Iran*. Oxford: Oneworld Publications.

Mould, Tom. 2005. "The Paradox of Traditionalization: Negotiating the Past in Choctaw Prophetic Discourse." *Journal of Folklore Research* 42 (3): 255–94.

Mullojonov, Parviz. 2001. "The Islamic Clergy in Tajikistan since the End of the Soviet Period." In *Islam in Politics in Russia and Central Asia (Early Eighteenth to Late Twentieth Centuries)*, edited by Stéphane A. Dudoignon and Hisao Komatsu, 221–50. New York: Kegan Paul.

Myer, Will. 2002. *Islam and Colonialism: Western Perspectives on Soviet Asia.* New York: RoutledgeCurzon.

Nadkarni, Maya. 2010. "Politics of Authenticity in Post-Socialist Hungary." In *Post-Communist Nostalgia*, edited by Maria Todorova and Zsuzsa Gille, 190–214. New York: Berghahn Books.

Nadkarni, Maya, and Olga Shevchenko. 2004. "The Politics of Nostalgia: A Case for Comparative Analysis of Post-Socialist Practices." *Ab Imperio* 2:487–519.

Narayan, Kirin. 1992. *Storytellers, Saints, and Scoundrels: Folk Narrative in Hindu Religious Teaching.* Philadelphia: University of Pennsylvania Press.

Naumkin, Vitalii Viacheslavovich. 2005. *Radical Islam in Central Asia: Between Pen and Rifle.* Lanham, MD: Rowman & Littlefield.

Niyazi, A. 2000. "Migration, Demography, and Socio-Ecological Processes in Tajikistan." In *Migration in Central Asia: Its History and Current Problems*, edited by H. Komatsu, O. Chika, and J. S. Schoeberlein, 169–78. Osaka: Japan Center for Asia Studies.

Nodiri, Saidaxmad Xodizoda. 2004. "Mavlavi dzhuni i ego masnavi 'Ma'dan-ul-hol.'" PhD diss., Tadzhikskii Gosudarstvennii Natsional'nii Universitet.

Nourzhanov, Kirill, and Christian Bleuer. 2013. *Tajikistan: A Political and Social History.* Canberra: Australian National University Press.

Noyes, Dorothy. 2003. "Group." In *Eight Words for the Study of Expressive Culture*, edited by Burt Feintuch, 7–41. Urbana: University of Illinois Press.

———. 2009. "Tradition: Three Traditions." *Journal of Folklore Research* 46 (3): 233–68.

———. 2016. *Humble Theory: Folklore's Grasp on Social Life.* Bloomington: Indiana University Press.

Nozimova, Shahnoza. 2016. "Hijab in a Changing Tajik Society." *Central Asian Affairs* 3 (2): 95–116.

Nozimova, Shahnoza, and Tim Epkenhans. 2013. "Negotiating Islam in Emerging Public Spheres in Contemporary Tajikistan." *Asiatische Studien Etudes Asiatiques* 67 (3): 965–90.

Nuraliev, Îu. 1991. *Luqmoni Hakim.* Dushanbe: Irfon.

O'Brien, Tim. 1998. "How to Tell a True War Story." In *Postmodern American Fiction: A Norton Anthology*, edited by Paula Geyh, Fred Leebron, and Andrew Levy, 174–83. New York: Norton.

O'Dell, Emily. 2017. "Subversives and Saints: Sufism and the State in Central Asia." In *Islam, Society, and Politics in Central Asia*, edited by Pauline Jones, 99–126. Pittsburgh, PA: University of Pittsburgh Press.

Ohlander, Erik S. 2008. *Sufism in an Age of Transition: 'Umar Al-Suhrawardī and the Rise of the Islamic Mystical Brotherhoods.* Leiden: Brill.

Olcott, Martha Brill. 2012. *Tajikistan's Difficult Development Path.* Washington, DC: Carnegie Endowment for International Peace.

Olszewska, Zuzanna. 2015. *Pearl of Dari: Poetry and Personhood among Young Afghans in Iran*. Bloomington: Indiana University Press.

Page, Mary Ellen. 1979. "Professional Storytelling in Iran: Transmission and Practice." *Iranian Studies* 12 (3–4): 195–215.

Pasilov, B., and A. Ashirov. 2007. "Revival of Sufi Traditions in Modern Central Asia: Jahri Zikr and Its Ethnological Features." *Oriente Moderno* 87 (1): 163–75.

Paul, Jürgen. 2002. "Contemporary Uzbek Hagiography and Its Sources." *Hallesche Beiträge Zur Orientwissenschaft* 32:621–28.

Paul, Jürgen, and Baxtiyar Babadjanov. 2002. *Katalog sufischer Handschriften aus der Bibliothek des Instituts für Orientalistik der Akademie der Wissenschaften, Republik Usbekistan*. Stuttgart: F. Steiner.

Pedersen, Morten Axel. 2011. *Not Quite Shamans: Spirit Worlds and Political Lives in Northern Mongolia*. Ithaca, NY: Cornell University Press.

Peirce, Charles S. 1955. *Philosophical Writings of Peirce*. Edited by Justus Buchler. New York: Dover.

Perry, John R., and Rachel Lehr. 1998. "Introduction." In *The Sands of the Oxus: Boyhood Reminiscences of Sadriddin Aini*, 1–25. Costa Mesa, CA: Mazda.

Peshkova, Svetlana. 2014. *Women, Islam, and Identity: Public Life in Private Spaces in Uzbekistan*. Syracuse, NY: Syracuse University Press.

Piot, Charles. 2010. *Nostalgia for the Future: West Africa after the Cold War*. Chicago: University of Chicago Press.

Privratsky, Bruce G. 2001. *Muslim Turkistan: Kazak Religion and Collective Memory*. Richmond, Surrey: Curzon.

Radner, Joan N., and Susan S. Lanser. 1993. "Strategies of Coding in Women's Cultures." In *Feminist Messages: Coding in Women's Folk Culture*, edited by Joan N. Radner, 1–29. Urbana: University of Illinois Press.

Rahimov, Dilshod. 2009. *Folklori Tojik*. Dushanbe: Ėjod.

Rahmon, Emomalī. 2009a. *Merosi Imomi A'zam va Guftugūi Tamaddunho*. Dushanbe: Sharqi ozod.

———. 2009b. *Muhiti Zindagī va Olami Andeshahoi Imomi A'zam*. Dushanbe: Sharqi ozod.

Rahmonī, Ravshan. 2008. *Ėjodiëti Guftorii Mardumi Tojik*. Dushanbe: Sino.

Rahnamo, Abdullohi. 2009. *Ulamoi Islomī dar Tojikiston: Kitobi 1*. Dushanbe: Irfon.

Rasanayagam, Johan. 2006. "Introduction," in "Post-Soviet Islam: An Anthropological Perspective." Special issue, *Central Asian Survey* 25 (3): 219–33.

———. 2011. *Islam in Post-Soviet Uzbekistan: The Morality of Experience*. New York: Cambridge University Press.

———. 2014. "The Politics of Culture and the Space for Islam: Soviet and Post-Soviet Imaginaries in Uzbekistan." *Central Asian Survey* 33 (1): 1–14.

Rasanayagam, Johan, Judith Beyer, and Madeleine Reeves. 2014. "Introduction: Performances, Possibilities, and Practices of the Political in Central Asia."

In *Ethnographies of the State in Central Asia*, edited by Madeleine Reeves, Johan Rasanayagam, and Judith Beyer, 1–26. Bloomington: Indiana University Press.

Rashtī, Shaïkh Davlatkhojai Mirzokhojai. 2005. *Dunëi fonī va uqboi boqī.* Dushanbe: Devashtich.

Remtilla, Aliaa. 2012. "Re-Producing Social Relations: Political and Economic Change and Islam in Post-Soviet Tajik Ishkashim." PhD diss., University of Manchester.

Roche, Sophie. 2013. "Continuities and Disruptions in Islamic Education: Biographies of Shogirds from Tajikistan." *Anthropology of the Contemporary Middle East and Central Eurasia* 1 (1): 23–53.

Ro'i, Yaacov. 2000. *Islam in the Soviet Union: From the Second World War to Gorbachev.* New York: Columbia University Press.

Roy, Olivier. 2000. *The New Central Asia: The Creation of Nations.* New York: New York University Press.

Ruffle, Karen G. 2011. *Gender, Sainthood, and Everyday Practice in South Asian Shi'ism.* Chapel Hill: University of North Carolina Press.

Rūmī, Mavlānā Jalāl al-Dīn. 2005 [1383]. *Kullīyat-e Dīvān-e Shams.* Edited by Badī' al-Zamān Furūzānfar. 2 vols. Tehran: Nashri Rabī.

Rumi. 2007. *Masnavi, Book 2.* Translated by Jawid Mojaddedi. New York: Oxford University Press.

Safī, Mavlono Fakhriddin Alii. 2009. *Rashaḣot.* Edited by Abduḣalimi Ḣusaïn. Dushanbe: Irfon.

Saïfulloev, Atakhon. 1956. "Saroïandai Ideïaḣoi Kommunizm." *Tojikistoni Soveti,* December 29.

———.1983. *Mirzo Tursunzoda: Ocherki Ḣaët va Ėjodiëti Shoir.* Dushanbe: Irfon.

Saltzman, Rachelle Hope. 2012. *A Lark for the Sake of Their Country: The 1926 General Strike Volunteers in Folklore and Memory.* New York: Palgrave Macmillan.

Saroyan, Mark. 1997. *Minorities, Mullahs, and Modernity: Reshaping Community in the Former Soviet Union.* Edited by Edward W. Walker. Berkeley: International and Area Studies, University of California.

Sartori, Paolo. 2010. "Towards a History of the Muslims' Soviet Union: A View from Central Asia." *Die Welt Des Islams* 50 (3–4): 315–34.

Schimmel, Annemarie. 1975. *Mystical Dimensions of Islam.* Chapel Hill: University of North Carolina Press.

———.1983. *Die Orientalische Katze.* Cologne: Diederichs.

Schoeberlein-Engel, John. 1994. "Identity in Central Asia: Construction and Contention in the Conceptions of 'Özbek,' 'Tâjik,' 'Muslim,' 'Samarqandi' and Other Groups." PhD diss., Harvard University.

Schubel, Vernon James. 1999. "Post-Soviet Hagiography and the Reconstruction of the Naqshbandī Tradition in Contemporary Uzbekistan." In *Naqshbandis in Western and Central Asia: Change and Continuity,* edited by Elisabeth Özdalga, 73–87. Richmond, Surrey: Curzon.

Schwab, Wendell. 2011. "Establishing an Islamic Niche in Kazakhstan: Musylman Publishing House and Its Publications." *Central Asian Survey* 30 (2): 227–42.

———. 2012. "Traditions and Texts: How Two Young Women Learned to Interpret the Qur'an and Hadiths in Kazakhstan." *Contemporary Islam* 6 (2): 173–97.

———. 2015. "Islam, Fun, and Social Capital in Kazakhstan." *Central Asian Affairs* 2:51–70.

Schwartz, Christopher. 2013. "The Relics of 1991: Memories and Phenomenology of the Post-Soviet Generation." In *Social and Cultural Change in Central Asia: The Soviet Legacy,* edited by Sevket Akyildiz and Richard Carlson, 188–200. New York: Routledge.

Scott, James C. 1985. *Weapons of the Weak: Everyday Forms of Peasant Resistance.* New Haven, CT: Yale University Press.

———. 1990. *Domination and the Arts of Resistance: Hidden Transcripts.* New Haven, CT: Yale University Press.

Sebeok, Thomas A. 1994. *Signs: An Introduction to Semiotics.* Toronto: University of Toronto Press.

Sefatgol, Mansur. 2003. "Majmū'ah'hā: Important and Unknown Sources of Historiography of Iran during and in the Late Safavids, the Case of Majmū'ah-I Mīrzā Mu'īnā." In *Persian Documents: Social History of Iran and Turan in the Fifteenth to Nineteenth Centuries,* edited by Nobuaki Kondo, 73–84. New York: RoutledgeCurzon.

Semenova, A. A., ed. 1954. *Sobranie Vostochnyx Rukopisei Akademii Nauk Uzbekskoi SSR.* Vol. 2. Tashkent: Izdatel'stvo Akademii Nauk UzSSR.

Seremetakis, C. Nadia. 1994. "Memory of the Senses, Part I." In *The Senses Still: Perception and Memory as Material Culture in Modernity,* edited by C. Nadia Seremetakis, 1–18. Boulder, CO: Westview.

Shafiev, Abdulfattoh. 2015. "A 'Last Prophet' Faces Jail for Land-Grabbing and Polygamy in Tajikistan." *Global Voices,* February 9. https://globalvoices.org/2015/02/09/a-last-prophet-faces-jail-for-land-grabbing-and-polygamy-in-tajikistan/.

Shahrani, Nazif. 1991. "Local Knowledge of Islam and Social Discourse in Afghanistan and Turkistan in the Modern Period." In *Turko-Persia in Historical Perspective,* edited by Robert L. Canfield, 161–88. New York: Cambridge University Press.

Shaw, Rosalind. 2013. "Provocation: Futurizing Memory." *Cultural Anthropology.* https://culanth.org/fieldsights/376-provocation-futurizing-memory.

Shryock, Andrew. 1997. *Nationalism and the Genealogical Imagination: Oral History and Textual Authority in Tribal Jordan.* Berkeley: University of California Press.

Shukla, Pravina. 2015. *Costume: Performing Identities through Dress*. Bloomington: Indiana University Press.

Shuman, Amy. 2005. *Other People's Stories: Entitlement Claims and the Critique
of Empathy*. Urbana: University of Illinois Press.

Shutika, Debra Lattanzi. 2011. *Beyond the Borderlands: Migration and Belonging in the United States and Mexico*. Berkeley: University of California Press.

Silverstein, Brian. 2008. "Disciplines of Presence in Modern Turkey: Discourse,
Companionship, and the Mass Mediation of Islamic Practice." *Cultural
Anthropology* 23 (1): 118–53.

———. 2011. *Islam and Modernity in Turkey*. New York: Palgrave Macmillan.

Silverstein, Michael. 1987. "Monoglot 'Standard' in America." *Working Papers
and Proceedings of the Center for Psychosocial Studies* 13. Chicago: Center for
Psychosocial Studies.

Silverstein, Michael, and Greg Urban. 1996. "The Natural History of Discourse."
In *Natural Histories of Discourse*, edited by Michael Silverstein and Greg
Urban, 1–17. Chicago: University of Chicago Press.

Simons, Greg, and David Westerlund, eds. 2015. *Religion, Politics, and Nation-
Building in Post-Communist Countries*. New York: Routledge.

Sitārzādih, ʿAbdālnabī, and Maḥmūdjān Tūrahjānzadih. 1997. "Mavlavī Junūnī ū
kitāb ʿishq īshān." In *Ma ʿdan al-Ḥāl*, by Mavlavī Junūnī. Tehran.

Sklar, Deidre. 1994. "Can Bodylore Be Brought to Its Senses?" *Journal of American Folklore* 107 (423): 9–22.

Soucek, Svatopluk. 2000. *A History of Inner Asia*. New York: Cambridge University Press.

Stahl, Sandra K. D. 1989. *Literary Folkloristics and the Personal Narrative*.
Bloomington: Indiana University Press.

Stenning, Alison, and Kathrin Hörschelmann. 2008. "History, Geography, and
Difference in the Post-Socialist World, or Do We Still Need Post-Socialism?"
Antipode 40 (2): 312–35.

Stephan, Manja. 2010. *Das Bedürfnis nach Ausgewogenheit Moralerziehung: Islam
und Muslimsein in Tadschikistan zwischen Säkularisierung und religiöser
Rückbesinnung*. Würzburg: Ergon-Verl.

———. 2017. "Studying Islam Abroad: Pious Enterprises and Educational Aspirations of Young Tajik Muslims." In *Islam, Society, and Politics in Central Asia*,
edited by Pauline Jones, 263–89. Pittsburgh, PA: University of Pittsburgh
Press.

Stewart, Kathleen. 1988. "Nostalgia: A Polemic." *Cultural Anthropology* 3:227–41.

Stewart, Susan. 1991. *Crimes of Writing: Problems in the Containment of Representation*. New York: Oxford University Press.

———. 1993. *On Longing: Narratives of the Miniature, the Gigantic, the Souvenir,
the Collection*. Durham, NC: Duke University Press.

Stewart, Tony K. 2010. "The Subject and the Ostensible Subject: Mapping the
Genre of Hagiography among South Asian Chishtis." In *Rethinking Islamic*

Studies: From Orientalism to Cosmopolitanism, edited by Carl W. Ernst and Richard M. Martin, 227–43. Chapel Hill: University of North Carolina Press.

Stoler, Ann Laura. 2016. *Duress: Colonial Durabilities in Our Times*. Durham, NC: Duke University Press.

Stoller, Paul. 1995. *Embodying Colonial Memories: Spirit Possession, Power, and the Hauka in West Africa*. New York: Routledge.

———. 1997. *Sensuous Scholarship*. Philadelphia: University of Pennsylvania Press.

Sultanova, Razia. 2000. "Qâdiriyya Dhikr in Ferghana Valley." *Journal of the History of Sufism* 1–2:531–38.

———. 2011. *From Shamanism to Sufism: Women, Islam, and Culture in Central Asia*. London: Tauris.

Taneja, Anand Vivek. 2012. "Saintly Visions: Other Histories and History's Others in the Medieval Ruins of Delhi." *Indian Economic and Social History Review* 49 (4): 557–90.

Tasar, Eren. 2012. "Soviet Policies toward Islam: Domestic and International Considerations." In *Religion and the Cold War: A Global Perspective*, edited by Philip Emil Muehlenbeck, 158–81. Nashville, TN: Vanderbilt University Press.

———. 2017. "Unregistered: Gray Spaces in the Soviet Regulation of Islam." In *Islam, Society, and Politics in Central Asia*, edited by Pauline Jones, 127–48. Pittsburgh, PA: University of Pittsburgh Press.

Taylor, Diana. 2003. *The Archive and the Repertoire: Cultural Memory and Performance in the Americas*. Durham, NC: Duke University Press.

Tedlock, Dennis, and Bruce Mannheim. 1995. *The Dialogic Emergence of Culture*. Urbana: University of Illinois Press.

Thibault, Hélène. 2015. "The Soviet Secularization Project in Central Asia: Accommodation and Institutional Legacies." *Eurostudia* 10 (1): 11–31.

Thompson, Stith. 1955. *Motif-Index of Folk-Literature: A Classification of Narrative Elements in Folktales, Ballads, Myths, Fables, Mediaeval Romances, Exempla, Fabliaux, Jest-Books, and Local Legends*. Vol. 4. Bloomington: Indiana University Press.

Thum, Rian. 2012. "Beyond Resistance and Nationalism: Local History and the Case of Afaq Khoja." *Central Asian Survey* 31 (3): 293–310.

———. 2014. *The Sacred Routes of Uyghur History*. Cambridge, MA: Harvard University Press.

Tilley, Christopher. 1999. *Metaphor and Material Culture*. Malden, MA: Blackwell.

Titon, Jeff Todd. 1988. *Powerhouse for God: Speech, Chant, and Song in an Appalachian Baptist Church*. Austin: University of Texas Press.

Todorova, Maria. 2010a. "Introduction: From Utopia to Propaganda and Back." In *Post-Communist Nostalgia*, edited by Maria Todorova and Zsuzsa Gille, 1–16. New York: Berghahn Books.

———. 2010b. "Introduction: The Process of Remembering Communism." In *Remembering Communism: Genres of Representation*, edited by Maria Todorova, 9–34. New York: Social Science Research Council.

Togan, Isenbike. 1999. "The Khafī, Jahrī Controversy in Central Asia Revisited." In *Naqshbandis in Western and Central Asia: Change and Continuity*, edited by Elisabeth Özdalga, 17–45. Richmond, Surrey: Curzon.

Trix, Frances. 1993. *Spiritual Discourse: Learning with an Islamic Master*. Philadelphia: University of Pennsylvania Press.

Turajonzoda, Ḣojī Akbar. 2007. *Shariat va jomea*. Dushanbe: Nodir.

Urban, Greg. 1996. "Entextualization, Replication, and Power." In *Natural Histories of Discourse*, edited by Michael Silverstein and Greg Urban, 21–44. Chicago: University of Chicago Press.

Valeri, Valerio. 1990. "Constitutive History: Genealogy and Narrative in the Legitimation of Hawaiian Kingship." In *Culture through Time: Anthropological Approaches*, edited by Emiko Ohnuki-Tierney, 154–92. Stanford, CA: Stanford University Press.

Varisco, Daniel Martin. 2005. *Islam Obscured: The Rhetoric of Anthropological Representation*. New York: Palgrave Macmillan.

Verdery, Katherine. 1996. *What Was Socialism and What Comes Next?* Princeton, NJ: Princeton University Press.

———. 2002. "Whither Postsocialism?" In *Postsocialism: Ideals, Ideologies, Practices*, edited by Christopher M. Hann, 15–28. New York: Routledge.

Voloshinov, V. N. 1986. *Marxism and the Philosophy of Language*. Translated by Ladislav Matejka and I. R. Titunik. Cambridge, MA: Harvard University Press.

Waugh, Earle H. 1989. *The Munshidin of Egypt: Their World and Their Song*. Columbia: University of South Carolina Press.

———. 2005. *Memory, Music, and Religion: Morocco's Mystical Chanters*. Columbia: University of South Carolina Press.

Weber, Max. 1963. *The Sociology of Religion*. Boston, MA: Beacon.

Weismann, Itzchak. 2007. *The Naqshbandiyya: Orthodoxy and Activism in a Worldwide Sufi Tradition*. New York: Routledge.

Whitesel, Jason, and Amy Shuman. 2016. "Discursive Entanglements, Diffractive Readings: Weight-Loss-Surgery Narratives of Girth and Mirthers." *Fat Studies* 5 (1): 32–56.

Wilson, William A. 1976. *Folklore and Nationalism in Modern Finland*. Bloomington: Indiana University Press.

Woolard, Kathryn A. 1998. "Introduction: Language Ideology as a Field of Inquiry." In *Language Ideologies: Practice and Theory*, 3–49. New York: Oxford University Press.

Yamamoto, Kumiko. 2003. *The Oral Background of Persian Epics*. Boston: Brill.

Yanagihashi, Hiroyuki. 2014. "Abū Ḥanīfa." In *Encyclopaedia of Islam*, edited by Kate Fleet, Gudrun Krämer, Denis Matringe, John Nawas, and Everett Rowson. Leiden: Brill.

Young, Katharine Galloway. 1987. *Taleworlds and Storyrealms: The Phenomenology of Narrative*. Boston: Nijhoff.

———. 1993. "Introduction." In *Bodylore*, edited by Katharine Young, xv–xxiv. Knoxville: University of Tennessee Press.

———. 1994. "Whose Body? An Introduction to Bodylore." *Journal of American Folklore* 107 (423): 3–8.

Yurchak, Alexei. 2006. *Everything Was Forever until It Was No More: The Last Soviet Generation*. Princeton, NJ: Princeton University Press.

Zanca, Russell. 2004. "'Explaining' Islam in Central Asia: An Anthropological Approach for Uzbekistan." *Journal of Muslim Minority Affairs* 24 (1): 99–107.

Zevaco, Ariane. 2014. "From Old to New Macha: Mass Resettlement and the Redefinition of Islamic Practice between Tajikistan's Upper Valleys and Cotton Lowlands." In *Allah's Kolkhozes: Migration, De-Stalinisation, Privatisation, and the New Muslim Congregations in the Soviet Realm (1950s–2000s)*, edited by Stéphane A. Dudoignon and Christian Noack, 148–201. Berlin: Klaus Schwarz Verlag.

Zubaïdulloh, Qori. n.d. *Ghazalʰo az ėjodiëti Mavlavi Jununi*. DVD.

Index

Abdurahmonjon: hagiography of, 54–56, 72, 87; as Soviet-era *pir*, 26, 33–34, 179n4; successor to, 47

Abdurashid, Qozidomullo, 54

Abuhanifa: poetry about, 130–31, 140, 142, 194n5–6; prayers to, 148; and the state, 96–98

Abulabbos (caliph), 97

adab: differences in, 34, 152; embodied, 168; in lodge, 27, 123; manuals for, 105; and the mind, 159; as mystical disposition, 155, 161; and politics, 169; requirements of, 32–33, 34, 180n9; and sociality, 165; during Soviet period, 26; Sufism as, 29, 154–56; and time, 17–18, 162–63. *See also* dress

Adham, Ibrohim ibn, 82

Afghanistan: books from, 118; experiences in, 4, 27; and Hamadoni, 38; *pirs* in, 32, 57, 75, 85, 121–23; Sufis in, 21, 32–33, 100, 181n15; war in, 6, 152, 171–72

Ahror, Khoja, 111, 150–54

Aini, Sadriddin, 188n16, 190n1

Albania, 198n11

Alexander the Great. *See* Iskandar

Alexievich, Svetlana, 12

Arabi, Ibn, 161, 198n10

Arabic, 41, 78, 124–26, 136, 161, 168

Arendt, Hannah, 59

Asad, Talal, 197n2

Attor, 79, 105, 183n5

avlie: Abuhanifa as, 97; and agency, 191n10; dreams and, 66; genealogy of, 192n15; graves of, 53, 108–9; Hofiz as, 65–66; lionization of, 17, 74–75, 81–83, 86–87; memories of, 80; and nostalgia, 55; *pirs* as, 7; and power, 15, 32, 39, 53, 73, 87, 103, 120–21, 161; secrets of, 139; stories about, 70, 88–89, 146; in Tajikistan, 21, 177n3; writings of, 38. *See also* *avliegi*

avliegi, 64, 85, 103, 177n, 185n24

Badakhshan, 194n7, 195n11

Bahodir, Abdulvakil, 31, 85, 121–23, 171

baiat, 111, 167, 199n15. *See also* initiation

Bakhtin, Mikhail, 141, 191n5, 192n14

Basri, Hasan al, 66

Bedil, 119–20, 135–36, 160

Bektashi (Sufis), 198n11

Benjamin, Walter, 83

Bolshevik, 4, 79

books: and agency, 108, 134; and authenticity, 124; and authority,